Christmas 2011

"Never Give

Marcy AKA
"Handy"

Nancy Hillis:

The Vamp *of* Savannah

As told to Mary Anne Street

Dedicated to:

Wes, my inspiration and who always makes me laugh;

And

Jacob, who taught me patience and to wait on the will of God.

FriesenPress

Suite 300 - 990 Fort St
Victoria, BC, Canada, V8V 3K2
www.friesenpress.com

ISBN
978-1-4602-7969-4 (Hardcover)
978-1-4602-7970-0 (Paperback)
978-1-4602-7971-7 (eBook)

1. Biography & Autobiography, Personal Memoirs

Distributed to the trade by The Ingram Book Company

Nancy Hillis:

The Vamp *of* Savannah

As told to Mary Anne Street

FriesenPress

Suite 300 - 990 Fort St
Victoria, BC, Canada, V8V 3K2
www.friesenpress.com

ISBN
978-1-4602-7969-4 (Hardcover)
978-1-4602-7970-0 (Paperback)
978-1-4602-7971-7 (eBook)

1. Biography & Autobiography, Personal Memoirs

Distributed to the trade by The Ingram Book Company

Table of Contents

Nancy Hillis book – August 15, 2013 – related at her home on St. Simons Island.

Cover photo used with permission from Carol Shaw, publisher of *Big Beautiful Woman.*

"There's only the trying again, and again, and again

To win again what we've lost before."

T.S. Elliott

Midnight In The Garden of Good and Evil
A song by Rick Burris - 1995
Used with permission of the writer's family.

A certain midnight dawns on the garden of good and evil,
In the presence and the company of the somewhat stranger people.
The good comes with catches…the evil is abound.
Then you'll find that evil is all there is around;
Yes, you'll find that evil is all there is around.

Nineteenth century charm, twentieth century alarm,
That sounds its warning too late to react.
Resulting in a role that really takes its toll,
You lose yourself in the final act; you lose yourself in the final act.

Privileged characters over time exempt themselves from rules,
Given inches they take miles, rules are for the fools.
The time proven tangled web that is always weaved,
Presents itself so prevalent when deceit is up their sleeves.

Chorus
Intoxicating pleasures and financial treasures,
Like charms on a bracelet marking time,
Then walking all too bold, into an abysmal hole,
Then find the exit much too high a climb;
You'll find the exit much too high a climb.

Preface

You may think being a character in a bestselling book would be great, especially a book that sold close to three million copies in 23 languages, that was made into a movie, and now is soon to be a Broadway show (this thing will live on way past me). But I'm here to tell you, it can be good and it can be evil.

I was Mandy in the bestselling book *Midnight in the Garden of Good and Evil*—John Berendt's book about a fatal shooting in beautiful Savannah, Georgia. Don't get me wrong, it was a great book—intriguing, interesting and a good read; but, as far as my character Mandy was concerned, well, Berendt didn't get it quite right. In fact, he didn't know or write the half of it, because my real truth is much better than his fiction.

I have stories, some good and some not so good, and my life has been a roller coaster of ups and downs. I've been thrilled to the highest heights and knocked down lower than low, but I've never been down and out. I have found that success is how many times you get up when you're knocked down over and over again. And that's what you do—keep going, and never, never, never give up.

I'm going to tell my story. I want to have it all down in black and white with splotches of color thrown in, and believe me, I've had a lot of color.

Every person gets defined by events that happen in their life from their earliest childhood to their old age. The smallest compliment, a look, a touch (good or bad), can leave an imprint that follows you your whole life and makes you the person you are. I'm no different. My life offered a myriad of experiences that molded me into who I am, and I'd be amiss to leave them out as I tell you my story.

I hope this book will impact other lives in a way that might inspire them to be strong, positive and kind to their fellow man, and not to judge people by their faith, color, sexual preference, nationality or money (or lack thereof). This is my wish and here is my story.

My trademark song was *Hard Hearted Hannah the Vamp of Savannah* and it was the first song I learned when I started the Dixieland Jazz part of my singing career. It was always my opening number. Because I sang it so much, my friends, family and fans started calling me the Vamp of Savannah. Many people have asked me what the word means and it has many meanings and connotations, but the ones most attached to the word are seductress, temptress, femme-fatale and sex kitten; but none of those describe me. If you define Vamp as a strong, assertive woman, who is comfortable in her own skin, then I am a Vamp with a capital V and that explains the title of this book. That's my definition.

So, in your eyes, am I the Vamp of Savannah? I leave it to you, dear reader, to decide.

Chapter 1

The Green Room

"Nancy, the phone's for you!"

I was upstairs in my private space in the historic Hamilton-Turner Mansion in Savannah, Georgia, which I bought in March of 1991 and owned at the time, trying to steal a few minutes of peace for myself as it was a few days before St. Patrick's Day and I was swamped trying to get ready. You may ask why this is such a big deal, but in Savannah it is a REALLY big deal. Hundreds of thousands come from all around the world to see the second largest (some years) St. Patrick's Day parade in the United States. New York or Chicago might have the first largest, but their firemen come to march in ours—that's how big and important our parade is.

The Mansion was next door to the Cathedral of St. John the Baptist Catholic Church where the holiday mass started the big day, and the parade participants geared up to put on the best show in front of the reviewing stand. The bands, majorettes, Irish clans all dressed in their family colors and plaids, the Clydesdale horses, the Shriners, the floats, cheerleaders, celebrities, beauty queens, singers, and firemen and police officers from everywhere put on their best show when they rounded the corner of Lafayette Square, right in front of my property. So I was neck deep in decorating the Mansion with shamrocks, leprechauns and anything else green I could find. My famous sign that traditionally hung from the roof and went from one side of the Mansion to the other read, "The Hamilton O'Turner House Wishes You a Happy St. Patrick's Day." And, of course, there would be a real live leprechaun dancing on the roof of my 10,000 square foot Mansion. Oh, and did I mention that I was cooking for 74 people who were to feast on a proper Irish breakfast, complete with green grits and a delicious casserole prepared by my friend, and then "unknown," Paula Deen?

"Tell them to call back," I hollered down. All I needed now was someone calling me with something else to do.

"You'll want to take this one, Nancy; it's Oprah."

"Oprah who?" I asked, barely paying attention to what she was saying. Then it dawned on me just who this might be. "Not THE OPRAH?" My mind raced; why would Oprah want to talk to me? Perhaps it had something to do with St. Patrick's Day, or maybe it was because the character, Mandy Nichols, in John Berendt's book, *Midnight in the Garden of Good and Evil* was really me, Nancy Hillis. I took the call and sure enough, Oprah's people asked me to appear on her show to talk about The Book. The episode was to be titled, "Cities and Their Claim to Fame." The mayor from Selma, Alabama was going to be there to talk about the Civil Rights' march as well as John Lewis, the man who lead the march 25 years earlier and who was now a U.S. Representative from Georgia; Punxsutawney Phil was to be there; and Chablis, (another character from the *Midnight* book) John and I were to appear to talk about Savannah and Berendt's book.

Now you have to understand, I was a grown up version of the country girl from "Plum-Nelly." For those of you who don't speak "country," "Plum-Nelly" means "almost" or "just-as-far-as-you-can-get-to;" so for example, "Plum-Nelly dead" would mean you are almost ready for the funeral. It also means "Plum outta Tennessee and Nelly out of Georgia." Our farm was three miles from the Tennessee-Georgia state line, in Georgia. Our address was listed as Chattanooga, Tennessee. Our post office was Tennessee, but our car tag said Walker County, Georgia since we paid state taxes to Georgia. The fact is, I guess I was a Georgia "cracker" mixed with a fair amount of Tennessee "hillbilly." How could such a person grow up to be worthy of a spot on the Oprah show—Oprah, who was recognized and loved by the whole world. Needless to say, my stress level put me in a full blown panic attack.

I had flown in the evening before the show (only a day after I'd received her call). I was at the Omni in downtown Chicago, and I hadn't slept since the call and I certainly wasn't going to get any sleep now that I was there. I tried a hot bath with lavender to calm my nerves with no results. My eyes looked back at me in the mirror with that "deer in the headlights" look. I had thrown three of my favorite outfits in my bag and I spent hours deciding which one would make me look the skinniest (television really does add about ten pounds and I was not one you'd call petite). My oldest outfit seemed to work the best. Next, I worked on my make-up.

My friend, Tara, from Washington, Georgia introduced the name "My Face" for her suitcase full of cosmetics. If it was ever lost, God help the one who lost it. Well, I had "My Face" bag with me, and staring at it I put myself in another tizzy. Should I put on heavy make-up or do light make-up? Maybe Oprah's make-up artist would do it for me; "in your dreams, Nancy," I thought. I began to give it my best attempt and ended up doing light make-up, just in case. I waited until the last minute to unroll my hair curlers. Big mistake! Big. The result was a curly, blond, pigtail effect all over my head, and it was too late to do anything about it. Oh God!

Aunt Evelyn, the matriarch of our family, and the one person in the world I wanted to please most had given me the strict directive that, "Our family does not air its dirty laundry in public, especially not on national TV." She was not happy that I was going to talk about The Book on Oprah at all. One would say she perceived that the lifestyle I was living at the time The Book was written was a grave embarrassment (she did relent some when about a year later her high falutin' friends kept talking about how great this Book was). I worried how Aunt Evelyn would take my appearance on the show and I told her ahead of time because I knew she would find out eventually. She told me to keep my mouth shut.

There were my two sons, Wes and Jacob. All along I had tried to keep them out of any publicity having to do with the Book, but now they wanted me to mention their names on TV. I couldn't just stop and wave and say "hi" to them like I was on the Price is Right. How was I going to bring their names in on the show?

The conversation I had with myself over all of these variables was exhausting so you can see what kind of shape I was in.

So here I was, shaking like a leaf and standing in the Green Room, THE GREEN ROOM at Harpo (Oprah spelled backwards) Studios and my little country-bumpkin self was about to walk through the door and be on millions of televisions across the country. Of course, you know (I didn't know) the Green Room is like a holding room where guests await their stage call. Green, I'm told, gets rid of evil spirits, but an evil spirit was just about to walk in the door and stare me in the face.

John Berendt didn't know I was coming so when he walked in he liked to have dropped his jaw. He began bouncing all over the room with what looked like nervous anticipation because he was afraid I might expose the truth about his book on national TV. You see, in his book, John strongly suggested that two of his characters, Joe Odom and Mandy Nichols (me) were involved in an intimate relationship. As handsome and charming as Joe was, he was not someone I was interested in in that way. Besides, Joe was, I guess, bi-sexual, and I was not.

John finally came over to me and began to lecture.

"Now listen," he started, "I am the reason you got to be here. I told the producer you would be good on TV. If Oprah asks you if you and Joe ever got married or were engaged to be married, just laugh and say Joe was going to marry everybody. You really need to follow the story line, Nancy."

I was puzzled and wasn't sure what he was talking about. Even though he had me living in Savannah some six or seven years before I was actually there—what difference did it really make? He also had himself there years before he actually came to Savannah, but so what?

Then he said, "They have talked with me, and 'they' do not want any negativism." I wondered who "they" were.

"John," I responded, "I have never been negative about The Book."

"Oh, yes, you have," he said. "You deny the fact that you and Joe had a relationship, and…." He was talking, of course, about Joe Odom, my former partner in the Dixieland Jazz Club called Sweet Georgia Browns.

"No, no, no. I don't deny we had a relationship, John, but we didn't have a romantic relationship and you know that. We were good friends and business partners. Period!"

He answered that it would just be better if I followed the story line, and by all means, he said, "If anybody asks you what caused Joe's death, say leukemia. That's what I say and that's the least you could do for Joe's poor family."

"I think they know that Joe died of AIDS," I said, "and secondly, I am not going to lie. It's public record that he died of AIDS, and why do you want to say leukemia?"

"You don't know that for sure," he said.

I asked him if he'd like to see the death certificate.

"How did you get the death certificate?" he growled as if I had committed some crime.

"It came in the mail to the Hamilton-Turner House. I guess they thought Joe was still there—it was probably the last address they had on file and I opened it—I had gotten so many pieces of mail and wanted to make sure none of them concerned Sweet Georgia Browns (which remember I had been a partner in). I will be glad to get you a copy. It's public record and anyone can get a copy."

John really got testy then, so much so he was almost stuttering. "You know I've never even told my mother and father, Nancy, what Joe died of; if it were to come out that Joe was gay I...I.... Just let me tell you this, Chablis got a book deal with a division of Random House and I hope to sell the rights to my book for a movie. There's a lot of money to be made and…and… you better follow the story line or you'll be sorry," and with that threat he walked away from me. I sat there in shock, feeling sick to my stomach. I didn't know whether to go on, or just run and get the first cab back to the airport. Then I began to get mad. I had known for a while that he didn't like me and I wasn't sure why, but now he was telling me what I could and could not say about my life; how dare he try to tell me what to say about my own personal history.

"John, you're not going to dictate to me what I talk about today or in the future. I don't ever offer negativism, but I do tell the truth and I'll do that today." Then as I went out the door to be with Oprah I said, "I was somebody before your book, John, and I'll be somebody way after it's gone. I don't need your book to be somebody. I'm all I want to be, so you give it your best shot, OK?"

I turned quickly and walked regally onto Oprah's stage to face the cameras and millions of television viewers, but I was shaking in my bones!

John, Chablis and I were seated and graciously welcomed by Oprah. I kept praying she would not ask me any direct questions. My head was spinning, and then it came.

"How has your life changed, Nancy, "Mandy," since this book has come out and now that you are known around the world in 23 different countries?"

I took a deep breath and began to speak. "One thing that has changed is how my children, Wes and Jacob, react," I said. "They come home sometimes and there's a group outside waiting to speak to me or get my autograph in their copies of The Book. They would kid and say, 'Mom, you've made us backdoor kids!' and then we'd all laugh."

"The second thing that changed," I continued, "was my appearance. Lots of times I would go out with no makeup on, wearing a baseball cap to cover my not-yet-styled hair. I didn't care because no one took a special interest in me as I went from place to place running errands. My new persona now required me to be dressed up and made up at all times—no more thrown together, unkempt hair and makeup. Now I don't go anywhere without being fluffed up."

Thank goodness Chablis was there. If you are ever on a stage with Chablis, you can count on her taking over, and you won't be in charge. You will relinquish your spotlight quickly—she just eats up the stage.

Chablis broke in, "I've never seen this girl when she wasn't fluffed up," and off she went. I wanted to hug her. Oprah didn't ask me any other questions and all-in-all I thought the experience was positive. I have to say that Oprah was real, just like she comes across, and she didn't disappoint me. You could just feel the kindness and honesty in her demeanor—such a dynamic person with a very kind and caring spirit.

John just didn't like me. There's just no other way to put it. He had loved to be around Joe Odom and I believe that's part of the reason why he disliked me—I was in Joe's life and the apple of his eye when John was around gathering material for his book, and he was jealous because I had unintentionally cut off his source of information. Joe just didn't have time to tell him stories any more. Also, Joe was bi-sexual and it was a rumor that John was homosexual so they had some things in common.

Looking back, I realize that without the romantic, made-up "sexual" relationship of Joe and Mandy, The Book would be a story of homosexual relationships, and about a female impersonator, or as Chablis said after Oprah asked her what she'd like to be called, a Drag Queen. I don't think in 1992 it would have appealed to a wide audience so in my opinion, the story of Mandy and Joe was probably a good business decision.

Chapter 2

The Great and Complicated Joe Odom

The Oprah Show, while undoubtedly a big deal, wasn't the most important event in my life which was well storied before and after that show, as you will learn through the pages of this book. But it was my relationship with Joe Odom that defined the latter part of my life. The time spent with him was pivotal, so I must talk about it first so you, dear reader, can understand how he impacted my life and events to come.

I had drifted into the strange and tangled life of Joe Odom on the tails of a nasty divorce (more about this later). I was living on St. Simons Island, singing professionally with a group called the Good Ole Boys and we got a gig at the luxurious Cloister on Sea Island, quite a famous and expensive place where the G8 summit was held one year, and where Presidents and their families have vacationed. (It still is a holiday magnet for the rich and famous.) A friend of mine who worked as a bartender in another room asked me to come over to his bar and have a drink before I went home. So I did, and that's where I was introduced to Joe Odom.

There sat, according to my friends, the "wealthy attorney from Savannah that lived in one of those gracious, beautiful historic houses, and played a mean piano." That's the way he was introduced to me—a wealthy attorney. I met the debonair Joe Odom and he was indeed debonair: tall, handsome, blonde haired, blue eyes, smart, talented, and he was bowled over by me. It was instant attraction and he was smitten. I found him attractive, but even then in the beginning, I thought there was something different about him and I had the feeling that he was a very complicated person. I did find out that Joe had had three marriages: two to a woman named Anne that he married, divorced, then re-married and divorced; and one to Mary, his third wife from whom he was divorced.

Later on, Joe and I moseyed over into the foyer where we had our picture taken together. The thirty-year, well known Cloister concierge, Houston, later reminisced, "Who knew that your chance meeting that night would become the basis for a storyline in a bestselling novel and it would start this whole "*Midnight* madness?"

Later, as expected, Joe offered to take me home. Always the gentleman, at least always the gentleman with a plot and a plan, he said, "Would you mind coming by where I'm staying first? I have two beautiful pianos and I want to hear you sing." He was the guest of a neurosurgeon and his wife, it was late, and I was afraid we'd wake them. "Not to worry," he said, so I cautiously agreed and off we went. Joe sat down at one of his baby grand pianos and I began to sing. I sang everything I could think of and he played as if we had been a duo forever. I complimented his playing and he shared with me that he had been taught by the well known Savannah pianist and songstress, Emma Kelly. I had not met her yet, but we were destined to spend many hours with her entertaining the visitors and residents of the fair city of Savannah. (I am honored to say that several years later she did play at my son's wedding reception.) Her piano style was called stride piano, wherein the bass goes back and forth creating the Dixieland sound.

After a few hours of mixing our extensive musical talents, Joe stopped playing and looked up at me. "Nancy," he said, "you and I are magic together. What do you say about coming to Savannah and opening a place together?" I said, nonchalantly, OK, thinking that it was just the booze talking. I said, "You set it up and I'll do it," never expecting it to come to fruition.

Joe said, "Just come to Savannah and get a feel for the city,"

"How will I find you?"

"Get off the interstate and it will spit you right off at Oglethorpe, then take a right, go on down and I'll be standing on the corner."

"What corner?" I asked. I had already made it clear that Savannah was not one of my regular stomping grounds.

"The corner at 101 E. Oglethorpe and Drayton," and that was the end of that; or so I thought.

Joe lived in a big, historic four-story house, and Jerry Spence, his friend, lived on the fourth floor. Jerry was a hairdresser, handsome, gay and he drank too much, and he loved Joe. I'd learn more about Jerry later.

Besides playing the piano, Joe had his broker's license and he was a tax lawyer, with his practice in the basement of the house where he lived. (He had received his law degree from the University of Georgia, and his master's in tax and law from New York University.) When I was there, no one would answer the phone, and they'd tell me not to answer it, either. They certainly used it to call out, but took no incoming calls because it was a "party-line." Later, I heard rumors that Joe sort of just moved in when the owners were gone, but I don't know. He was their realtor/broker and at that point I didn't ask too many questions.

One day Joe asked me how I felt about alternative clubs. "You mean like a gay bar?" I asked. That's what he meant and I said I was fine with that; that I didn't judge people by their sexual preference—I looked to their heart and soul instead. I wasn't sure at the time what he was saying, but I had no qualms about alternative clubs.

"I want you to meet Emma," Joe said and we went to her place on the river near Jere's Antiques. It was called Emma's, and he took me in and I met Emma Kelly, known as the Lady of 6,000 Songs and one of Joe's really good friends. Afterward, we went lots of places, and everywhere we went everyone knew Joe. He introduced me to Wanda Brooks and I sang for her and she said, "That'll work." I think I was auditioning for his circle of friends.

Later we went to an Irish pub called McDonough's. It was past two in the morning but it was still open and all of a sudden someone turned out the lights and said, "Get on the floor. If y'all want us to keep our license, get down on the floor and be quiet." Joe pulled me down to the floor. Jerry was with us, and he grabbed my shirt and told me to follow him. We crawled on the floor to the bathroom and turned on the light and Jerry asked me if I was in love with Joe. I'm not sure if Jerry and Joe had a thing (Jerry would tell people that he was more than a friend but less than a lover to Joe), but Jerry did everything for Joe, and I think he would have loved to have had a thing with Joe, but I wasn't sure Joe would want one with him. They were like a couple. Jerry cooked, cleaned, cut his hair and mustache, and took care of him; he did everything that a wife would do. I asked him why he wanted to know about Joe and me and he said because "you don't seem to know everything." When I asked about that he said, "It'll all unfold, it'll all unfold." That's about all I knew about Jerry Spence at first, but I liked him a lot. He was quick and very funny, and he started the term, "over-served;" no one was ever drunk, they were "over-served."

Joe started calling me all the time, and he took me to meet his best friend, Kenny Rudd. Kenny was quiet, a bit younger than Joe but just as cute. I said, "Let's go to Orlando to see Ruth Crews and Rosie O'Grady's." I knew Ruth, and had been to Rosie O'Grady's several times, so we went. I took them all in, and introduced them to the lady who had graciously taught me how to sing real Dixieland Jazz, Ruth Crews. Joe was enthralled with the place and talked about how our Club should be patterned after this successful one. Unbeknownst to me, this was my approval dinner for his friends—Billy, who had been in law school with Joe, and his wife Suzanne; Dr. Steve and his wife who owned the house with the two pianos; and Kenny Rudd and his wife. They were seeing me as his girlfriend.

I called a friend from Orlando to tell her that we were spending the night and I said, "You know we're in separate rooms." She said, "What do you think about that?" I said, "Well, I'm glad because to be honest with you, as wonderful as he is, he just doesn't appeal to me that way, and I don't want to hurt his feelings." Joe was very polished, very debonair, very much a southern gentleman, but there was something about him. At the time, I didn't know what it was, but I figured it was that I was from Tennessee and I loved a polished man who treated me like a lady. But I also wanted a man to have a little redneck in him; a man who was real; they had to be able to maybe go hunting and fishing sometimes and not worry about getting their hands dirty, and I could never see Joe Odom like that. He just was never going to get his hands dirty at all, which is not a bad thing, but he just didn't appeal to me as a love interest or romantic interest. I really enjoyed being with him, and I never laughed so much; I felt like he was one of the most intelligent men I had ever met, but the sexual attraction just wasn't there. I found out much later that it was good that the sexual feeling wasn't there—in spite of his having been married, he was gay.

We got serious about a place and decided to call it Sweet Georgia Browns and we were raring to go, but we had one problem: money. We didn't have any, so I asked Joe how in the world we could open a club, and put in all the needed equipment without any money. He said, "Nancy, have you not ever heard of OPM (other people's money)?" Because I was involved in selling real estate, I thought maybe it was a new loan package that I didn't know anything about so I didn't question him.

Joe was very good at getting OPM and he used that talent to find a place in City Market. The area had been an old market where in the 1800s people would sell their fruits and vegetables, but now it was nearly vacant. There was one Mexican restaurant there, a small Polk's vegetable market, and a bar/restaurant called Malone's—that was all. He found a vacant building that had nothing but a concrete floor that rocked and rolled. It had two Savannah gray brick walls, no ceiling, no heating and air, no bar, nothing, but Joe thought it was perfect. He set up a corporation and set aside the name for the club. He had grand ideas that as soon as we got this one off the ground, we would franchise and we would have Sweet Georgia Browns all over the state of Georgia.

As he showed me all of this I told him I didn't have any money but he said not to worry. The city of Savannah wanted to bring life back into the area so they offered up-front money for people who would open a business there—they would match money that the City Market owners would give. At that time it was, I think, $75,000, so the final amount would be $150,000, but City Market gave Joe only part of the money promised. I was told all of this but never saw it in writing as Joe was in charge of the money and all legal issues, so I never really knew much about it and why we didn't get the whole amount.

Joe's good friend wrote a very good story to put on our brochures about how Miss Hard Hearted Hannah and Miss Sweet Georgia Brown knew each other, and how they came to Savannah—you know, he gave us a history for our bar, because you can't have anything in Savannah that doesn't have some history. In the meantime, I was selling real estate, working at a boutique, being a single mother, running back and forth from St. Simons to Savannah (about a one and one-half hour drive) and things were rolling along.

Our target date for opening was just before St. Patrick's Day in 1988. In Savannah, everyone is Irish on St. Patrick's Day and the party's on, so it would be a perfect time to open our place.

All my friends started coming up from St. Simons to Savannah to meet some of Joe's friends, and at the same time, I was meeting this person and that person, and I was finally getting to know Joe's house mate, Jerry Spence. We had met briefly, of course, when I first came to Savannah, but Joe had really kept me from him for about four months. Jerry was a wild, flaming homosexual who drank too much and who could be obnoxious, but I really liked him. He was a hairdresser, but his real claim to fame was that he dressed in drag and did a show at Club One, calling himself Judy Delight. I'm told he was wonderful, gorgeous, blonde, blue-eyed and sexy. I found it a little strange that Jerry was with Joe all the time, but all of Joe's friends, all the married well-to-do friends said, "Poor Jerry, you just have to overlook Jerry," and "Oh, let's wait a while before you get introduced to Jerry." They were warning me and trying to prepare me for the up and down experiences with him. It soon became obvious that Jerry considered himself everything to Joe. There's no doubt in my mind that he loved Joe.

In the meantime, Joe and I started the search for antiques for our club. We had the diagram and had the architect draw up what we wanted to do and how we wanted it to look. We'd break out a wall here, put a new wall in there, and raise the floor, which we actually had to build. We went to Atlanta to purchase antiques. I had background experience in interior design, helping my Aunt Evelyn, so I knew a lot of antique dealers and fabric houses in Atlanta. We went from one place to another, and we found out later that the shops thought we were Ted Turner and his wife. No wonder we got such fast and good service.

I also noticed as we walked around the shops, homosexual guys took a very keen liking to Joe. He was just so likeable anyway, but I was getting my first real idea that maybe Joe might walk on a little bit of the "left side of the street." It was just that they took to him so quickly, and one particular fellow who worked at one of the galleries was particularly charmed. He walked up and said, "So, you play the piano?" and with that Joe sat down and played. I started singing and before we knew it, we had a crowd around us. The guy said, "This piano is just what you need for your opening." Joe agreed and off-handily said, "Send it right on down."

It just so happened that the day before the grand opening, the truck came down from Atlanta with some of our antiques, and guess what was on the truck—the $50,000 signed Steinway.

Then City Market threw a kink in everything. They decided that after they gave us our first money, they weren't going to give us any more. Their excuse was that the City had not given them their share of the start-up money so they would not continue. Joe started a lawsuit for breach of contract.

In the meantime, we had to go up to Atlanta to get the rest of our things and we were going without a penny in the bank. We were in a borrowed van, and I said, "Joe how in the world are we going to pick up anything without any money?"

"Well, honey, what would you have me do? We're damned if we do, and damned if we don't. If we don't go ahead and get the things, we can't open. If we don't open, we can't pay anybody anything, and we already owe a lot. If we can get open, we can get to making some money and pay folks we owe and get going."

"Joe, how are you going to write a check for anything?"

"Well, I don't know. Let's just go to Atlanta and go see Johnny (not his real name)."

Johnny was an attorney friend of Joe's and we thought he might have an idea. He was gorgeous, gorgeous, gorgeous; blonde hair, blue eyes, all-American looking. Johnny sat down and we told him our plight. I said that I had never written a bad check in my life and I wasn't about to start.

"You can't go into these places and write checks that aren't any good," I said. They both laughed and laughed, like I had said something really funny.

"Don't you love it?" Joe said.

Johnny laughed, "Joe, you've got a gold mine here."

I wondered about the whole conversation; was I that naïve that different people wrote checks all the time without money in the bank? It sounded like I was the only person in the world that never bounced a check.

Joe said, "All right, Nancy, when we go into these places we'll show them our contract with City Market. Will this suit you if we show them that, and say that the check we're giving them is not good at this point, but as soon as City Market pays us our money, the check will be good?"

That made sense to me, and I felt it was honest so we went in every place and said just that. They took our checks, knowing they weren't any good at that point. Joe assured them that they would get their money, so there was nothing to fear. That was the magic of Joe Odom.

We opened Sweet Georgia Browns two weeks before St. Patrick's Day in 1988. The opening occurred over three nights and it was wonderful. My son, Jacob, who was about eight years old at the time, passed food for us, and he was so cute with his little striped shirt, garter on his sleeve, and straw hat. My other son, Wes, also helped.

At one point, Joe looked around and said, "Boy, we've got the A group tonight."

Gary Strickland showed up one night at Sweet Georgia Browns with his trumpet. He wanted to sit in and he was the nicest guy, so we let him. He wasn't great at first, but he kept getting better and better, especially when Kenny Palmer—probably the best musician Savannah ever had—started teaching him and helping him. Gary always showed up—he didn't drink—he loved to play and Kenny took him aside and he got better. He'd blow the heck out of that little horn. He had gone through a bad divorce and he was a spiritual guy, and when he found us, he said he was just saved—he had something to do that he loved and it kept him busy. He became a part of our core, which included Gary, two bartenders, Val who played and sang, Joe, and me.

We were busy and many people came every night. I know we were making money, but our agreement was that most money would go back into the bar as there were a lot of things we needed to pay for, especially all those antiques. The Steinway also had never gone back, and we started getting little phone calls about that along with others about payment for this antique or that antique. Before I knew it, Joe was being arrested. Every other night he would be arrested for writing another bad check, and every other night he would dip into the cash, or I would to hand it to someone who would go and bail him out. Sometimes he just took the cash with him. It was almost costing us more to bail Joe out over the bad check charges than we were making.

I was back and forth from St. Simons a lot. I would work the bar until midnight, get in my car and drive the one and a half hours home to St. Simons because Jacob was still in school. I would do breakfast, work at my various jobs, do homework and prayers with Jacob, then jump in my car and drive to Savannah to sing. I would sing until 2:00 am, especially on the weekends, and then drive back home to St. Simons, sleep for a while, get up and the day would start all over again. I really didn't know about the money situation or what was happening with Sweet Georgia Browns because Joe was in charge of that part.

There was always an entourage of people around Joe. If it wasn't Jerry and all his friends, it was other people and all their friends. It was always a party with Joe; and the music from midnight to two or three in the morning was some of the best you could ever hear anywhere. Some of the best jazz musicians in the world would drop by just to jam with us. The music would go on and on, and sometimes, even though we had to close legally at two in the morning, the party would go on wherever Joe was going. It might be his Oglethorpe place, or it might be a late night bar, but it would be somewhere because they were not ready to stop the party. Sometimes I'd stay, but most of the time I had to get back to St. Simons to keep my life going down there. It was like I had two lives; but, I must say, this time was magical.

Chapter 3

I Drive With My Knees

One day, among the entourage of people around Joe, I met John Berendt. He was born in Syracuse, New York, and moved to Manhattan after college. He was an intellectual who went to an Ivy League school, and came South because a friend had asked him to come. John would go back and forth from New York to Savannah, and he was always hanging around our place. He was a feature writer for *Esquire* magazine at that time, but he didn't have a car, and he was the only one of Joe's friends that we never borrowed much money from because he rarely had any. In fact, he lived in a dumpy apartment building near Forsyth Park, in one room with a bathroom, mattress on the floor, hot plate, typewriter, fax machine, and folding chair. Once in a great while Joe would ask John for $50 to open the bar and if he had it, he'd give it to us, but he was always there, counting the money, demanding his $50 as soon as the cash drawer had it.

John was always asking questions. He came in one night and asked me if it was boring driving all the way from Savannah to St. Simons and back all the time. I said that it really wasn't boring, that it gave me time to get ready.

He asked, "What do you mean, get ready?"

"Well, I put on my makeup and get ready," I said. "I don't have any other time to do it, so I do it when I drive." I told him about my family in St. Simons, my other jobs, and that I only had time to grab my stuff, get in the car, and get ready while on the way.

"Well, I don't understand how you do that."

"Well, John, you just drive with your knees."

"You actually apply makeup while you drive with your knees?" he said. "And you wear a lot of different colors on your eyes? How do you get that done?"

"John, let me tell you," and I told him the story about when I was modeling for Hanes Just My Size pantyhose, I'd often get a call to be in Atlanta in just a few short hours. "If I couldn't get a flight out of Jacksonville or Savannah, I would jump in the car and drive. I had my hair in those little, pink sponge rollers, and I'd put my makeup on the seat and have everything right there that I needed to get ready. I'd plug a VCR player into my lighter, and put a movie in so it would help keep me focused and awake, as the drive on I-16 from Savannah to Macon was so boring. I wouldn't always watch it, but I'd listen. One of my favorites was *Raiders of the Lost Ark*."

I told him about the time I stopped at Dublin to get gas and go to the bathroom. When I pulled over, a truck driver pulled up beside me. He got out and pecked on my window and said, "Excuse me, but I've been behind you since Brunswick, and I just had to get a look at you. You know, you pulled those pink things out of your hair, then you put on makeup and I saw all those brushes you were using; then it looked like you were painting your fingernails. I've just got one question: When you have both hands up in the air doing your stuff, how in the world are you driving?"

"Oh, I drive with my knees," I said.

"Oh my God, and there's a TV on the seat; I should have passed you, you could have killed us all."

John, of course, found the story most interesting, and later wrote about it in his book. He put that I watched soap operas, which wasn't true, but I had no idea at the time what he was doing.

Life rolled on and I began to see things in Joe that would make me pause. He would disappear and come back in a much better mood. With my background in drug abuse (more later), I was suspicious. Also, a couple of nights I saw people hand him things, and he immediately would put it in his mouth and take a drink. I knew he drank too much—he woke up drinking Savannah Sweet Tea (sweet tea and vodka)—but he seemed to handle it. He seemed to be able to just drink and drink and drink and still be sensible.

One Saturday night we didn't close the bar until three o'clock in the morning, and we had a morning gig on River Street the next day. It was ridiculous for me to drive back to St. Simons, so I stayed in Savannah. I had had three drinks, and the next day I was so sick I couldn't do the first two sets. Joe said later, "Nancy can't drink. Don't expect Nancy to try to keep up any more." I never did drink much.

Joe and I had also landed a job singing on a cruise ship that docked in Savannah. We'd go on board the ship, me in my red hot mama outfit and Joe in his gambler outfit, and we'd sit down and sing to them for a while and we got paid very well. In the meantime, Joe would say to me, "Nancy, you know I love you." And I would say, "Joe, I love you, too." I would tell my girlfriend that I didn't know what I'd do if he ever got really romantic with me—he just wasn't my type, and I had started to really suspect he had homosexual tendencies, and I was scared of that. We were as close as any two people could be, but it was like brother and sister. We danced together; we entertained together; Joe introduced me as his "fourth wife in waiting" and we were King and Queen of Savannah. People would say, "You are a gorgeous couple," and some would say things like, "I don't know how you stand it when that good-looking thing sings to you. Oh, it gives me the chills." His friends would say, "You know, Joe is deeply in love with you; when are y'all going to get married?" We never talked about it though until one night.

The bar had closed and we had something to do on Sunday at 9:00 am, so I spent the night. Joe had found himself homeless again and had no place to live. The top realtor in Savannah was a friend of his and she owned a house on Jones Street. It was the house Joe and Mary had lived in when they were married. Mary had been a socialite in Savannah, daughter of the president of a bank, and she was gorgeous, tall, blonde and the debutante of the South. They had had a beautiful wedding and a good life, but after seven or eight years, they divorced, Mary left town and Joe got the house. He couldn't afford the payments, and the memories made him so sad, so he said he "gave it" to his realtor friend if she would just take over the payments. Well, this particular night she put us up in the carriage house in back.

Joe had a bit too much to drink that night or as he always said, he was "over served," and while sitting in front of the fireplace he said, "Nancy, you know I really do love you."

As usual, I told him I loved him too.

"Well, no, no, I really do, and do you think that if the bar works and we make some money—because you know you are not cheap to keep—you would marry me?"

I said, "Joe, you've been over served!" About 30 minutes later he asked me again.

"You know, I'm a very complicated person and there are a lot of things I can't explain to you, but you are just everything I have ever wanted, and will you please marry me?"

I was feeling uncomfortable at this point and didn't really know what to say.

He continued, "What's the matter? Is it that sex business? Nancy, don't you know that all that sex business just does nothing but ruin a good relationship."

I said, "Joe, I just kind of want the whole ball of wax, and you don't do little girls,"

He looked at me with a puzzled look on his face and said, "Well, Nancy, I may not do little girls, but I don't do little boys, I don't do little sheep, I don't do little goats, I don't do nothing."

I repeated that I really needed the whole ball of wax.

He said, "I was afraid you would say that." The whole thing struck me as ironic. Here I was telling a man that because he won't have sex, I won't marry him. All the times I had to run around the room to try and get away from a man and now I was saying no because of the no-sex thing. I know it hurt him too, because I was telling him he really didn't appeal to me that way. I really loved and cared about him, but I couldn't marry him.

The next day he said, "I'm sorry I got all bent out of shape last night, but it's OK. Things will all unfold." That was one of his favorite sayings.

Chapter 4

Trouble All Over

The devil will always come for his due, and he began showing up in spades! In our standoff with City Market, Joe said we had the best case. We had worked for three months on that case and I took his instructions and went to the Law Library in Savannah and researched everything he requested. Remember that City Market had given Joe $75,000 start-up money with the other $75,000 coming later. Joe decided that "later" was here and it was time for City Market to honor their side of the bargain. He had filed a motion for breach of contract and it was time to get our money.

We were ready, and I arrived at the court house a little earlier than our scheduled time. I looked around the room but there was no Joe. Our case was called and then dismissed because our lawyer, Mr. Odom himself, was not present. The legal term the judge used to find in City Market's favor was "non-performance." To say I was upset would be an understatement. I stomped over to the Hamilton-Turner House, expecting to find Joe sleeping off a hangover, but instead, I found him naked and in bed with a man who was also naked! There may have been non-performance at the courthouse, but Joe was putting on a performance at the House. My senses were whirling and I must say, I was dumbfounded! As I've said, I had my suspicions, but to see the blatant reality of the homosexuality in my face was devastating. I just shut the door—slammed it.

He hollered out, "Nancy, is that you? What's the matter?"

"Joe, did you forget about court?" I yelled from the hallway.

"Oh no," he yelled.

That was the first time I saw that he was openly gay—the first time I actually saw him with a guy in bed, naked. We lost the case because Joe didn't show up to court; Joe dropped the ball for a roll in the hay.

[By the way, my curiosity drew my eyes to the exposed, rather large package that Joe had (I had always wondered). I was ashamed of myself after a moment or two but thought if he ever did girls, he would be wonderful.]

I did go to court with him the day that the judge was going to sentence him on bad check charges. A nice antique dealer, who had sold us several things, had come down from South Carolina to testify that Joe's checks had bounced. The man didn't have all his paperwork correct and he began stumbling through it.

Joe said, "Your honor, I can help him—he comes all the way down here and he deserves to get his money and a judgment. I would like to help him and the fee will be pro-bono." The judge thought it most unusual for the defendant to help the plaintiff, but that was Joe. When he was together, he was the biggest hearted person, and he was sorry he took advantage of the man; Joe truly thought he would have the money to pay him eventually.

That night a really good friend of Joe's gave him some money to pay off the bad checks debt so he wouldn't have to go to jail. Joe gave him a piece of paper that said the friend now had a lien on a certain piece of property somewhere that Joe owned (I doubt that he did) and also on some of the antiques at the Club. Of course, he neglected to say that they weren't paid for and they really still belonged to the antique dealers that had sold them to us, so now, this friend really had two pieces of paper that weren't worth anything. Joe also gave him a lien on Emma's grand piano which he said he had promised her before we started Sweet Georgia Browns. Well, Emma still had it, but Joe gave the friend the lien on it, even though she was still playing it at her bar on River St. All of the liens, which were worthless, seemed to satisfy the friend, but I don't think he cared if he ever got anything back or not. He cared about Joe that much, and that night as they walked out with their arms around each other, a friend turned to me and said, "Hummm" and I thought, "Hummm."

Later on Jerry Spence said, "Nancy, are you so stupid that you didn't realize why that friend does everything for Joe? Don't you know there's a whole lot more to that situation than meets the eye?"

I said, "Well, Jerry, I don't have a clue," but I sure had an idea.

Jerry kept on badgering me, and one night he came into the club, bringing a lot of people with him and serving them all drinks for free.

He said, "Come on, I own half the place. This is mine," and he jumped behind the bar and Joe said, "Nancy, get rid of Jerry."

"Joe, it's your place to get rid of him. He lives with you and he's your friend."

"Well, he needs to leave and you know it."

"Well, what do you expect me to do?" I thought Joe should be the one to take care of it, but he couldn't hurt his friend.

Jerry kept coming in and it became a habit that he'd bring friends and serve drinks for free. One night, when I got to the bar from St. Simons, the bar was full of gay men. That night after we closed I asked Joe if he really wanted a gay bar."

"What do you mean, Nancy?"

"Well, if you want us to have a gay bar, that's fine with me. I don't mind. We can have the best damn gay bar in Savannah, if that's what you want to do—we'll put the other two gay bars out of business."

"You know I don't want to fill up the bar with all those queers," he said and those were his exact words. I was a little shocked at his reply.

"You can't let Jerry come in here and serve all of his gay friends," I said, "because then they start making out at the bar and all the straight people leave. It just won't work."

"Don't you think we can do both?"

"Not in Savannah. Maybe in New York, but not here."

"OK," he said, "but you handle it."

In the weeks to come I had to handle it. One night it got so outrageous with Jerry behind the bar, wheeling and dealing drinks, and he was spilling as much as he was pouring. I finally told him he had to leave, "and get out from behind the bar right now and go." He got mad and said, "Nobody likes a drunk bitch and I can out-bitch you, bitch." He was just as awful as he could be and lit into me. I had a glass of water in my hand and I poured it on his head. He always worked very hard to get his hair just right because he had a thin spot in the front that he wanted to cover. When I poured the water, he got livid and left.

We had several more episodes like this, and in the meantime, we were still having money problems.

One time a girl walked in for a job. Her name was Kathleen McNamara Smith, an Irish lass with bright beautiful red hair; a complexion as white as the driven snow; long painted fingernails; and an Irish smile. She also had three boys and two other jobs and she was trying to keep the boys in private schools, so she needed a third job. She and I hit it off right away as she wasn't a drinker and she just liked to work and make money to keep her family well. She eventually ended up as one of my best friends—she still is to this day.

Kathleen was drawn into the "Joe appeal" just like everyone else. There were times when she would give Joe a check to open the bar, and she didn't have the money for it, but we would float that check long enough to get us open, then the first money that came over the bar that night was always Kathleen's. Our bar manager made sure Kathleen's money got hidden first before anybody got a hold of it, and she'd hide it in the blender. One night though, someone ordered a blended drink, which no one ever did, and we all screamed, "DON'T MIX IT IN THE BLENDER."

In the meantime, Joe had to leave the realtor's carriage house because he said it just had too many memories for him. One day he called me to say that I didn't have to worry about his being homeless any more, as he had a home now. "Come and see my new place," he said. "and just wait until you see it because it's the nicest house in Savannah." His friend, "cousin" Buzz Harper, happened to own a place called the Hamilton-Turner House, a 10,000 square foot, second French empire Mansion on Lafayette Square. It was presently an eight-unit, two bedroom apartment building and he said he'd let Joe have one of the apartments if he'd get rid of the guy on the parlor floor who hadn't paid rent, and if he'd manage it for Buzz. It didn't take long for Joe to get rid of the man who wasn't paying, and Joe moved in. It was the last house Joe would live in.

Buzz was 6'3", and had been a juvenile judge from Jonesboro, Arkansas but now owned Harper's Antiques and Interiors on Royal Street in New Orleans. He was just an amazing person. He wore three-piece suits, had a cane and a watch fob, diamonds on all his fingers, and he rode in a chauffeured, white Rolls Royce. One night Buzz took a bunch of us to dinner at 45 South, a really hot place at the time, and he ordered champagne, wine, and the best food. I sat next to Joe, and on the other side of me was someone I had never met and knew nothing about. His name was Jim Williams, and he was very attractive, with dark piercing eyes that you really couldn't read at all. I talked with him briefly as he seemed a bit quiet, and he mentioned he was an antiques dealer. We had a great dinner then all went back to our Club where Joe and I played and sang a while. All of a sudden, Mr. Williams looked at his watch and said he had to go—that he wasn't even supposed to be in a place like this.

I later asked Joe who he was and what did he mean. Joe smiled and said, "Do you like him?"

"Well I don't know if I like him or not, I just met him, but it was strange he had to leave all of a sudden. What's up with him? Did he get a DUI? He looks too cosmopolitan for that."

Joe laughed and said, "There's a bit more to it than that. One night this guy gets a little bit ugly and Jim had to shoot him."

"Shoot him?! You don't mean he killed him, do you?"

"Yes, that's what happened and he's got a fourth trial coming up. Sonny Seiler is his attorney and John Berendt is directing the defense, and we're all going up to Augusta to support him; he'll get off this time."

"When did this happen?" I asked.

"I think it was 1982, several years ago."

"Did he intentionally kill him?"

"Well, I don't know, Nancy, I wasn't there. Did you like him?"

"Joe, he killed somebody!"

"He is one of life's most interesting individuals and that's all you need to know." Joe kind of smiled and took another drag from his cigarette.

Joe, of course, was talking about the case that was the centerpiece of the book, *Midnight in the Garden of Good and Evil.*

One day, Joe said he was at the end of his rope and he went to visit his friend in New Orleans for Mardi Gras. He left Kathleen and me to handle the Club. There was no money with which to open the bar—no money to buy liquor for the night, and we needed at least $250 to buy enough to get started. By nine or ten o'clock we would have more money and we'd be all right. We borrowed ice from Club One, the way we usually did, to open the night up, but we still needed the cash. We took all of the silver we could find, plus my silver and the silver that Joe had at the

Hamilton-Turner House, and took it to the pawnshop. We got all the money we could for it and we had enough to open the bar. The next day we bought the silver back. We did things like that all the time, just to keep going to the next day. Things got worse and worse and one night Joe told me he was throwing us into bankruptcy to protect us from our creditors. At that point we had to have three checking accounts: one for the bankruptcy court, one for payroll, and one for the business. Joe had tried going to every bank in Savannah to get a new account but no one would give him one. The judge said we had to have three or we would be in contempt of court so I took the money we had to St. Simons, and opened three checking accounts there. I thought that finally I would have some control over the money, but wrong again! Before the night was out, instead of the money going into the bank, it went into Joe's pocket and where it went from there, I don't know. I do know Joe seemed to be using a lot more drugs, staying out a lot more, and spending a lot more money.

Chapter 5

The Last Stand

There came a night where we had taken in several thousand dollars. It was three in the morning and we were having a hard time getting people to leave. We had a gig the next day, so I had to spend the night. I went to the house, showered, climbed into bed and went to sleep. I woke up and there was no noise. It was about five in the morning and Joe wasn't home. "Oh my God," I thought, "Joe has been killed. Somebody has knocked him over the head and taken the money." I got dressed, jumped in the car, and went back down to Sweet Georgia Browns. I opened the door and went to the bar and saw about two dozen people, most of whom I didn't know, and more white powder than I had ever seen in my life, all over the bar. The people were standing there, snorting cocaine through straws and rolled up money. Joe saw me and I gave him a look and walked up to him and said, "I don't believe you. You know how I feel about this stuff and my God, if you are going to do it, don't do it in a club that partially belongs to me."

Well, he was so high, he said, "Oh, Nancy, you're mad aren't you?" I walked around the corner and saw a very young guy—I don't think he was 17 years old, and he worked across the street as a bus boy at the Mexican restaurant. Several gay guys were egging him on and obviously this kid had no business in there to start with, much less with the crowd that was there. The way I felt about kids and drugs made me sick to my stomach and I turned and left. I sat in my car for a few minutes, trying to decide what to do, and I finally decided to call the police. I realized that I could get killed if I did that, but, I went to a pay phone and called the police and told them that my husband was still in the club, Sweet Georgia Browns and they were still in there partying way past closing time. The dispatcher suggested that maybe they were just cleaning up.

"Well, my husband is in there and he doesn't work there. Please go see about it!"

She said she'd send someone so I drove back to the Club and waited. The police went by as they do on patrol and nobody stopped.

I was so frustrated with the police, and I had to do something, so I went back to the pay phone and called again. This time I said, "I looked in the window and I saw people using cocaine in Sweet Georgia Browns."

"How do you know this ma'am?" she said. "Where are you located at this point?"

I yelled to just send someone and go and see about it. I hung up and got scared; I had actually reported the cocaine use and it was done now. I went back over there and sat outside the bar and in about ten minutes a patrol car came by, and a policeman got out and knocked on the door.

Joe came to the door and said, "Well, hello, John. How ya doing? And he shook his hand. "How's your mama 'n all," Joe continued. These are the words I could actually hear. "Oh yeah, we are just in here cleaning the place up, you know."

I couldn't hear everything, but the police officer never went into the club. I sat outside not believing what had just happened, then, here comes the entourage—a couple of dozen people, all happy and going across the street.

Joe saw my car and said, "Hey, Nancy, this party is going over to the Hyatt. Want to come with us?"

"No, Joe, I don't. Where are the receipts from tonight?"

"Oh, I've got them," said Joe. "Everything is just fine. You go on. We're just fine. You mad?"

He was so high he could hardly see. They all walked on over to the Hyatt and I was so angry, I drove to a hotel to spend the night. The next day I called a psychologist friend of Joe's and told her what was going on.

She said, "You know, Nancy, Joe is either the sweetest, most innocent man I have ever met in my life or he is the devil himself. I'm not real sure. I have tried to counsel him, and it's just like a beautiful piece of silk with a fatal flaw running right down the middle. He is either an angel sent from

God or the devil incarnate, and he's got me baffled. I'm not sure what he is or what to do with him."

From that day forward, I began to detach myself from Joe. He was getting in and out of more trouble, and he was up to about $25,000 in bad check charges. But more than anything, he was involved with drugs and I didn't want a club that even hinted of drugs in any form.

One night, the girls put the receipts in my purse because they knew that the phone and electric bills were due on Monday and if they weren't paid, there'd be no jobs. The fellow I was dating at the time (we'll call him Mike) and I started to leave, but one of Joe's cronies saw what was going on and told Joe.

Joe said, "Nancy, where are the receipts?"

I told him they were in my purse because I was going to pay bills.

"The hell you say," he said, and he went for my throat. He said later he was trying to get the purse off my shoulder, but he had his hands on my neck and he knocked me down. Mike pulled him off and held him, and Joe got this look of horror on his face. He had been so buzzed he didn't realize he had tried to choke me. I ran out the door and Mike came after me with my purse and we drove back to St. Simons and I said I'd never go back.

All of Joe's friends began calling me, asking me to forgive him and come back. Joe's ex-wife even called and said he hadn't been himself that night, that he'd never hurt me. She told me he'd been out of it because of the problems with the bar. I knew this wasn't like Joe, but I also knew if he did it once, he could do it again and I just wanted to be out of the picture.

I asked Joe to buy me out, and of course, he laughed.

"I would be glad to, but I can't."

I finally went to the people at City Market and asked them to close the bar, that I would let them in. There had just been too much going on and it was frightening, and Joe was like a monster that I didn't know how to stop. So they padlocked the bar and confiscated everything that was there, saying it was all theirs for back rent. I moved back to St. Simons vowing never to go to Savannah again.

Chapter 6

A Fully Fledged Bona Fide Diva at Age Two

For the first half of my life, I had basically always been cared for by a man. That's what women were expected to do at that time—marry well and be cared for. The first that cared for me was my controlling Granddaddy, Lee A. Brown. He controlled everything and always carried a gun in his belt, which no one doubted he would use (and he did several times) if he had to, but I loved him. He was strong, confident, my protector, and I went everywhere he went and I adored him and he adored me.

My Granddaddy, known by everyone as Papa Lee, was a steamboat captain. He would come around the bend on the Tennessee River in Meggs County, Tennessee and blow the whistle. My Grandmomma Myrtle, at age 14 or so would jump bareback on the horse and meet him. He was 22, and I guess they fell in love. The steamboat industry went under, so Granddaddy married Grandmomma, and they settled in Chattanooga, Tennessee. They opened a sandwich joint on Broad Street, and Granddaddy hired the steamboat's chef, to cook in the restaurant. With time he became known for his barbecue and they renamed the shop Browns BBQ—one of the first real pit barbecue restaurants in Chattanooga. Granddaddy would start biscuits at 4:00 am and not close until midnight. Grandmomma worked alongside him, and when my real mother was old enough, she waited tables.

By the age of 16, Grandmomma had two children, Leland A. Brown, Jr. and Betty Eloise Brown, my mother, and they bought a farm over the Tennessee-Georgia line. Everything that was cooked in the restaurant was raised on that farm. They ended up opening a second restaurant located at the foot of Lookout Mountain and began making money.

Mother, Betty Eloise Brown, born in 1922, ended up being the poor little rich girl. Due to the restaurants' success, the family had a lot of money, but mother's parents had little time for her. She was a beautiful Southern belle, and she loved music so she started singing and playing piano and saxophone in an all-girl band in high school. Mother's brother, Leland, also had a band, and Grandmomma would also sing upon occasion, so the family was very musical. Music was always there in one way or the other.

Eventually, my mother fell in love with a man, and Granddaddy said that if she married him and moved away that she was never to come home again. This man was a Yankee from New York, and they didn't like him (I understand that he wasn't very likable). You have to understand that this was the hard South—Yankees were frowned upon and still were considered the enemy. No Yankee was good enough for Granddaddy's little girl. I don't know much about this time in mother's life, but I think she was in her early 20s when she met and married the Yankee and went to New York. According to my Aunt Evelyn, Leland's wife, he was abusive and it wasn't long before mother knew she had to leave him. She saved money, a little at a time, and finally had enough to get away.

Aunt Evelyn said that the day mother left, she walked down the street, hiding along the way since her husband drove a city bus and might see her. She had on a sharp, winter white suit with brown and white spectator pumps, seamed stockings, an alligator bag, a red fox stole (the kind that included the heads, tails, and feet of the fox and draped over the shoulder), and hat which matched her auburn hair. She hid several times as she walked around back streets to get to Union Station. In her train case was one pair of shorts, a top, and her cosmetics—that's all. She entered Union Station, and I can just imagine the shock and awe this small town Tennessee girl experienced, entering the grandest place she'd ever seen, scared to death, but determined. I'm proud that she had the courage to go on.

She walked over to the teller, put her money under the cage, and said, "How far away from New York will that get me?"

The teller told her she had enough money to get her to the end of the line.

"Where's that?" she said.

"Miami, Florida."

"I'll take one ticket, one way."

She changed her name to Sandy Brown and got off the train in Miami and headed to the Fontainebleau Hotel, the finest of its kind in the day, and there was a sign that said, "Waitress Wanted." She went in and got the job. According to Aunt Evelyn, the very first day on the job she met my father, a very good-looking man who just kept staring at my mother. His name was Delmus Burl Long, but everyone knew him as Nick. He was a middleweight boxing champion, on his way to becoming champion of the world, of course. After about three months, he asked mother to marry him and she did, and never mind that she was already married. After about a year—when Granddaddy and Grandmomma calmed down from the calamities of mother going to New York—mom and dad found it safe to come back and visit everyone in Tennessee. She was proud to have this wonderful, handsome husband, but Aunt Evelyn asked mother when she had gotten the divorce from the first guy.

"I didn't," mother said.

Aunt Evelyn told her that she couldn't do that and mom responded, "Why the hell not? It's nobody's business."

Aunt Evelyn informed her that it was the government's business, and what she was doing was against the law, so mother gave in and Granddaddy obtained the divorce from mom's first husband, and she and Nick were remarried.

From what I gather, mother and daddy were passionately in love and they were both just so good-looking. I have only one picture of them together, and they look so young and in love in that picture, but in reality the marriage was awful. Every time they got into a big argument, they got divorced. In fact, they were married and divorced five times. The last time they got remarried it was a family joke that Granddaddy was getting them a new house and he'd just wallpaper the bedroom with the divorce decrees.

As I said, my Granddaddy was a very controlling person and he thought that if he controlled everything, then all would be better. One restaurant was close to the newspaper and was therefore called the *Daily*

News, and he set up the family members, mother, daddy, Uncle Leland and Aunt Evelyn, to run it. Back then, there was a lot of activity around the newspaper, so it was a great restaurant place and very successful. But, of course, it was the wrong move, as the relatives argued all the time. Dad wanted to go back to Miami to get out from under Granddaddy's control, and mother didn't want to, especially when she got pregnant with me at age 26.

I was born Nancy Lee Long on March 19, 1948, and almost from the first, my grandparents began raising me in their home. Papa Lee Brown and Myrtle were my "mother and father." My birth mother, Betty, would disappear for a while, but then would show up from time to time and live in an apartment behind my Granddaddy and Grandmomma's home. My grandparents always had to take care of her, but I always was their little girl.

Eventually, dad left the restaurant business and traveled back and forth between Chattanooga (to be with us) and Miami (to box and work). He'd finally had enough though, and said to mom, "I'm not living up here under the control of your father, so I'm going to Miami to stay, and if you love me you'll come too." She didn't want to go, so he left for good without her.

I have one video of my parents with me. I was in a Little Miss Miami pageant at about 18 months old, and I was walking, but not that well. I had on this little outfit that was silver and white that scratched me to death, a scepter, crown, and I was in a Gladiola float with my trophy, because I had won. The film shows my dad pulling the float with his Harley, and mother is beside the float with a rolled up newspaper, which she slapped up against her hand meaning I needed to throw kisses, so I threw kisses. That's the last and only picture I have of them together with me because shortly after that they divorced for the fifth and last time and dad left.

I looked like Shirley Temple, I really did, and at a young age I had a knack for show. I was a cute little girl and everyone was crazy about me; hence, I was a fully fledged, bona fide diva at the age of two. I learned early on that I could wrap people around my little finger (spoiled would be the word for it). Granddaddy and Grandmomma took me everywhere, and I became their second chance at having a daughter that might turn out well. My mother was working in the restaurant but she was distant and as time went by, it was evident that she had some mental issues, so

Nana took care of me. Nana was a wonderful black lady who was there with me consistently and I loved her.

As a child, I wondered about my daddy, why he never came to see me or never called, and I wasn't allowed to talk about him or ask questions. If I did, everybody'd get real quiet, so Aunt Evelyn told me not to ask about him. It became a family secret and I was very confused as to what was going on. Years later, I found out that my Granddaddy had every intention of killing my real daddy when he told me the story of why he didn't come around. It seems that one day when Nana was taking care of me she called my daddy and said, "Mr. Nick if you want to see Nancy Lee, ride your motorcycle down here and come in the side porch; don't come to the doors; come through the window and you can see her. I've got her here and I'm alone."

Daddy came to the house and he said he put one foot through the window and there was a mirror in the hallway where he could see my Granddaddy sitting in a chair with a big gun. Daddy told me, "I knew he was going to shoot me, so I just pulled my foot right back out as easy as could be and left. I spent a year driving around everywhere, doing whatever—just kind of lost." It was clear I was under Granddaddy's thumb, and my daddy better not come near me.

I had a lot of good women in my life that I considered my mothers. Besides my Grandmomma and mother, I had Aunt Evelyn who was the one who was really able to relate to me as a mother. She was the right age, whereas Grandmomma was older and old fashioned. Aunt Evelyn provided a realistic, modern eye to dressing me and teaching me in relation to the times.

I also had all the waitresses at Granddaddy's restaurants: Irene, Vivian, Patsy, Frankie, and Laverne, and they probably went to work for Granddaddy at age 14 or so, coming from bad homes, and they worked for him for 40 years or more. Granddaddy actually took care of them. On the side of the mountain, about a mile up, there was a stone tourist home. It was run down and probably one of those places that sell by the hour—if you know what I mean. One day, Granddaddy went up and talked to the owner and said, "I can keep this motel open and full 365 days of the year, because I'll put my waitresses in here to live, and I'll send all the tourists that come through my restaurant to y'all, but I want you to clean it up, make it a nice place and we'll have a deal." The guy said OK and he fixed it up and the girls lived there. Granddaddy bought the girls a truck, and Irene, our main hostess, drove them where they needed to go. They started to call Granddaddy "Papa Lee" because he was like their papa, and soon everybody called him "Papa Lee." It was great what he did for the girls, but he did control them. They did have the choice to leave, but they stayed.

I have a strong memory from kindergarten, believe it or not, which caused great confusion for me in my early years. It was my first day of kindergarten at Chattanooga Bible School. Aunt Evelyn and mother took me to sign-in at school, and they began arguing about my name. Mother put down Nancy Lee Renshaw.

"Her name is not Renshaw," said Aunt Evelyn.

"That's who she's going to be," mother insisted. Mother was dating a man named Buster Renshaw.

"No, Betty, you can't put that down. Her last name is Long."

"Well I'm not putting that down there," mother retorted. "Buster would be mad."

"Her daddy's name is Long," continued Aunt Evelyn, "and whether you like it or not, she's a Long. She's not been adopted by anybody, so it's Long."

"How about Brown?"

"You can't put that down either," answered Aunt Evelyn.

Teachers were looking, other people were looking, and I was embarrassed. No one else was arguing about what their name was; what was my name? I was really confused.

They finally decided on Nancy Lee Long.

Chapter 7

This Won't Get me Down

I was assaulted at the age of seven by my mother's fiancé, Buster, who was a fireman and a drunk, and he was trouble. One day, mother and Buster came to the restaurant and mother asked me to get in the car for a ride with her and Buster. She was driving, and Buster scooted over next to me. She was trying to tell me that she was going to marry him but he reached over and kissed me on the mouth with that drunk's alcohol breath and that ugly, awful tongue. Mother told him to stop, but he just kept grabbing me all over, and I was twisting and crying and she finally pulled over so I could get out. I felt awful. I ran back and into the bathroom of the restaurant, locked the door and sat there. I actually washed my mouth out with that white, awful hand soap and I'm surprised I didn't throw up. I just waited there until I knew they were gone. To this day, if someone tries to kiss me and I smell alcohol on their breath, it's like having a dart go through me.

Even at that young age, I knew that Buster would have molested me if he ever caught me alone, so I made sure I was never alone with him. In fact, I avoided any contact with him, but every once in a while, an incident would occur. I remember one time I was in the restaurant. Granddaddy would let me take the customers' money and lay it in the cash register, and I had a little stool so I could reach it. Well, Buster and mom had three kids and one day one of the boys was on my stool and I had to take a customer's money. I pushed him to get up on the stool and with that, Buster hauled off and hit me, sending me across the room. I had a big welt on my cheek, but if my Granddaddy had seen it or found out, he would have killed Buster, and it would've been my fault, and I'd be in trouble with momma, so I went back to the bathroom (again) to hide out until the welt was gone. I never told Granddaddy. I slipped upstairs and stayed in my room. If he had asked what happened to my face, that would've been it for Buster. He was evil, but since I loved my mother in a strange way, I wouldn't risk having her angry with me. I learned to hide my feelings and sweep things under the rug.

Mother and Buster had three other children, Sam, Webb, and Ricky. Ricky didn't grow—he had so many things wrong with him—and basically was a baby all his short life. In those days we said that he was retarded, and he went to a school for handicapped children. Buster used to put little Ricky in a wagon and go down the street and cry and beg for money to "buy his medicine," but he was only getting his alcohol money. Grandmomma saw him doing this one time and put a stop to it. Ricky lived to be only nine and then he died.

How he died is a tragic story. The drunk, Buster, rolled over on him and smothered him. Of course he said it was unintentional, but I've always had my doubts. Years later, when I married my second husband, Charles, who was a doctor, I brought him to our house for the first time. He kept saying he'd been there before, but couldn't put his finger on it. We went to the garage apartment where Buster and mom lived and it suddenly hit Charles—he was the coroner that was called in to examine Ricky's body. Charles said, "When I did the autopsy on the boy there was absolutely no brain matter there. When police asked me about prosecuting Buster, I said, 'No, it was a blessing the boy was gone.'" Those were different times then.

As a child I never really knew my other two stepbrothers, Sam and Webb, which was a shame because they were both great guys. They lived in the garage apartment, and I was in the big house. Buster would say terrible things to them about me—how I was a little spoiled rich girl and how I thought I was better than everyone else. I was never able to establish any kind of relationship with them in my younger years; however, years later, I did become close to them. They seemed to get mixed up with bad women and had a rough go of it, but Sam later moved back to Chattanooga to open a repair shop, and I saw them occasionally. They both died early, but I loved them.

Buster continued to be a problem. One time, after Granddaddy had his stroke and was mostly bedridden, Buster came over and wanted to borrow the car. Granddaddy said no and Buster started to hit him and Grandmomma called the police. After the incident with Granddaddy, I started fighting back. I could go out my bedroom window on the roof and there I stacked up rocks, and as Buster walked by, I threw them at him. I carried my baton with me and if he got anywhere close to me, I knocked the heck out of him. I broke his glasses and made his head bleed and he'd go home to mother, mad and complaining, but she did nothing and he couldn't get to me. I locked the door, and he'd holler about it, but I did everything I could to stay out of his clutches.

I was scared, and I didn't understand why my mother wouldn't do anything and I came to resent her for not helping me. She was mentally ill, but I was young and didn't understand what that meant, and as time went on, she became more and more distant. Aunt Evelyn explained that she believed all of the marriages and divorces threw her in a deep depression from which she never really recovered. She said that one time, mom stayed in her bedroom for two months and hardly came out, and she never quite got herself back to where she should be. Buster contributed to the problem, too. He'd insist they come to the restaurant all the time to get free food, and I think mother thought that he married her for a free ride. By then her "cheese had slid off her cracker," as we say here—meaning she was a little daft. Our Uncle, who was a psychiatrist, diagnosed mom as mentally ill, saying she needed to go into a place for help, but my Granddaddy wouldn't hear of it, so she languished. She didn't speak to me much; she was sweet but just disconnected, and that's hard to understand when you are young. Was there something wrong with me? She was raising my half brothers, why didn't she want to raise me? Don't get me wrong, I was being raised by my Grandparents and they took great care of me and I loved them, but why wasn't my mother doing it? All Grandmomma would say to me is, "Remember to just respect your mother. She's just not right, but you should respect her." Mother and her family lived in the garage apartment on the farm property, but her distance, and the situation, drove a wedge between us and the whole thing was just sad.

Mother let life beat her, and so many women out there let life beat them. But I learned, and the lessons made me resilient. I'm not about to let the downs keep me down—I think of my mother when I want to give up, and I fight against those feelings. I also often look back and think what would've happened to me if she had raised me after all? It probably wouldn't have been good, so thank heavens, God was looking after me.

I'm happy to say that later in life when I married Charles, the doctor, he checked mother out, gave her some medicines and she got better, so we were able to salvage a relationship. But, in my early years, seeing my mother beaten down made me want to rise up, fight, and use whatever means I had to survive. Unlike my mother, nothing was going to beat me down.

I do have a couple of memories that stand out from my childhood. We lived on top of the restaurant when I was younger (before we moved to the farm) and it had one big room that was round like a tower. Granddaddy and Grandmomma slept on one side and I slept on the other. One Christmas, I woke up in the night and I saw the presents that Santa had left that weren't wrapped. I saw a doll with a pink trunk full of clothes (my favorite color) and it was the best thing in the world. I sat there astonished for a while, and then crawled back in bed and acted surprised in the morning. I felt that was a special moment.

I could walk out on the tower which had a balcony all around it where you could walk. There was a hot pink neon sign, with a little black boy chasing a pig to advertise the BBQ. Every time the black boy's hatchet would come down to get the little pig's tail, the tail would go in and he would go "He-he-he." When his hatchet would come back up, all the corkscrews on his head would come out, and so would the pig's tail. I loved that sign and I wished I knew what happened to it. My favorite color is hot pink—from that sign.

I always loved clothes. Grandmomma did too and she made my clothes until I was in the 5th grade. She was so artistic; she dyed her own wools, hooked rugs, and could do just about anything with a sewing machine. My fancy dresses, though, we would buy. I remember one favorite outfit that we bought for a junior high banquet. It was made of a purple fabric that changed from purple to pink as it moved, it had a rhinestone broach and drop waist with a ruffled bottom and long sleeves. I kept that outfit way past the time I was able to wear it. I wish I knew what happened to that dress.

I had a Shetland pony named Cocoa and I rode him all the time on the farm. I came to love horses and down the road was a stable that trained

Tennessee walking horses. I loved those horses, and they were really my only hobby early on. I got to ride them when I was older and when you ride a Walker, it's like riding a Cadillac—they flip their feet out so you just roll.

Chapter 8

Opera and Twirling

For a while, it looked as if I might become an opera singer.

Since the house was sad, I became very active in school. I ran track and played basketball. I was smart, popular, and I worked at being perfect. My Grandmomma had said that if I was going to do something I should try to do it better than anybody else, and I took that to heart and became competitive and ambitious. I won trophies and medals—more than you could count.

Maria Ransom, who trained at Julliard, was our music teacher at Chattanooga Valley High School. I was in the chorus and she said that I had a really nice voice, so she began working with me to train me as an opera singer. I entered some competitions and eventually received several awards. It was wonderful. I liked it but I would go upstairs to run scales and try to sing arias, and the dog would howl downstairs and Grandmomma would be laughing. "I know you are getting better," she'd say, and as my pronunciation of words changed, Granddaddy would accuse me of sounding like a damn Yankee. I guess I was awful sounding if it would make the dog howl and Granddaddy call me a damn Yankee; but I continued to work hard. Ms. Ransom would tell me to hold the mirror in front of my face and if it fogged up, I was letting out too much air. She also said, "I want you to pretend you've got a dime in between your hienie cheeks and you've got to hold it through the whole song—hold that dime between your cheeks." Later, she'd be pretending to pick up something from the ground and I'd say, "What are you doing?" "I'm getting rich picking up all these dimes off the floor," she'd say.

Ms. Ransom was a good teacher and she did a lot for my self esteem. She cast me in all the plays at school. I played the lead in *Madame Butterfly* and in *Bye Bye Birdie* and I got involved in acting on the stage and in theater. She even got me an appointment for an interview for a scholarship to Julliard, but I didn't go to the appointment. I loved singing opera a whole lot, but I knew it wasn't for me because I loved twirling more. Twirling came easy, and all I had to do was just smile, keep my mouth shut and twirl that baton.

I began taking twirling lessons from Imogene Collins and her sister Diane, and they taught me all they knew. I became an award winning twirler, but I had exceeded beyond their capabilities and needed a more experienced teacher. Soon, I began lessons with Betty Ann Epperson who was the solo twirler for the University of Georgia. I competed in everything I could, and won many contests including Ms. Majorette of the Southern States.

Chattanooga had a semi-pro football team called the Chattanooga Cherokees and because I had learned to twirl fire batons—two at a time— and my reputation as a great twirler was growing, they asked me to be their mascot and star twirler at all the games. I was in high school and I was being paid to twirl for a semi-pro ball team. I dressed like an Indian with long pigtails and twirled two fire batons. I concentrated on my twirling because I thought I had a chance to get a scholarship to the University of Georgia or the University of Tennessee for twirling. However, being paid to twirl for this team almost got me in trouble: You couldn't be a professional and get a scholarship, so they started paying me by starting a scholarship fund in my name, and I eventually received my college scholarship to the University of Tennessee for twirling.

I would've never gotten there if not for Betty Ann, Imogene and Diane.

While still in high school, I won Miss Congeniality in the Junior Miss Hamilton County contest. I was on the Miller Brothers teen board and I modeled for them. I marched in all the parades and if there was a pageant, then I'd be in it. There were border wars between schools in Tennessee and Georgia, and I was selected by schools on both sides to be in their pageants, and in every one, I was selected Miss Congeniality—always.

Chapter 9
My Real Daddy Shows Up

When I was 16, two things happened: my Granddaddy died, and I heard from my real daddy.

Granddaddy's stroke finally took him and I was devastated. Then, two months later, I was in class and someone came and asked me to go to the principal's office. I couldn't imagine what I had done. My Granddaddy's death had made me a bit fragile and I thought the worst. Once at the principal's office our secretary was crying, and she sent me to "the back room" which meant you were in deep trouble.

"Nancy, you have a phone call," said the Principal.

I picked up the receiver, and a voice said, "Hello, honey, is this Nancy Lee? This is your daddy."

Now growing up, I made up stories about my dad. When people asked me where he was, I said he was dead because no one would tell me anything about him or where he was. Aunt Evelyn would say, "Don't bring him up around anyone; it'll just make them mad," so I said the only thing that would make them stop asking questions: he was dead. I said it so much that I really believed it myself. Now here he was; I was horrified, but also shocked and I didn't know what to say. I cried.

"I want to explain things to you," he said. "I'm married to a nice, special person and her name is Marian and we live in Ft. Myers, Florida, but I would like to drive up to Chattanooga to meet you. Is that OK?"

I didn't know what to think, but I said yes.

"I know you are 16, do you have a car? If not, can someone bring you and meet us?"

I said that I had a boyfriend, Sonny, and he could bring me.

"Can you do that in a week? Honey, I love you, I didn't desert you. It wasn't my choice, and I want to explain things."

I hardly said anything back because I didn't know what to say.

"Promise you'll come," he said, and I promised.

"How will I know you?" I asked.

"Oh, honey, don't worry, I'll know you. Just park on Broad St. in downtown Chattanooga, close to Mr. Silverman's bike shop."

"I'll be in a '57 red and white Chevy," I said.

Sonny took me and I met my daddy for the first time since I was a baby. I could look at him and tell he was my dad right away. We just looked at each other for what seemed like a long time. I didn't say much but I started to cry. Sonny put his hand over the front seat to hold my hand to reassure me that I would be OK. We sat in the car and we talked for a long time and dad told me about coming to see me when Nana had called him, and seeing my Granddaddy with a gun. That was the first time I had heard that story.

He said, "I don't want to go into everything, but I have books and books on you because Mr. Silverman, the owner of the bike shop, sent me clippings and things about your life, and he helped me keep up with you. Every time your picture was in the paper, I got it."

I had so many emotions that day and I couldn't understand why my family lied to me all this time about him. Why didn't dad go to court and fight to see me? Why had he not called me in 16 years? It was a lot to take in.

After a while, daddy sent me a ticket to come to Ft. Myers to stay a week. I was scared to tell my Grandmomma but I really wanted to go, so I finally got the nerve to tell her and she cried and cried. She called Aunt Evelyn who came down from Kingston, Tennessee and started telling me stories about my daddy—how he hit my mother, shot a gun at Uncle Leland, and other horrible tales. But, she was sure to tell me how good-looking he was. I felt guilty that I was hurting my Grandmomma, but I got on the plane and went to Ft. Myers.

There I met all my other relatives—daddy's wife and his sister, and a girl and boy from the wife's first marriage, as well as a boy who was daddy's son. It was great to meet everyone.

We sat up all night and talked, and it was then he showed me the picture of mother and him. He also showed me a picture of mother that was hidden in his wallet. It was of her in the white suit that she wore to "escape" in New York. He looked at the picture and said, "That is the most gorgeous woman I have ever seen—before her or after! To this day, I have not seen a woman who comes close."

I felt so odd seeing my dad, and it was different being with him than with my grandparents. Obviously he didn't have as much going for him as they did, and he had had a heart attack so he wasn't boxing or working any more. His house was very nice, but it just wasn't like my home.

"I was three matches away from being Southern States champion," he said. "I was ready to fight and some men came into the dressing room and they said I was to go down in the third round. 'The hell you say,' I said. They laid a pack of money on the table and explained that if I went down in the third round the money was mine, and if I didn't, I'd be dead. Needless to say, I went down."

He explained that the fights were controlled by the Mafia, and he had become disillusioned and went on to do something else. He said he'd become a shrimper and he had two boats and sailed out of Ft. Meyers. He told me stories of being out in storms where he could've drowned, of things he'd seen in the ocean, of horrible things; but he was successful as a shrimper and he accepted his work. He complained about the government making him change his nets; complained how the government took all his money.

Then, daddy asked me that when it was time to go to college would I come down to Florida, that if I came and lived with him he'd get me any car I wanted. I explained that I expected a scholarship to the University of Tennessee at Chattanooga, that my friends were going there, and I would get to be the featured twirler. He accepted it, but I could tell he was hurt and mad. "They had you all this time," he said. "I just want to know you."

During the visit, I had a hard time calling him dad, the feeling just wasn't there. It was a good visit and I met and liked everyone, but I had a hard time calling him dad—I did use the word, but my heart just wasn't in it.

I didn't see him much after that. However, when I was married the first time, we went down to see him and attended a Miami Dolphins game together. Later, when I married Charles, the doctor, daddy's wife had cancer and the doctors there had done everything they could. Daddy asked Charles to get her some medicines that were not approved by the FDA yet. Charles said he couldn't, that it was against the law, but dad might have some luck getting the drugs in Mexico. Daddy got mad and dropped out of my life. I'd call him, but he was always so angry at Charles, it was never a good conversation. I called and called and left messages and after a couple of years, I quit calling. I didn't even know that he died until five years after it happened. I had called to say hi and the youngest son called back to say he had died.

"Your dad's been dead five years," he said with anger.

"Why didn't you tell me?" I said.

"We thought that since we hadn't heard much from you through the years, you weren't interested. We didn't think you cared a flip about any of us." All I could say was that I was sorry and I hung up.

I just thought it was all so sad; it hurt my feelings and I felt guilty for not keeping in touch more, but I did wonder why dad never got in touch with me earlier. I know he was afraid of Granddaddy and all, but he could've written.

Anyway, after the trip to Florida, I returned to Tennessee. I had no idea what I wanted to be yet, but I was twirling, I was popular, and I was having fun. I was also in love.

Chapter 10

The Love of My Life

The real first love of my life was Sonny Day.

Sonny was in high school with me and he was captain and quarterback of the football team; so handsome, smart, and of course, he had been the one that took me to see my daddy for the first time. We dated for several years, and in my junior year we broke up. He went off on vacation with his mom and dad and when he got back, we were going to go on a date. There was a picture on the visor of a girl that he met on the trip. I asked him about it and he said it wasn't anything—just a girl, well I flipped out and I broke up with him. We argued for a few weeks, but it was done.

I regret that because looking back, I believe he was *the* love of my life. I think he and I would have been good together. We both enjoyed the same things, and worked so well together, and the experience with my dad gave our relationship special meaning. I'm sorry it ended. I often wonder how my life might have been different had I stayed in the relationship, but with all that had gone on in my life thus far, I think I just didn't trust anyone or anything, and Sonny caught the brunt of it all.

Years later, both Grandmomma and mother were living with me and at her request, I put Grandmomma in a nursing home that happened to be near Sonny. I would go back to visit and spend every other weekend with her, and one time I called Sonny's best friend, who I dated after Sonny, and asked about him. He suggested the three of us get together so the three of us went out. Sonny was married at that time, and evidently happy and that was that.

When his dad died, I went by his mother's house to talk. She wasn't home so I left a note on the car. Sonny called me shortly thereafter and said that his mom had died, as well, and he was divorced. We chatted some, but we were never able to get back together—the timing just wasn't right.

After Sonny, I started dating Sonny's best friend. I liked him but I was still in love with Sonny. He hung in, waiting until I got over Sonny, but I never did. He later said that I was the love of his life, and I did love him back in a way; he was so kind and caring, but I guess I wasn't able to get over Sonny, my first real love, very easily. I stopped seeing him.

Through the years I attended and was baptized in the Church of Christ. The director of the choir, we'll call him Rocky, liked me and we started dating. I was a senior in high school and he was a sophomore at the University of Tennessee at Chattanooga and quite industrious. He was talented—played timpani for the Chattanooga Symphony (I met him when I sang for the Chattanooga Opera Guild), played guitar, and he could sing. He played the drums for *Bye Bye Birdie* when I starred in that show. My Grandmomma really liked him—thought he was perfect—and that made him not perfect for me (you know how that goes). He had a band that had a bass, a banjo and two guitar players, and they'd joke about how there was only four of them but the "fifth" was in the car. They played folk music like Peter, Paul and Mary and when I was a senior, Rocky asked me to sing with him some. Besides singing in church, it was my first real experience with this kind of professional singing.

I loved singing in the band, and we did well until I started college at the University of Tennessee at Chattanooga. Rocky and I started having trouble, not getting along, and he was very jealous. He also did not question the religion of the Church of Christ like I did. I didn't like the fact that no musical instruments were allowed at the services. We had a special funeral chorus and one that would sing at weddings, but they performed a cappella—no instruments, just voices. Also, you could not be divorced and get remarried in the church unless there was proven adultery by one party. I began attending the First Presbyterian Church in Chattanooga which I liked better. A fine gentleman was the choir director and I really admired him, as I did the minister. I really felt something in that church and wanted to join. Rocky couldn't believe I would leave "the one true church—the only one whose members were going to heaven." We broke up, I joined the Presbyterian church, and I played, twirled and did my college thing.

Chapter 11

The Real World

I was popular, fun, and had lots of friends—the whole nine yards, and I even pledged Pi Beta Phi. Twirling was my first love, and though I wasn't necessarily boy crazy, I dated a fair amount.

One day at a game in Knoxville, Tennessee a guy came down where the band was waiting to play, and he gave me a note that said a certain gentleman would like me and my family to be his guests at his restaurant in Knoxville. I didn't know who he was and wondered why he asked me to be his guest, so I called one of my friends. She knew who he was. She said he had been a former professional football star and now he owned a very hot "Go Go" club in Chattanooga, and lived on Missionary Ridge, a ritzy section of Chattanooga. I decided to go and went with Uncle Leland and Aunt Evelyn as it felt safer to have them along. The man had on a white suit, I remember, and looked about 15 years older than me. He said he had watched me on the football field and thought I was a good twirler. Ha!

Well, this guy started sweet talking me and saying things like, "If you have a need to go back to Chattanooga, I'm up here all the time. I can take you back in my private plane." Aunt Evelyn had looked into his background and discovered he had "girls in cages" at the Go Go Club and that his background was rather colorful, so she had her suspicions and told me to be careful. After the date was over, I forgot all about it until one day when I was in Rossville, Georgia getting in my car, a Cadillac pulled over and it was him. "Why don't we go out for a Coke or something," he said. I went and he said he was having a party and he wanted me to come. "Wherever you are I'll have the helicopter come pick you up," he said. He wasn't that handsome and I was a bit afraid of him, but I was young and flattered, so I went by myself to the party.

The party was at his house on Missionary Ridge, and when I walked in, I was astonished. The place had beautiful views, and the whole house was built around a pool in the shape of a Playboy bunny head. The ears, which were filled with water, went off into the bedrooms, and in one bedroom there was a mirror over the bed, a shower with all kinds of different nozzles, big enough for six people, and a Jacuzzi which was the tip of the bunny ear. One whole wall in the living room housed a saltwater fish tank that went to the ceiling, (which, by the way, looked like a double cathedral ceiling about 25 or 30 feet high); a huge polar bear leaned over the pool; there was a big, long bar; and animal heads were mounted all over the place. There was also a helicopter pad on the roof. I was about 19 and so naïve; I had never seen anything like it in my life except in James Bond movies, and you can see where this is heading.

He had been a gentleman so far, but said he had to do something but he'd be right back. His security guard walked up to me and said, "Little lady, you are in way over your head. I'm through in an hour and I'll take you home before you get into something you don't know how to get out of." I took his advice and let him follow me home. He ended up being my first husband, Chuck Bonner, a former police officer who was now a private detective and guard for this famous gentleman. He started calling, but the gentleman was also after me so Chuck had to break his relationship with him so he could date me. It was nice of him to "save me." Can you imagine what might have happened if Chuck hadn't come along that night?

We started dating and all of a sudden it was like I stepped into a world of intrigue, meeting bad guys and people I thought only existed in the movies. When Chuck had been with the police department he had an altercation (that I knew nothing about) in Chattanooga with a Mafia man whom we'll call Sal. Sal had been parking his wreckers on the sidewalk where old people needed to walk and get by, and they were forced into the street. The police had on occasion asked him to remove his cars and he refused, so they sent Chuck to deal with him. Chuck dealt with it all right—he beat the devil out of him and nearly killed him. Sal filed charges and Chuck went to jail for a time. The trial was occurring just as I started dating him and it was in all the papers, a real scandal, and it scared me. Chuck told me all was going to be fine but it was something he had to go through. I went to one of the hearings, and to hear Sal tell it, he nearly died and it's kind of embarrassing, but all I could think of was, "that's a lot of power," and it scared me. Chuck was acquitted, and we went to the Hyatt in Atlanta where he asked me to marry him. He didn't buy a ring as he had gone to Grandmomma for permission to marry me, and Grandmomma had given him a ring she said she'd been saving for just such an occasion. I got the ring and I said yes.

He was the first man I gave myself to. Rocky and I almost "did the deed," but we didn't go through with it because it hurt too much. Chuck was my first.

It was 1968 and we were preparing to be married in the Church of Christ but they found out a week before the wedding that he had been married before, so they wouldn't allow it. We moved the wedding to my Grandmomma's house and all of Chuck's police friends took over getting guests to the house, and we were married. Grandmomma gave us land on the farm with a garage apartment, as it was part of my inheritance from Granddaddy, and we decided to build our dream house onto the garage. It had a beautiful view of Lookout Mountain and I was putting everything I ever wanted into that place. One whole wall was made out of mountain stone. The great room we added was larger than our current apartment, and it had exposed wood beams which they had floated down the river from the Tennessee Mountains. The whole thing looked like a hunting lodge—just beautiful and I was living there with Chuck. But then, we started having trouble.

Chuck went to work for a guy who had a club called the Play Late Club. It was a big club and Chuck was the bouncer. The owner's wife liked me and on some nights she'd call and ask me to come keep her company at the Club and I'd go. Chuck became very jealous of any attention I received. He started hitting me, sometimes throwing me against the wall. One day I'd had it and I went to my Grandmomma's to stay because I now had a child, Charles Wesley Bonner, Jr. who was born July 12, 1969. He was the cutest and most precious little boy that ever existed, and I needed to protect him. If Chuck came around and started being ugly, Grandmomma would call the police, and I felt safe at her home. I was married to Chuck for two years before I realized I needed to leave. I sued for divorce and had trouble at first getting him to sign the papers, but then he got a new girlfriend so the papers were signed without incident. (He even brought her to the signing!) But my mountain house was left unfinished; it was all I ever wanted, but I had to give it up.

Needless to say, I went into a depression thinking that I ruined my life. Aunt Evelyn came down and said, "I'm not going to let what happened to your mother happen to you. You need to realize this is not the end of your life, and you need to go somewhere where people really have problems." She picked me up and made me go with her. We ate lunch and then she took me by the Tri County Hospital in Ft. Oglethorpe, Georgia to the Walker Catoosa Day Medical Center. "Now, go in there and apply for a job," she said. I had never been in a hospital except to have Wes and I just kept thinking, 'What am I going to do?'

They had cafeteria work, which I knew I didn't want to do, but one post caught my eye—a job as a floor secretary. I thought I could do that, whatever that was, so I applied and got the job. It was in pediatrics, which helped me a lot because it was breaking my heart to be away from Wesley. My supervisor was Linda Cleghorn. I was about 21 and I didn't know what in the world I was doing but Linda taught me how to do the duties and run the floor. This was back when nurses had to wear white dresses, white shoes, big caps, and white hose; there were no computers; and I took orders from charts and made sure they happened. If someone wanted something, I got it; I put in requisitions; I posted them when they came back; I answered phones and kept charts—all by hand. It was a busy job and I liked it as the girls were great and it got me out of my depression. Aunt Evelyn was really smart because I saw children die and in terrible shape, and it put my problems into perspective. It also gave me my confidence back, and gave me a way to support my son and I.

At this time, I also went to Disney World for the first time. It was like I had gone to heaven.

When I am depressed or down about something, I do one of three things: I fold in my "tent", cry, pray and try to get through it; I work hard and long hours to get my mind off my problems; or I go to Disney World (as a matter of fact, after we closed Sweet Georgia Browns, I found a way to go see The Mouse again).

During the time after my divorce, my nurse friend, Bobbie, who also had a child about Wes' age, asked if I wanted to go to Disney World with her. I said yes, and we got in my little Opal GT, put the kids on pillows in the back, and took off. We didn't have much money so we stayed in a hotel in Kissimmee which was a ways from the park, and got in line early. The only part of the park open at that time was The Magic Kingdom, and as we waited at the gate for the park to open, we stood at the top of the monorail station and looked over Main Street. I have a picture of little three year old Wes at that exact spot. I call it, "A child's first look at Disney." He was mesmerized and so was I.

It was magical and I learned that it was impossible to be sad at this wonderful Park—everyone walks, talks, and breathes magic. When the doors open, Tinkerbelle flies to the castle, the parade comes down the street, people are kind, the world is happy, and you are swept into a different world. It's hard for people to be ugly at Disney World. I find peace there, and believe it or not, I pray there. It's my happy place and all of my friends know that if I am upset, I'll be at Disney World. All my boyfriends have been three or four times over our courtship time and when my friends first meet them they ask, "Have you been to Disney World yet?" I have taken my boys many times; I've taken friends who couldn't necessarily afford to go; I've taken my employees; I've treated other people's children to a trip or two; and I just love it. In fact, I'm hoping to get one more trip there before all is said and done.

Chapter 12

The Great Dr. Hillis

I heard a huge crash down the hallway and here comes a stainless steel bedpan a-flying, clicking and clacking and making a racket. Someone had thrown it, and with that I hear in an angry voice, "Do you all not know what input and output is? I want everybody here on the double so I can train them what this means." All the nurses came running down there and I was scared, so I went to the restroom and hid. "Why isn't it posted?" he screamed. "Why isn't it on this chart? What good will it do me if it's just in your head. It's very important to the life of this patient." He was mad, and I tried to stay out of his way.

That was my first introduction to Dr. Charles Hillis, my second husband. While it took a while before we actually started dating, I had met my future.

Dr. Hillis had a practice in LaFayette, Georgia with two other physicians. One of them was cute, cute, cute, and he began paying lots of attention to me. He had been a witness to the bedpan incident and one day he came in and said, "You've got to excuse Dr. Hillis. He gets a little upset when you don't follow his orders. We'll talk soon." I figured this doctor was not married because where his wedding band would be there was a University of Georgia ring. I asked Linda if he was married, and she said she didn't know but I should ask another nurse who evidently had been dating him. She told me that he was supposed to be getting a divorce and that he and his wife didn't live together. Ha!

This doctor, whom we'll call Rudolph, was in his early 30s and he began taking a stronger interest in me. "You are so beautiful," he said. "Are you married? How about we go to dinner?" Well, I went and we started dating.

He had me drive to LaFayette at night when he was on call and we'd sit and talk, then I'd go back home. He took me to Augusta two or three times for medical meetings. He wanted me to meet his three children but said, "I don't want to upset them, so come to the restaurant and I'll come by your table and you can meet them." So I went to the restaurant and sure enough, he came by and I got to meet his two sons and his daughter and they were cute kids. He told me they liked me, and that he loved me. We went everywhere in public and I thought all was up to par. He had an apartment in East Ridge in Chattanooga and he gave me a key, but I noticed that there weren't many clothes there and he "explained" that it was because he was in the process of moving stuff. He went to church with me, and he seemed very spiritual. He met my Grandmomma and Wes, brought his brother over to see my unfinished home to tell me what I could do to sell it, and more; it all seemed so real.

In the meantime, at work I was noticed by a supervisor and he said he needed a director for a new area called Traffic Control. It was a new concept for this 368-bed hospital. Everything that moved in the hospital was moved by this department—the garbage, the trays, the mail, the charts. We had to have a plan for the movement of everything except blood—that was the only thing we didn't move. This new method could keep skilled nursing on the floor where they were needed, so it was a good move. We had carts go to nursing stations every hour and they made rounds and took all the requests, notes, and reports. We did all the Xeroxing, handled calls, did stats, did the paging—we did everything. If they had an emergency, I'd call for the machine named Big Mac. I was so busy, but I loved it.

One part of the job was taking the doctors' mail to their boxes in the doctors' lounge. One day, I'm doing that job and I overheard the doctors talking about a party, and one of the doctors there was Rudolph, the guy I was seeing. One person was saying something about Rudolph's wife and the party. I waited until they finished talking then I walked where Rudolph could see me and just looked at him. He knew I had overheard them. "He was talking about something else," he said.

"I can't believe you lied to me," I snapped. I felt like a creep. We had gone everywhere together and I don't know how he got away with it. I found out he did live with his wife in LaFayette, way back a long drive and I went there and found it. It was a big house with a pool, and it had his last name on the mailbox. I was tempted to knock on the door and tell her what a creep he was, but I felt so bad for us both, I couldn't do it. That was my first (and last) experience with dating a married man and I felt like an idiot. He was married and I don't think he had any prospect of getting divorced and I had wasted two years of my life. I felt so humiliated. I was also brokenhearted, and I felt like the biggest sinner and home-breaker in the world. I broke it off.

Shortly after, a fellow asked me out. He was a hospital administrator and a big football star from Georgia Tech. We only had one date, but it was significant because it is where I was officially introduced to Dr. Charles Hillis, my future husband. My date took me to the Fairyland Club on Lookout Mountain, which was a nice dinner club, and in walks Dr. Hillis and his date. (Charles had gotten a divorce and was now dating again.) My date and Charles knew each other, so Charles came over to chat a bit. I was introduced to his date and she had peacock colored eyes like Elizabeth Taylor and she was blonde, beautiful and very young. She didn't have much to say and just didn't seem "with it." I thought she was either uneducated or very shy, but she just didn't seem like Charles' kind of girl as he was very gregarious and she was just quiet. Charles didn't know I worked in his hospital where he was chief of staff, but as we talked he found out. The following Monday, he popped his head in and said, "Just thought I'd say hey." He started coming by every other day.

One night I was really tired and depressed because Rudolph wouldn't leave me alone, so I took two sleeping pills to get some rest. My sister-in-law, Gwen, tried to wake me and I wouldn't wake up. She panicked and called the doctor's office. Rudolph wasn't there but Charles was. He rushed to the house and administered an IV.

After that incident, my Grandmomma got worried and she called Aunt Evelyn and they made me quit my job. They shipped me off to Kingston to live with Aunt Evelyn for a while so I could get away from Rudolph. She asked me what happened, and I explained everything, including that Rudolph was married.

"Men do that," she said. "They know how to do that."

"I was with him more than his wife was," I cried.

I stayed in Kingston about six months, and Aunt Evelyn tried to bring me up to date on my naïveté. She also kept Rudolph away from me, not letting him know where I was. Then, one day, Charles called Aunt Evelyn to find out how I was and she invited him up. She liked him instantly and since she had always wanted me to marry a doctor, she welcomed him right in. I thought he was awful nice, but I really had no other feelings for him at this point. When I came back home, I found out that Charles had gone to Rudolph to tell him he was going to start dating me. Rudolph had the audacity to get really mad and he found the number where I was, picked up the phone and called me, madder than a wet hen.

"You are married," I screamed at him and hung up. (It was time to go to Disney World.) Charles and I started dating then, but we didn't become a couple yet, as I wanted nothing to do with the Doctor's Clinic where Rudolph worked.

An emergency room physician's wife introduced me to her brother, Clint Willingway (not his real name). She and her whole family were from Salt Lake City and were Mormon. Clint was so handsome, dedicated and he'd passed his MCATS and was going to medical school. He had taken two mission trips to Germany for the church, spoke fluent German, and was just so interesting to be around. He was a nice package and I really, really liked him. I started dating him seriously, and quit seeing Charles, although we remained friends. Charles didn't like Clint, and he called him "Apostle Clint."

One day Clint said, "Would you mind going to temple with me?" There was a temple in Washington, DC and I went there to see his church. We went everywhere and we were like really good friends who were also attracted to each other. He was very devout, and there was no sex, and at that time in my life I was so appreciative of that. I had had enough of it and loved being respected like this.

Charles wouldn't give up all this time and he would call me and say funny things, never really pushing, but just being present. He hung in there, but I was serious with Clint.

One thing I learned about the Mormon Church was that the only way to get a divorce recognized was if one party committed adultery. My first husband, Chuck, had committed adultery, but I just wanted out of the marriage so I had put something else as grounds for divorce. "In order to marry someone and go to heaven with them, you'd have to go back and change it to adultery," said Clint. So, I did. Chuck had married soon after the divorce and he didn't care.

Then Clint went away to medical school—away from Tennessee. I had gone back to my job at the hospital so I threw myself into my son and my work. Clint called me all the time but he was going to be gone for four years, I had a small child to raise, and I was lonely, so I began dating Charles again.

It was at this point I began wearing false eyelashes, for which I am known. Linda Cleghorn, my former supervisor at the hospital, found a place that put individual false eyelashes on you, so she asked if I'd go with her to the Ace Harris Beauty Salon in Chattanooga to have them done. It cost $50 and was too expensive to do often. "I can do it for you if you do it for me," she said one day, so we began putting each other's false eyelashes on, and I began wearing them all the time. (Linda and I are still good friends to this day, and I admire her character and her faith.) One day early on, when I was dating Charles, I cried so much over what was happening in my life and the lashes came off. I asked a friend what I was going to do—Charles had rarely seen me without my eyelashes. She said, "Well, you're going to learn to do them yourself." It took me an hour and a half to do one eye and it was exasperating, but I did it, and then did the other one, and got them on. I started doing my own and until my illness, I could do them in about 30 minutes.

Chapter 13

If You Can't Marry a Doctor Marry a Minister

My first real date with Charles was significant; there were brains all over, the smell was horrific, and I fainted dead away.

It was Christmas time and we were having dinner at a restaurant when Charles received a page saying they needed him to come to the hospital to check out the body of a very prominent man from Chattanooga who had been in a plane crash the week before. They had a time finding the wreckage site, but they finally did and the FAA and GBI all wanted the coroner right there when the body arrived to draw blood for alcohol and drug evidence.

"It won't take long," Charles said. "I may have to look at his skull and draw blood, but you can go with me and then we'll go back to dinner, or I can take you home and we can have another date next week."

I decided to go with him. When we arrived at the autopsy room in the bowels of the hospital, Charles found he'd forgotten his Dictaphone.

"I have this pad," he said. "Can you go in and write down what I tell you? He'll be covered up and you won't see anything."

"What if I can't spell something?"

"I'll spell it for you. You can spell 'heart' and 'blood', can't you?"

We walked into the autopsy room. There were a bunch of men there in suits, one male orderly, and me—dressed to the nines. They flung open the door, and nobody had covered the body. Here's this body all banged up, brains hanging out, limbs at all angles, and the smell was horrific. I fainted and that's the last thing I remember.

I woke up in the hall on the sofa with a sheet over me (what a dangerous place to be with a sheet over you), and I was so embarrassed. They were all kidding me and Charles mentioned that I passed out so prettily. He suggested we go back to dinner, and not wanting to seem like a wimp, I agreed.

That was our first date.

With Clint gone, Charles was right there being attentive and nice. I still just liked him, and he was nice to be around, but there was no 'wow factor.'

He was living in a trailer, and his oven didn't work. Although he didn't have a grill, he invited me over for steaks.

I said, "Where's your grill?"

"Watch this," he said.

He proceeded to make a little grill on the ground with bricks and the iron shelves out of the oven, and cook the steaks. He told me he had been a minister for nine years, but that he decided to go back to Emory Medical School to become a doctor.

I asked him how he got "uncalled" from the ministry.

"The way I see it, I was called to preach. My father was a minister and retired as one, and maybe I was trying to follow in his footsteps. But I felt as if I was in the right church, but the wrong pew, so I became a doctor."

With Charles' temperament and personality, I could not see him in the pulpit.

After a bit I went to Atlanta and met his mother, Mamie Hillis. She was a true Southerner from Vidette, Georgia and she acted like she adored me, but later she didn't and we had a tough time of it. She'd say, "Charles is my only child whom I loved before he was born, and I knew he was destined for greatness as he served the church for nine years, and cured people's souls, then he went back to medical school and now he cures their bodies." Ugh!

I met his oldest son, who was at the University of Pennsylvania, and his next son who was at Darlington, a prep school. His baby was with his ex-wife. I then began to realize why he lived in a trailer—all his money went to his ex-wife and kids.

I knew Charles was still seeing the beautiful girl that was with him when I met him, so I asked about her. "She'd had an ulcer at young age and I was her doctor," he said, "and she was in my life eight years." He hadn't been divorced but one year so I knew what happened to his marriage. He told me she couldn't hold a conversation, that she was sweet, but not raised like he was, and she wasn't compatible with his friends.

Charles finally bought a little house in a nice neighborhood in LaFayette and I don't know how he had any money to do it as he was taking care of his children. I realized I was falling more and more in love with him, and then one day we went down to Vidette to his mother's house to pick-up some furniture. Mamie had lots of things she wanted to give to her beloved son to start again in his new house. We were out in the shed on the farm, looking for something Charles wanted, and I found an old filing cabinet and started looking in it to see what was there. I found some meditations from the 1950s when Charles was a young minister for the Methodist Church. He would type and file his morning prayers and talks with God. I began reading them and they were just beautiful, and that's the day I really fell in love with Charles. I realized then he was such a good man—even with the bedpan-down-the-hallway incident—he really was good and just wanted his patients taken care of properly. My friend Linda said that he was a good man and good doctor, and if she needed a doctor that's who she'd want. I was a goner and evidently so was he.

Charles gave me a beautiful, solitaire ring and asked me to marry him and I said yes. I don't remember how he proposed, I'm sure it was at dinner somewhere, but we became engaged. Then one night he disappeared. He usually called me before bed but there had been no call, and I couldn't reach him. The next day I saw him and asked where he'd been. "Well," he said, "My old girlfriend has an ulcer and she was bleeding and came to the emergency room and they were going to put her in the hospital but she had no insurance, so I said I'd be over to get her. I gave her some meds and stayed." At least he didn't lie but that was it! I didn't talk to him for a week and I knew she was trying to move back in.

One night, I saw his car at a restaurant in Chattanooga. It was a big Lincoln and you couldn't miss it. I walked in, and there he sat with the "old" girlfriend; I was so angry I went over and sat down and his eyes got really big.

"Hi," I said. "See this ring?" and I shoved the big diamond engagement ring in her face.

She replied, "Do you see all of these—these sapphires and diamonds?"

I shot back, "This is the one that counts."

"Nancy," said Charles. "Calm down and have a drink."

I ordered a Long Island Iced Tea and when it came I said, "This is all I have to say to you," and I poured the drink all over him and went out the door. They got up and followed me and he kept saying, "I can't believe you did this." Charles smoked a pipe and I slapped him and the pipe went flying. I took the ring and threw it in the front seat and as far as I was concerned, it was over.

I went on about my business and a couple of weeks later, he started trying to come around again. He called me and apologized and said he was going to a therapist and he'd like me to go with him. We went to see Dr. Neumburger who later officiated at our wedding. He was a Christian therapist, and we began going to him for relationship advice, and he was the first person to recognize that I had anger issues; I had a hard time controlling my temper. If any person was trying to hurt me, I automatically hit back. Anyway, we improved our relationship and soon, the "old" girlfriend went out of the picture, and to my knowledge, he never saw her again.

We were married at Lookout Mountain Presbyterian Church in the chapel the day after Christmas. Wes was about five; my mother and Grandmomma were there; my Grandmomma's brother, Raymond Exum, gave me away; my maid of honor was my sister-in-law and dad wasn't there. We honeymooned in Gatlinburg, staying our first night in the Chattanooga Choo Choo. I had done what my Grandmomma told me: "If you can't marry a doctor like Aunt Evelyn wants you to, marry a minister." I married both!

Our reception had been at Rock City, and under the napkin Charles had placed a pair of diamond stud earrings. My ears weren't pierced but Charles said he'd do them for me. He put ice on the back, then put a cork behind my ear and stuck the needle in and it hurt like the devil so I wouldn't let him do the other ear, it hurt too much. I said I'd just wear one. This went on for weeks, but finally, I did have the other one done at the mall and wore the earrings.

Charles wasn't the sexiest man or the handsomest, but he loved me and took care of me and Wes, and I loved the real person he was, and admired his confidence and intelligence. I moved into the little house he had bought in LaFayette, and Aunt Evelyn helped me decorate it, putting in book cases and a fireplace, and closing in the carport with glass. We also added a large deck and built a pool, and Wes had the time of his life playing with the kids in the neighborhood who lined up everyday to be in the pool. Soon a loaf of bread, a jar of peanut butter and a jar of jelly emptied in a day and I began letting parents know when the pool was "open" for visitors. Moms began sending sandwiches and snacks; I would provide lemonade, punch or water and Wes was king of the neighborhood.

I was still working at the hospital, but people began treating me differently. My friends knew I was the same person, but administration did not want me there. Charles was known for "blowing" the whistle and I was his wife. I think they were afraid I would see something and say something to Charles, and it just wasn't the same, so I left the job.

Chapter 14

Children

Charles and I were happy, but I wanted another baby and he didn't. "We have enough children," he'd say. Well, I got pregnant and he absolutely demanded I get an abortion. He wouldn't have it any other way, so I did it. That haunts me to this day and is still so painful that it is hard to talk about—it was hard to put in this book. That incident harmed our relationship for a while, but Charles was so good about so many things. For example, it was important to me that Wes attend a Bible school like I did—I wanted him to learn the Bible and not be afraid to pray. Public schools had changed so much, and I wanted better for my son, so Charles sent him to Boyd-Buchanan—my old Church of Christ School now renamed. Charles would get up every morning and carpool Wes and the boys to school, and in the afternoon I would pick them up. It was a long haul; it took 45 minutes to an hour to get there, but there was no Christian school anywhere else. This was important to me and Charles made that happen. Our relationship got better.

I got pregnant again and this time Charles agreed to keep the baby. When I was about eight and a half months pregnant, we were in Gatlinburg, Tennessee for a medical meeting and I walked out of the Civic Center, fell, and rolled down the steps. People came running to help and, of course, they got Charles. I was crying and quite embarrassed but he said the baby was fine, that I was the one that had the problem—a broken femur. I went to Maryville Hospital and Charles set the leg. That night there was to be a banquet, and I was determined to go. I needed to take a bath to get ready, so Charles helped me into the tub but when it came time to get out, he couldn't get me out. He pushed and pulled, and I pushed and pulled. We tried everything and it was hilarious. He finally gave me some clothes and he had two guys come in to help him get me out of the tub. I was in a lot of pain, but I couldn't have anything other than Tylenol because of the baby, so needless to say, I didn't go to the banquet.

At Christmas, I was shopping in a wheelchair with one leg up, and it came time for the baby to come. They had to take the cast off for the delivery because I was delivering by C-section, and I had a boy on December 27, 1977, and I was thrilled. We named him Jacob Exum Hillis after Charles' father, Reverend Jacob Hillis, and my Grandmomma whose maiden name was Exum. After the delivery, it came time to get me up and moving, but they hadn't re-cast my leg yet. An aide came in to get me up and she didn't know I had a broken leg. Ouch! They finally recast the leg, and I went home with our new baby boy, but not before we stopped by Wes' school to show him his new brother. Wes was nine and a half by now and was really excited and in awe of this precious baby.

Thank goodness I had help at home because I couldn't get around; I had my Grandmomma and my mother, and we hired some help, as well, so Jacob was well taken care of.

When Jacob was about one month old, Charles and I were scheduled to go on a trip to Hawaii with our good friends. We had already signed and paid for it a year before we knew about Jacob, but I didn't want to leave my new baby. Charles said that the best time to leave him was now while he was small, so I had a friend who was a nurse take Jacob to her home, and watch after my sweet, little infant. Grandmomma and Charles' mother, Mamie, came to stay with Wes. When I was on the plane, I wrote a letter to Jacob about how hard it was leaving him and I was writing and crying. Two other people asked to read my letter and both cried. I still have that letter somewhere.

We went to Hawaii and it was so nice, an unbelievably pretty place with happy people and we had a good time. While we were gone, though, Mamie evidently acted up. When we got back, Grandmomma said to not ever let that woman stay there again. Mamie went around to the neighbors and said, "I never thought Charles would marry a common girl," and it was never good between us after that. She talked about my family like they were low class, uneducated and trashy.

After the trip, we came home and lived in the little house in LaFayette. We had seen some land we both loved, though, and a house plan that suited us. The property came up for auction, and since I had sold the mountain house by this time, I bid on the property and got it. We were very happy. In the meantime, Charles' former wife was moving, and his youngest son, didn't want to go, so he came to live with us. At this point it was Jacob, Wes, Charles' youngest son, Charles, and me.

Meanwhile, Rudolph had left the practice so Charles and his other partner were running it. Rudolph's brother had been the business manager, and his job was to take the money and make more; he bought land for strip mining, bought pine trees and invested the money. But evidently there had been some problems and we owed big money. The new business manager, who had been Charles' nurse ever since he started his medical practice, was very fond of Charles and in her efforts to help him pay everything off, she made some bad decisions. One day the IRS knocked on the door and said they were shutting the Clinic down until all the social security was paid back. Charles commented that there might be "real good jobs for doctors in the pen." The IRS people were not amused, and this was very frightening.

Now we were broke. We had to sell our land, and we lost our money including that which was left over from my inheritance from Granddaddy. We extended our hours, laid off most of the employees, and the doctors put me and the partner's wife to work. I started out filing for Medicare and Medicaid, re-filing, talking to them all day—filing workman's compensation because all of it had been let go and we had to catch up. I learned to do all the jobs a nurse would do. I took temperatures, x-rays, gave injections, helped with vasectomies, did sutures, drew blood, and whatever else I had to do. I began to see why Charles loved the world of medicine so much.

Chapter 15

Murdering the Chickens

Being a rural, small town doctor can be interesting and there were some funny stories connected with Charles' practice.

There was the chicken lady. Charles' secretary was the Baptist preacher's daughter and she was cute, sweet, young, and shy. I went by her office and she was splotchy all over, obviously in some emotional discomfort and there was a woman in the chair in front of her. "Connie, can I help you?" I said. "Yes," she said. "Could you help this lady; she wants to talk to Dr. Hillis about a 1013." Charles was on the state board that could send folks off to the mental hospital if he thought they should be there. When you sent someone against their will it was a 1013.

The woman had a brown paper bag with her and I put her and the bag in another room and asked what the problem was.

"My husband is killing the chickens," she said.

"Do you own a chicken farm?" I said. "Isn't that what you do?"

"Yes, but he's fucking them to death," she said.

Oh boy, we either had a nutcase or something else was going on at that farm. I moved her to Charles' office and sat her down. I went to Charles and told him he just needed to talk with her; didn't tell him anything else. Well, he goes in, picks up his pipe and she starts on the story. He's patting down his tobacco as she talks.

"I told your nurse he's screwing the chickens to death," she said.

He kept right on packing his pipe and then lighting it. This is what he did when he needed to think about something and needed to stall, and you could tell he was trying to think of something to say to the nice lady.

"So now you're telling me, let's see, you're saying that your husband is having sex with a few chickens?"

"Not just a few," she said, " a lot and here's the bag to prove it."

"You have the dead chicken there?" Charles said.

"Yes, a bag full."

"OK, sit here and I'll be back."

Well, you never heard such commotion. He talked to the lab tech and told him to get the pap room ready and bring a slide. "She's crazy or he's crazy," Charles said. "If there's sperm in a chicken, then we'll know."

"How do you do a pap on a chicken?" said the tech.

"We're about to find out," said Charles, and sure enough, when the tech put the slide under the microscope, there was sperm in the chicken.

"We will send the police out to collect your husband," Charles told the woman.

He later said to us, "If my choice would have been her or the chickens, I would have screwed the chickens, too."

Another time, a little lady came in and I asked, "Ms. Brown what can we do for you?" She said, "It's my pocket book." I looked down on the floor and saw her pocket book and it looked fine! I told her I'd be right back because I had no idea what she meant. As I said earlier, Charles was on the board of the local psychiatric hospital and he could send mentally ill patients there and I was convinced we had a case right here. I called the real nurse and told her what Ms. Brown had said, and what could it possibly mean. She said, "It's what old people call their privates!" I had never heard such a thing and we all got a kick out of my naiveté. We got her ready for a pap.

While we were working long hours, we had some fun and wonderful times together, with many varied and poignant stories about our patients. It was hard, but I wouldn't trade that time for the world. Eventually, we paid back all the social security withholdings. We also had paid back alimony for Charles' first wife, so we finally were out of our hole.

Chapter 16

At That Price They Can Puddle a Little More Than Normal

In the south we have a way of dressing our windows in our homes. We buy curtains usually too long for the window, and let them "puddle" on the floor, that is, we let the extra material bunch up and lay on the floor. This is very fashionable, especially in antique homes. The idea is to use a very expensive and beautiful material that showcases the windows and rooms.

There was a woman named Mackie Bell Shepherd whose husband had been a doctor and he died. She remarried and wanted to sell their early 1930's, big, two-story Federal style house in LaFayette. We bought it for $64,000 and put another $80,000 in it, and Aunt Evelyn, who was an interior decorator, helped us redo it. She used this very expensive leopard toile fabric that was an adaptation of an old antique print, and it cost $150/yd but Aunt Evelyn could get it at cost. It was gorgeous. I've had it made into curtains for every house I've lived in, including the Hamilton-Turner House, the Savannah mansion I once owned. When I left there, I brought the curtains with me and they are now in my house in St. Simons. They are way too long for my windows, but at that price, they can "puddle" a little more than normal!

Charles was a terrific doctor and he just had a natural knack for it. Heart doctors would come to Charles and ask his opinion about EKGs and he won all kinds of awards for outstanding doctor; for saving lives; for going beyond the call of duty. He was named family physician of the year from the American Academy of Family Practice, and the AMA gave him a national award for Outstanding Physician of the Year. He was kind and took whatever time it took with his patients. The girls in the front office took a lot of grief because of the long wait to see him, and if a patient needed help and couldn't pay, no problem; Charles would take whatever payment they had—eggs, a ham, cords of wood, and once a live pig and some chickens. I never knew a doctor kinder to his patients.

Because our house was easier to get to than the hospital, and everyone knew where we lived, we often delivered babies on our pool table. People would come by the house just ready to deliver, and we'd throw down plastic bags on the pool table, put a sheet down and tell her to put one foot in the pocket of the table. There she'd have the baby. We also treated patients with minor problems at the house. For example, one time a young man came in with a dislocated shoulder. Charles gave him a shot to knock him out, and I supported him while Charles put his foot in the boy's armpit and jerked the shoulder back into position. So our house was more than just a home and I have happy memories of it.

Recently, my friend and former close employee found an article about the now historical Shepherd-Hillis house—Shepherd for Dr. Shepherd and Hillis for Mandy of *Midnight in the Garden of Good and Evil* fame. There wasn't a word about Charles. I guess I finely became more famous (or infamous) as Charles was in LaFayette, Georgia.

I was married to Charles from 1971-1989—18 years. We were happy until a disturbing incident occurred that forced me take hold of my own life. At the same time, a chance occurrence sent me in a whole new direction.

Chapter 17

My Greatest and Best Achievement

Our best friends with whom we went to Hawaii, had a son that overdosed on drugs and died. Charles spoke at the funeral, and as I sat there, it struck me that although there were some 200 kids there, and they were upset he was dead, there wasn't any real sorrow. It was as if they were saying, "We all do this," and they accepted it as part of the game! It made me sick and concerned so I decided to look into the drug scene and learn about it.

When in college, I had volunteered at a methadone clinic where the state of Tennessee substituted methadone for heroin (and other opioids) addiction. Patients would come in and be tested, and if they were found clean of opioids, they'd get a dose of controlled methadone; this worked well. Usually the patients who came in were raised on the streets. They often didn't know who their parents were, and they had had a terrible life. I could almost understand why they were addicted to something that would alleviate their pain and help them forget. Also, because there were studies that showed that drug use helped cut down on crime rates, the law didn't want to particularly rock the boat. It seemed to me even back then, nobody cared or seemed to know how to handle drug addiction.

Things were different, too, since I was in high school. Drugs weren't used in high schools during my days, but now drug use was trickling down to middle schools and even elementary schools. We had teenagers ourselves, so that gave me more reason to want to be informed.

I took a course at Georgia State from a group called PRIDE (Parents Resource Institute of Drug Education), which educated parents about drugs so we might know what to look for and understand what we were fighting. The last day, people could stand up and speak. I stood up and said

I was in the medical world, and it seemed that doctors were the first line of defense, and why wasn't the medical community checking into this? Why weren't doctors and society looking at this as a medical problem instead of a social problem? Why weren't doctors doing drug screens as part of primary health care physicals for young people?

A doctor came up to me after the session and asked me to serve on their team as it seemed I was passionate about the problems. "You struck a nerve," he said, "and you can reach people." I was awfully shy then and told them I wasn't particularly good at public speaking. "We will send you to school," he said, "teach you every fact, and arm you with results from every study if you'll work with us." So, I volunteered with no salary and only my expenses being reimbursed, and the first thing I got to do was sit down with Nancy Reagan.

Every first lady has a program and Ms. Reagan's was adolescent drug abuse. She was gracious and caring and I served on a panel with her. We were bantering back and forth as to what to call our project and we said, "Why can't they just say no?" That stuck and the slogan became, "Just Say No."

Charles supported this work and I helped to start the first treatment program in the country for adolescents. It was called Charter Brook and it was located in Atlanta. Up until then, there was no treatment facility for a child. All addicted people were thrown in together, children and adults alike, but the illness and treatment is not the same for children as it is for adults. Adults can make life changes; kids can't; they need another kind of help and intervention. I began visiting towns and schools to talk about drugs, and I bought paraphernalia in the towns' actual shops to show adults where kids were getting their stuff. I had suitcases full of facts and I had a special license to carry the things around so I could talk to parents and teachers. I'd burn marijuana so they could smell what it smelled like and know what it looked like. I showed a film about how one young boy lost his brain function from bad marijuana that had been cut with P.C.P. I did a lot to make people aware, and get kids to facilities that would help them.

My work with drugs helped our own family, too. Charles' youngest son was in Baylor High School in Chattanooga. We had a charge account for him at the dry cleaners and we had one at the bookstore. The bills began doubling, and it didn't make sense so I told Charles I thought he might be charging to the accounts and buying drugs with money he made off of cleaning everyone's shirts (the dry cleaners), and selling Cokes on the dorm floor (the bookstore). Charles couldn't believe it, but that's exactly what was happening. His son was on drugs. I wanted to put him in Ridgeview Hospital in Atlanta, but his mother wanted him with her, so he went there to live because we were "crazy" (especially me, the wicked stepmother). About six months later, she called Charles asking about drugs in general. It seemed the son had charged $6,000 on her credit card and that got her attention. She took him to Ridgeview and admitted him to the psychiatric floor, and after a drug screen, he was transferred to the drug and alcohol addiction floor. He stayed for months and then finished school in Atlanta, and went on to have a good college experience, and by the grace of God, went on to have a wonderful life and family. He is a very kind young man.

If I hadn't been doing my work on drugs, we might have never known before it was too late.

PRIDE had a conference every year and it started with 300 people at Georgia State University in Atlanta. The last one I attended was at the Omni World Congress Center and there were thousands of people there. Ms. Reagan attended, and it was the third time I got to be in her company. She was just wonderful. I served on committees with governors and dignitaries; I received letters of commendation; I was named one of the most outstanding young people in Georgia; and I received awards from communities and organizations. The best rewards were letters from young people, writing about how I'd helped them and how they now had a life; but I was getting burned out and some of the stories were becoming too horrific. For example, one little 4-year-old was addicted because his parents would blow marijuana smoke in his face to calm him down. It worked, but at what price? It was heartbreaking. Also, I was aware that addiction and recovery were more difficult for kids than for adults, and it seemed I was losing more kids than I was helping. One day, in front of the Capital building in Atlanta, a TV interviewer picked up a guy yelling at me, "Just how much good has 'just say no' done? You've only helped about 300 kids. Just what have you done?" That drained the rest of the life out of me, and I backed off the drug work. (It was time to go to Disney World.)

That work I consider my greatest and best achievement, and even if I only helped to save one child, it was worth it.

In the meantime, drinking became a way of life for Charles. He went to lots of parties and meetings, and there was always alcohol served because in that day and age, it was standard to serve alcohol at most events. It began to be that every night he'd have four or five drinks. I'd mention it to him that maybe he was drinking too much, but he'd insist he was OK. I began to find out that there were many physicians who were abusing alcohol like Charles, and decided to try and do something to help them. I got a group together and we went to the Medical Association of Georgia (MAG) and they set up a program with Ridgeview: if a physician decided that alcohol or drugs were a problem, he or she could go to the program there. We'd have a doctor run their practice, telling people they were on a mission; and we took care of the family so the doctor could get the help that was needed. When the doctor completed the program, he could step back into his practice if he stayed in recovery. It changed a lot of lives, but my Charles, who needed the program desperately, would not go. He didn't think he had problem and I knew that programs only work when someone admits to themselves that they have a problem. Charles wouldn't admit it yet. To his credit, he never missed a day of work, but it sure got dicey at times.

Since I had worked for him, I knew most about what to do when patients called for help. The emergency room at the hospital would call for Charles after business hours and he'd be passed out in bed. I'd cover for him by saying he was in the bathroom or downstairs, and through the door, I'd get instructions from him and tell them what to do. I know it wasn't right for obvious reasons, but I loved Charles and wanted to help him all I could but I now know I was enabling him.

Chapter 18

The Swing Set

The year he was made Chief of Staff, Charles started bringing home magazines about swinging, that is, switching partners for sexual pleasure. Our marriage had been deteriorating because of the drinking, and now he was interested in swinging and I would have no part of it. I'd ask him how he could be a minister and rationalize this thinking, and he'd give me church history, turning everything around where it would sound sensible—he was so smart—but he couldn't talk me into it. I also didn't know that Charles was seeing other women; I guess I could guess, but I didn't want to know. That's another indication of the time—you turned your head the other way when it came to husbands' extracurricular behavior and I guess I turned mine.

One night I developed an awful cough and it progressed to where I was coughing all night for two weeks. Charles wasn't one for giving me medicine, but he gave me a shot for my cough so I could rest. The next morning our babysitter, woke me up and said that there wasn't any food to feed Wes and Jacob. It was Sunday, and she had said Dr. Hillis went to church, but left the boys home which was unusual. If only one of us was able to go to church, we'd take the kids. I was still pretty groggy and not feeling well so I told her to call Dr. Hillis at the church. A little later, she woke me again to say that the minister said Charles wasn't at church.

"Call the hospital," I said. She did and they said he was not there. I got up and called the hospital operator myself and asked her to find Charles. I was on hold with the operator as she called each floor, asking if they had seen Dr. Hillis. We had a second house phone (Chattanooga line) and it rang. The babysitter answered and gave it to me as I was still holding on the other line. It was Charles.

"Where are you?" I said.

"What are you doing awake!" Charles yelled and then said, "I'm at the hospital in the doctors' lounge."

I was still on the other line with the hospital operator so I asked her to ring the doctors' lounge where he said he was. I didn't hear a phone ringing so I knew he was not there. I confronted him by saying that I had the hospital operator on the other line, ringing the doctors' lounge phone where he said he was, and there were several lines there and none were ringing. His voice changed and I could tell he was scared. I felt as if someone had hit me in the stomach and I was wide awake at this point.

"Nancy, we need to talk," he said.

"Ok," I said, "but tell me where you are."

"I'll be home in an hour and we'll talk."

"An hour! It doesn't take but 30 minutes to get here from the hospital; where are you?"

"I can't talk now; I'll be home soon," and he hung up on me.

I knew as sure as I knew my own name that he was with someone and I couldn't turn my head this time. I told the babysitter to take Wes and Jacob to a local restaurant, and because I had no cash, she should tell them that Dr. Hillis would be by to take care of the bill tomorrow. A few minutes later, Aunt Evelyn called "out of the blue" and she sounded upset.

"What's going on? Are you ok?" Of course I started crying. She said that Charles had called my brother, crying, and told him to never mention the diamond necklace and earrings he had purchased, and that my brother knew about. He said it was a long story. Aunt Evelyn told me not to over-react and stay calm. She said that all men do this and I have a great life, and my children are taken care of and Charles will give them an education which I could never give them on my own. She asked me to go to her condo on Pawleys Island in South Carolina and think about everything and calm down. I told her I had only about $400 in the bank, and she suggested I use the business receipts, that they were just as much mine as Charles'.

About an hour later, Charles came home and into our Florida room which we called the Oval Office. We had some cocktail glasses that cost

$200 each, and I picked one up and threw it at him, asking him who he'd been seeing. "Do you know how much those cost?" he said. I grabbed another one, eventually breaking all of them, and then I grabbed a butcher knife, threatening him. He ran out to our neighbor's house, and he got him to call me.

"Now, Nancy, you'll have to give him some clothes so he can go to work tomorrow," the neighbor said.

"Don't call me anymore about Charles," I said. I didn't sleep that night and the next morning I got Wes off to school.

I told our babysitter, that we needed to go so I took the receipts from the weekend's business as Aunt Evelyn suggested, packed up Jacob, and headed to the bank. (I had to leave Wes with Charles as he was in school.) I had thousands of dollars in checks and cash, and I calmly went to the window and asked to cash them all. I ended up with about $15,000 so I got on a plane and went to my Aunt's condo at Pawleys Island. Our business manager called and said, "You can't do what you are doing," and I retorted, "Well, Charles can't screw around on me either," and I hung up. I wouldn't talk to them.

I was just so hurt and mad. I had Charles' doctor's bag, so I took some pills to let me sleep, and for two days our babysitter, who was like a daughter to me, took care of Jacob and I cried and slept.

I found out later that his affair was with our next-door neighbor. She was very sexy and thin and Charles had bought her the diamonds he had asked my brother not to mention. One day, before I knew about the affair, she came to our office, just hysterical. She was pregnant and I've always wondered if that was Charles' baby. She and her husband separated shortly thereafter, then divorced and she aborted the baby.

I had been at Aunt Evelyn's beach house for over two weeks, and I knew I couldn't stay away any longer. Charles' son was going to graduate from high school and I came home from Pawleys Island to attend the ceremony. Charles drove me home afterward and he and Wes asked me to stay at home, so I did, and I confronted Charles and he just kept saying how sorry he was. He didn't really talk about it much, but I kept hearing rumors about others he had been with. Somebody had told me he was with his nurse who was cute and married with two kids. I called her on the phone and told her she'd better leave the office right now because I had his gun and I was coming down. I was crazy. When I walked in the front door, she left and the entire office was trying to "reason" with me! Years later, she did admit to the affair and said that her husband had run around on her and now she knew how it felt, so she didn't blame me at all for my behavior.

I went to a lawyer to talk about a divorce, but Charles kept saying he'd do anything to keep the marriage together. We went back to our Christian psychologist and after some months of therapy, we were back together. I felt that if we moved, I could put everything behind me and move on so I asked Charles if he'd move, and he said yes. The best job offer came from Wayne Memorial Hospital in Jesup, Georgia so he sold his practice and we went to Jesup where he worked as an emergency Medical Director at Wayne Memorial. We went from the northwest corner of Georgia to the southeast corner, far away from my home town of Chattanooga. Also, as mother and Grandmomma were healthy at that time, they stayed in our house in LaFayette.

Around this time, we started having trouble with Charles' mother. One day a preacher from her church in Vidette called Charles to say that his mother had run into a ditch a couple of times, and it wouldn't be long before she killed someone or herself. We also knew she had an alcohol and drug problem. She could get drugs easily because her husband had been a minister at various parishes all over Georgia so she knew many doctors from those places. She'd call them for pain meds for all her aches and pains, and they'd give them to her. We took her car away and finally put her in Ridgeview in Atlanta. She was 74 years old, but she didn't see she had a problem, so they finally had to release her and she went back to her house. We had brought her to our home for a while, but she wouldn't stay. She died alone and no one knew for two or three days.

Things rolled on. I got into the Jesup Jollies, a singing and dancing show. There was a young guy who had just graduated from college, and he was trying to get into medical school. His name was John Smith (not his real name), and his mother worked in the ER. He was a nice looking guy and Charles told him one time that I was often without a car and that I needed someone to play tennis with and go places with. John and I went a lot of places together and it was nice. We took Wes and Jacob sometimes, and we were friends, but Charles was always trying to get it to be more. That should have been a clue.

Then the incident happened.

One time we went to Atlanta to a meeting and we were sitting in a restaurant. Charles said he had to meet a doctor there whom he was trying to recruit for the hospital, and the doctor would be bringing his wife. During the dinner, the husband paid attention to me and his wife paid attention to Charles. I saw what was going on, and started making a scene: "If you think we're going to have a party time, it ain't going to happen," I said, and the other couple left after dinner.

A man from across the room came over, complimenting Dr. Hillis on his beautiful wife, saying he wanted to meet us. He evidently was quite taken with me and he said, "I want you to try this bottle of rare scotch." It must have cost a fortune because it was locked in a cage that was soldered to the table. I had a drink and he then invited us to Zazoo's, so we went over there, and had more drinks—more than I was use to having. Obviously, I didn't remember much after that until I woke up in the hotel room and there was one too many people in the bed. I went to the bathroom screaming, yelling for them to get out. I stayed in the locked bathroom the rest of the night, wondering how I had led this man on enough to make him think he could get me and my husband in bed. What part had I played in what I considered rape?

In the morning I went to our car and started driving home, leaving Charles in Atlanta. He called saying how I just couldn't leave him there, that he thought I was liking it and we'd just had too much to drink. That was it. From then on I didn't want him to touch me. I was done. I drove and thought about how and if I might divorce him, and could I do it. I was a different person then and I was afraid of living alone and supporting my boys by myself. I decided to wait. I turned around and went back to get him. I had felt guilty and wondered what things I had said to contribute to that horrible scene.

Charles got offered a job at West Paces Ferry Hospital in Atlanta on the same road the governor lived on and he took it. I was glad to leave Jesup as the relationship with John was heating up. After the incident in Atlanta, John looked like an answer for me, but it would've ruined his life, so I left with Charles. I was now back north, closer to our house in LaFayette and my mother and Grandmomma.

Even though it was a great job, it was boring, so Charles drank more and began fooling around more. After the first year, there were rumblings that Charles' contract would not be renewed. I still cared for him, and still hadn't decided if I wanted to live on my own, so I called the administrator and asked if I could come in to talk. I asked what was going on and was there anything to the rumors. "Yes," he said. "Charles is drinking heavily and he is going to be let go." An ER nurse also told me that Charles had been messing around with the administrator's honey on the side, so that was it. He was going to be let go.

At this same time, Wes started having trouble with his grades. He had been in private schools but an incident made me move him into the public schools.

When he was 12 at Boyd Buchanan, he raised his hand to lead prayer as he did many times before. This time the teacher asked if he'd been baptized and he said no. She said, "Well, you are at the age of account-ability and if you haven't been baptized, you can't lead prayer." Wes looked around and asked if he could say his own prayer outside and she said yes (actually two buddies followed him out). At home that night, it came up at dinner, and the next day I called the principal and asked what was going on. He said that the school was based on the fundamentals of the Church of Christ and this was a rule. I argued that only two percent of the population of the school was from the Church of Christ denomination and probably the rest were not aware of any such rule. He said it didn't matter, the rule would stand. I asked that he send a letter to all parents, informing them of the rules and then I took Wes out of the school at the end of the year.

Now he was in a public school, and not doing well. His grades hit the bottom, and I was afraid that he was just slow, and if we were pushing him too hard it would push him into drugs. Charles suggested we take him to a place to have him evaluated. The doctor said his hearing, his speech, his athletic ability, and IQ were all normal, he was fine, just lazy and unmotivated, and there was no evidence of drugs. "It won't be easy for him," the doctor said, "he'll have to work at it, but there's nothing wrong with him," so we signed him up for Darlington, a boarding school in

Rome, Georgia and he pitched a fit. On top of everything, he had to go to summer school to get prepared for the fall. He went, and when I took him and said goodbye, he looked at me with tears in his eyes and said, "Mom you must hate me." All I could say was, "You know better than that," and then I walked out. As I drove home, I cried and stopped three times to call the headmaster—it was so hard for me to leave him. For a while he was depressed and mad at us, he wouldn't even come to the phone to talk with me—he just didn't understand tough love. But eventually he fit right in and began doing well. When he graduated, he even won the most prestigious award Darlington had.

One day I was implementing our drug program on St. Simons Island and overheard the ER doctor's wife mention that there was a job opening for a physician in the ER at the hospital. I told Charles and he went for the job and got it. He moved there and I stayed in LaFayette with the boys to see if I could live alone; to see what single mothers did. We were in the middle of the school year, so I could do this without upsetting anyone. Charles was so controlling, but he was paying the bills and my life revolved around him; I was also scared to death to be by myself. I often stayed up all night in the TV room, getting the boys to sleep with me in there because I heard noises all night and didn't sleep, but I knew I would have to be able to do this if I was going to get a divorce. I also didn't want to upset Charles until he was settled as I did still care about him. The boys were still in school so I told myself I'd wait to file the papers until June when they were out for summer. However, I didn't serve papers then, though, because Charles said he'd get help for his alcohol abuse and that he did not want the divorce. My lawyer, our Christian counselor and our minister suggested I give him a chance. It was the first time Charles said he'd get help, so I moved to St. Simons with the boys to give it a chance.

Charles did go to an outpatient program at Charter by the Sea every day, but it didn't set well with him. It made him angry and mean, and I could tell he was upset with himself. Facing his problems made him very sad.

A little time went by and Charles was still not doing well, so in September, I suggested that he move back to the house on the beach as this wasn't working. We separated and I stayed in the apartment and he went to the beach house. Charles kept trying to come back to the apartment, but I kept saying no. He called a marriage therapist in Jesup, and we worked on the marriage. I had never told a soul about the Atlanta partner swap business, not even my Aunt Evelyn, who thought I should stay with Charles no matter what. "All men run around," she said. "But he can take care of you and the boys. Stay with him, he really does love you."

She told me about how Granddaddy had run around, too. "Do you remember the egg woman at the chicken and egg supplier?" she said.

"Yes, I do." I remembered that she had been very pretty.

"Wasn't she always sweet to you, and gave you something while she and Granddaddy went off somewhere?"

"Yes, they went to get the chickens for the restaurant."

"No, they didn't! They went to make chickens, and when your grand-mother found out she took a gun down there and said 'don't you ever come around Lee A. Brown again.'"

I was shocked, since I thought my Granddaddy hung the moon and could do no wrong.

Aunt Evelyn said they almost called the police on Grandmomma. (I guess I take after my Grandmomma.)

Anyway, she wanted me to stay with Charles so I continued the counseling. I also was trying to make it work because Charles continued paying for Wes to attend Darlington, and he didn't have to. Wes wasn't his child but Charles had been a good father to Wes and loved and took care of him as if he were his own.

One day the psychiatrist talked to me alone and I told him what happened in Atlanta that night, and that I was so ashamed, felt so guilty and so sick with it, I felt responsible. How could I let that happen? How could I be so stupid? What part of 'no' did he not understand? I blamed myself, and the therapist said to just cry and get it out. That was the first time I told anyone about it. He confronted Charles with the issue and Charles tried to make excuses, but at least it was out. I was done though, and proceeded with the divorce.

You have to understand that Charles was a God in LaFayette. In the grocery store, for example, men and women of all ages would come up to me, telling me what a great man Dr. Hillis was and how he had saved the life of their children, mother, grandfather or sister. And because he still filled the pulpit of several churches on Sunday (remember, he had a

Doctor of Divinity degree from Emory), they would tell me what a great Christian-filled spirit he had.

I didn't have a prayer!

I knew that any judge in LaFayette would slant the settlement toward Charles so he would fight to have it take place there. Sure enough, as soon as I sued Charles for divorce in Glynn County (St. Simons Island) he countered for a change of venue to Walker County in LaFayette. The original decision by the judge was to obtain the divorce in LaFayette, but I told the lawyer that we had papers showing Charles' residence as St. Simons, so we appealed, appearing before the Georgia State Supreme Court in Atlanta, and we finally managed to prevent it from being moved to Walker County. This part of the process took a year and within that year, Charles tried to starve me to death. He had to pay the condo mortgage and fees, but he balked at everything else. I needed money so one day I went back to LaFayette and got in our safe. We had some gold coins in there and when we bought them, they were worth about $20,000; I figured they'd be worth a lot more now, so I went and got them, selling them one at a time as I needed money. Once he found out, it didn't buy me any brownie points with Charles, but at that point, I didn't care because I needed money to support myself and the boys. Besides, I didn't get much for the coins because I had to depend on a man in Atlanta to sell them, and he knew I was really desperate. He had me over a barrel, as they say, and I took whatever money he offered. When you have nothing, even a little amount is a lot!

The attorney wanted more money for the divorce, and I had none, so I worked several small part time jobs to try and make ends meet.

The divorce was proceeding, but Charles was dragging his feet. He wouldn't come and sign the papers and the cost kept going up, but I knew I should just wait. He was living in Alabama at this point and I knew that one of these days one of the women he was seeing would want him to get a divorce, and he'd do it. I just let it go, waiting him out, and that's exactly what happened. We decided on a settlement and he signed the papers and we were divorced. It had taken three years since the first filing.

It was time to start thinking about a real career and how to make a living and support the boys.

Chapter 19

The Last of the Last of the Last of the Red Hot Mamas

I got my first job as a hostess at Blanche's Courtyard on St. Simons, one of the best restaurants on the Island. Three days into hostessing, the owner realized I could sing. "Can you sing Dixieland, Jazz and Ragtime?" she asked me. At first I was going to say no, but when she said it paid three times the money, I said yes. Now, I had never sung anything like that before—remember the opera—but I was about to learn.

Whenever I let my mouth overrun my brain, I'd go to the Library to get it right, and that's what I did to learn about singing Dixieland. One of the Dixieland Jazz's Ragtime books noted a special lady called Ruth Crews. It said that she was one of the best ragtime singers ever, so I looked her up and found out she was in Orlando, Florida at a place called Rosie O'Grady's. I went to catch her act, sitting through all of her performances that night, taking notes and learning as much as I could.

Ruth was a big woman, maybe 350 pounds, platinum blonde hair, powder blue eyes, but dressed and fluffed up with feathers and boas, and when she came down the big stairs for her performance, in all her glory, with all the good-looking men helping her down, she'd say, "Honey, if you can't hide it, just decorate it." And she could sing! She had sung with Bob Hope and other Hollywood legends and she was mesmerizing. After the last performance, she came over and said, "Honey, I know I'm good, but what are you doing?" I told her my situation and she said, "Do you sing?" and I told her I sang opera. She said, "Oh hell," and took me back to her dressing room where she gave me advice on how to sing Dixieland and

Jazz. "Don't hold the notes a long time," she said. "Let 'em go, break 'em off. This ain't opera. You gotta be quick and happy. Also, breathe from the basement, not from the attic, and you've got to learn to sing everything in a lower key." I came home with three songs I could sing—*Hard Hearted Hannah, Sweet Georgia Brown,* and *Moon River.*

I started singing at Blanche's with a group called The Good Ole Boys. They wore red and white shoes, white pants, red vests, red bolo ties, and they were great. They opened every night to *Sweet Georgia Brown,* but their most requested song was *Butter Beans.* They asked me what song I would like to have as my signature song and I said *Hard Hearted Hannah* and they learned it in my key. But if it wasn't for Ms. Ginny Hammock and her husband, Reverend Julian Hammock, I would have never been able to sing Dixieland Jazz, even though I learned from the best. Ms. Hammock sat with me and got the songs in my key, and we worked together. Her husband played the hot pink, stand-up bass in The Good Ole Boys and Ginny played the piano. I did *Frankie and Johnnie* as an opener, and of course, *Hard Hearted Hannah,* and I kept sticky notes on my hand so I'd remember what songs were in what order. I look back and wonder how I did it.

I'd come in at 5:00 pm and work as a hostess then at 9:00 pm I'd go to change to get ready to sing. My dressing room at Blanche's was in the bathroom in the kitchen, about five feet from the broiler, and it was so small that I had to stand on the toilet to get dressed. The chef put a glittered, gold star on the door. There was no A/C in the area so it was hot and my makeup and hair would drop if I wasn't careful.

I always wore a black fringe dress which had layers of fringe in rows all the way down to the bottom. It had rhinestones on the straps and I always wore long, black gloves, a big boa, and pink feathers in my hair. It was my signature look when I performed and it captivated men and women alike. I still have the dress even though it's a bit faded now and it no longer fits. Anyway, the chef would put the boa in the freezer to keep it cold. I'd change, and he would help me get in the dress—bulging boobs in front as well as bulging in the back, but I got in it (I was always a little heavy for it, and David always said that the zipper was made of iron). Once I was ready, he'd get the boa out, I'd put it on and waltz on out.

They'd introduce me as "the last of the last of the last of the Red Hot Mamas."

We were an instant success, packing them in all weekend, and I became a singer. Lots of retired, wealthy folks hung out at Blanche's as it was their favorite spot and I did very well in tips. I also met the "mayor" of St. Simons, (of which there really wasn't one) Mr. Rowland.

Mr. Rowland had been a window dresser in New York and he came to St. Simons to live. He use to come to Blanche's some years before, and he began coming in again (after his wife died) every Saturday night with a lady from Sea Island. He called her Butterfly and she always wore a boa and a butterfly in her hair. People gave him a hard time and talked about him because he was with this "rich old lady," perhaps taking advantage of her. But if and whatever she was paying him, it was worth it, because her last years were just wonderful because of Rowland. He was a great dancer and they danced together beautifully. She eventually died and he was gone for a while, but then he came back.

Every morning he'd wear one of his many wonderful outfits with shoes matching and a different color dinner jacket—green, orange, coral, pink, purple, or red, and he would stop in the St. Simons' florist where he'd get a carnation to match his outfit. Then he'd go down to St. Simons' pier where he'd talk with everybody and tell who would ever listen about St. Simons. People began calling him the Mayor of St. Simons. One time as a joke, city hall held a race for mayor, running Mr. Rowland against a yellow dog. You paid to vote and the money went to charity; he won but it was a close race.

Every night I was singing, he'd dance one dance with me. The floor was brick and I about killed myself in my high heels, but it was just great as he was the ambassador of St. Simons, and he danced like Fred Astaire.

Chapter 20

Big Beautiful Woman

I came home one day and on my answering machine was a message from a girlfriend in Atlanta who had sent my picture in to *Big Beautiful Woman* (BBW). She said, "Have you ever been to Vegas? Well, pack your bags; you're going to be in the Ms. Big Beautiful Woman contest in Las Vegas." The only big beautiful women I had ever heard of were connected with wrestling, so I called my friend back to say I knew I needed a profession, but I just didn't think I was cut out to wrestle. She laughed and explained that it was a pageant for full-figured women and for me to get over it as that's what I was. "I know you said you don't want to be in any more pageants, but this one comes with the possibility of a modeling contract," she said, "so it might mean some money. Go get a copy of the magazine and look at it. It will be in the fashion magazines area."

"Oh, just one thing—the last time I saw you, you were maybe a size 14; you've got to be a size 18 or they will send you home! You've got a few months—eat."

The contest was held at the Dunes and it was just like a Miss America Pageant: you were awarded points for talent, interviewing, poise, fashion and figure competitions. Ages 18 to 50, married or single women were allowed. There were lots of rehearsals and big staged numbers, and it was a big deal—I was floored! I met some of the most beautiful women, inside and out, who had been denied jobs, school placements, medical school acceptances, a spot in the seminary, and other positions because of their weight. There was a general feeling in the 80's that if a woman was overweight, she was not worth much, she had something emotionally wrong with her, she was not very smart, and that she needed to wear oversized men's shirts and polyester stretch pants, preferably black, and try to fade into the background. She certainly wasn't desirable or sexy. Well, these women proved to the world that they were beautiful, smart, sexy, talented and confident, and they did so much to show bigger women that the world could be theirs. I never felt so beautiful and confident.

I sang *The Greatest Love of All*, and I won. I also was awarded Miss Congeniality. Emmy winner Telly Savalas of *Kojak* fame was there, and he hugged me and said, "Now this is my kind of woman; who loves ya baby!" and he gave me one of his lollipops.

Because of this pageant, new doors opened for me. I was awarded a modeling contract for "Just My Size Pantyhose," and did a lot of print work for "Hanes" Isotoner gloves, shoes and anything else "Hanes" owned at the time. Then Georgia Public Television also did a 20 minute segment on my life; in fact, the producer won an award for the piece, and Diane Sawyer gave her the award.

Carol Shaw, the founder of BBW, and the one who coined the phrase, wanted to show that being big is not bad, that life is what you make it, and to go for the gusto and live your life to the fullest. Weight should not be an issue at all. BBW celebrates who you are no matter your age, weight or looks, and Ms. Shaw was the first woman to recognize that, and she continues to be an inspiration to so many. I received many wonderful letters and phone calls from women all over the U.S. telling me what an inspiration the *Big Beautiful Woman* magazine and pageant were to them.

Shortly after my great time with BBW, I experienced firsthand how horrible some people can be about weight. I was driving a red jeep down in Boca Raton, Florida, and had pulled into a parking spot when a red Maserati pulled up in back of me, blocking me in. I didn't know if he had his eye on the spot or what, but I couldn't move my car and I needed to straighten it up a bit. I sat in the car, thinking he might leave. He got out of the car and walked up to my window and said, "Not only are you a bitch, but you're a fat bitch, a low-class, fat bitch." I was stunned. No one had ever said anything like that to me before (at least not to my face). The man looked to be in his 20s and he had a beautiful blonde with him, but he was rude as ever. I got out of the jeep and walked across the street. All the while he was yelling and blowing his horn, "Where are you going, bitch? Suey, suey, suey; fat pig; here piggy, piggy, piggy." I went into the first place

I saw and sat down in tears. The clerk asked if I was OK and I told her what happened. She called the mall policeman, but I told him there was no use; the kid wouldn't listen even if the policeman chastised him.

That young man made me feel humiliated, bullied and hurt, and it was the first (and only) time someone had been that cruel. I had to keep remembering that there were big beautiful women all over the place, and I had been chosen their top lady; but it took a while before I got my confidence fully back again.

Soon after, I met a woman we'll call Mindy Taggert. She was married to one of the most wonderful doctors in St. Simons and he was in charge of Charter by the Sea, the clinic for drug and alcohol addiction. Mindy and I had our hair done at the same salon, and there was a place next to the salon that was empty. Mindy suggested we lease it and open a boutique with fashions for women, including clothes for full-figured sizes. There was nothing like that on the island and she believed it would be successful. The hair salon was called The Main Event and our shop was going to be called The Sneak Preview. I was supposed to get a $10,000 settlement from the divorce, so I said yes. In the meantime, we used her husband's money and hired his CPA to help us, and before we knew it the CPA's niece was part of the business, too, as was the salon owner, so there were four of us: Mindy, me, the niece and the salon owner. No one put cash in it but Mindy (my money was tied up with Charles). We went to the merchandise mart, bought clothes and fixed up the space. We opened it and I loved it, but I was the only one putting any time into it. I worked nine to five, the only person doing so, and then I'd get dressed in the boutique and run over to Blanche's to hostess and sing. Jacob would come to the shop right after school and do his homework. Then my wonderful babysitter would come and take care of him until I got home. I still worked the other jobs, and I was studying for my real estate license. I was busy, to say the least.

I finally got my real estate license, passing my State Boards on my first try, and worked for a company called Litus. They liked that I had lots of jobs so I could meet people and sell property. I did sell, too, and I was an even busier girl.

Shortly after, I met Joe Odom and devoted by life to Sweet Georgia Browns of which you know the story (see Chapter Two). I was still trying to tie up loose ends from all the mess, but I thought I was through the worst of it until several events happened.

Chapter 21

More Troubles from Joe

After the bar had closed and I was back to St. Simons selling real estate and singing at Blanche's, there was a surprise. One day the police came to arrest me for writing several thousand dollars worth of bad checks. I went to the Savannah DA to tell him it was not my signature on the checks that had bounced and to prove it, I signed my name a bunch of times. They asked me whose signature it was and I said I suspected it was Joe Odom's. Faking a signature was a felony so Joe was to be arrested. The day they came to arrest him was the day of the Georgia-Florida football game, and he never missed one. When he saw the police coming, he snuck out the back window and went to the game. That was Joe for you.

Eventually they found Joe and he said that I had given him permission to sign my name, and now I was just angry and trying to get him in trouble. Well, that didn't fly, but Joe was such a brilliant attorney and such a mastermind, he could sit down at a typewriter and in 20 minutes he could have something typed out that would take five Philadelphia lawyers three months to unwind—he was that smart. He bought some time, and when the court date rolled around, he had paid off all the money except about $1,800. The judge reduced the charge from a felony to a misdemeanor and told Joe that if he didn't pay the rest back in a timely manner, he would go to jail. He started paying the money back to the court, but then there was one excuse after another why he couldn't continue, and in the meantime, the bankruptcy case was coming down on us.

I had lost the bar in Savannah, I was in financial trouble, I had lost my marriage, and Mike (my boyfriend) and I were having trouble; I couldn't sleep and I was plain worn out. Since Charles and I were still friends, I asked him for something to help me sleep, and he prescribed the new drug at that time, Xanax. I started taking it and in eight months I was taking twice as much as I was prescribed because I was waking up at one in the morning and not being able to fall back asleep, so I'd take another pill. Mike was going through a lot of personal problems himself and our relationship was strained. Jacob was feeling the effects of not having a father around and everything seemed to come crashing down. Before I knew it, it was close to time to go before the bankruptcy judge and I'd have to take a Xanax just to relax enough so I wouldn't hyperventilate about the upcoming event. One day I faced the fact that I was addicted to Xanax. I made arrangements for Jacob and went to the emergency room at Glenn County and told the physician that I thought I had a problem.

He looked at me and said, "I've seen you somewhere before. Yes, you're from Savannah and you had Sweet Georgia Browns with Joe Odom."

I said yes and he went on to say there was nothing wrong with me that, "Honey, Joe Odom has just about driven everybody crazy. You don't need to go to the drug unit; go home and rest." He wrote me a prescription for some sort of nerve pill and told me to go to the beach and relax. "It'll be better tomorrow." He wanted me to take a nerve pill to get over an addiction to another nerve pill!

I knew better and as I drove over the Causeway at St. Simons, I saw Charter by the Sea and pulled in. I went in and said I needed help for my addiction to Xanax. The next thing I knew I was in the 28 day program and this, of course, upset my whole family. I found out that coming off of Xanax causes sleep troubles: it doesn't allow you to sleep; it does the opposite; it keeps you awake. I had to let go of all of my jobs, but I knew my health had to come first. Also, Jacob was being cared for by friends, and Wes was away at Darlington, so they were safe and I could get the help I needed.

One night while I was wide awake I overheard the doctor at the treatment center desk, scolding Charles on the phone saying, "How dare you keep her on this drug for over two months. It is the most addictive drug in the world, and no, you are absolutely wrong, she is addicted. She needs help and she needs to be here."

Charles was very upset that I had checked myself into Charter as was everyone else. Mike was just in a rage; and then, during my stay at Charter,

Mike's father died in his arms and I wasn't able to be there for him. He was very upset and it was just a very, very bad time in my life.

On top of everything, while I was in Charter, someone called the Department of Family and Children's Services to say I was an unfit mother, and they were concerned for my child, Jacob. They came to see me (at Charter), and I told them Jacob was well cared for, that I had taken him to stay with good friends whom I trusted explicitly, whose two boys played baseball with Jacob, and that all the bases were more than covered. (After a few months, the social worker asked who in the world hated me to do this, as I was so far away from being an unfit mother.) They reported all was well, but they had to come and check on me for the next six months to follow through. It was humiliating, and I just wished we could've gone to Disney World.

Later, it came time to face the bankruptcy court, and, of course, I told them the truth. I thought we were incorporated; we were supposed to have been, and that's another thing Joe didn't follow through on; he didn't incorporate us. He set aside the name and meant to follow through, he just never sent the money to fulfill it. I told the judge about what had happened and that I was unaware of the business end of it, even though I was listed as a partner, and I didn't have much for the bankruptcy court to take, that I had just spent the last six weeks in Charter and I guess I more or less threw myself on the mercy of the court. All of the attorneys and judges in Savannah knew about Joe and his shenanigans, so the judge found me not guilty and dismissed my part of the bankruptcy, so that was good.

I was still getting phone calls from all of the people who needed to be paid for the antiques we bought for Sweet Georgia Browns. I tried my best to get the items back to them, but it was an impossible situation because City Market had attached everything for back rent that had not been paid. It was a legal battle, and I just did all I could to try to get the people their possessions back. I gave legal testimonies, written statements and depositions, telling what happened. I don't know whether everyone got their things back or not. I know the signed Steinway piano went with the next tenant at Sweet Georgia Browns, Ben Tucker, (he changed the name of the club to Hard Hearted Hannah's) and when he moved to the Pirate's House's upstairs room called Hannah's East, he took it with him. I don't know business-wise how that happened, but anyway it sat at Hannah's East at the Pirate's House for a while. I know Emma Kelly played it until she died and that just seems right. Maybe that is just the way it was meant to be.

After the judge had dismissed my part of the bankruptcy, I went back to trying to do my real estate business. I wanted to go back to singing as I loved it so much, so I asked for my job back at Blanche's. I also worked for Kelly Services, and I did several other little jobs, such as selling makeup at home, to try and make ends meet (Rose Marie was the brand). I also helped my real estate employer, Litus Real Estate Development, develop Hampton Point at the north end of St. Simons Island.

I began doing children's theater in Savannah. Gary Strickland, the trumpet player who became a member of the band at Sweet Georgia Browns, and who had the corporation called Hurray for Kids, asked me to help with the group. We did children's theater in different parks every day in Savannah, so I was driving up to Savannah to sing and entertain the inner city kids. It was one of the best things I ever did with my singing. We would dress up in funny costumes and tell stories to the children. We introduced the inner city kids to opera and to singing, and we saw so many bright little faces that were just in awe. I know we introduced them to something that they hadn't been exposed to before, and that some of them might even go on and get into it for their life's work—it was very fulfilling.

Mike, the Italian fellow I was dating, really wanted me to move back to Savannah. His best friend was Buzz Harper, the gentleman I had met before, and the owner of the Hamilton-Turner House on Lafayette Square, and Buzz was ready to sell his beautiful Mansion. The Savannah College of Art and Design (SCAD) had shown some interest in turning it into a dormitory and he really hated for that to happen, so he asked my boyfriend if I was interested. Well, this delighted Mike because he would get me to Savannah. I told Buzz that, of course, I was interested, but I didn't have the kind of money it took to qualify for a mortgage on a half million dollar house. He said he was sure we could work something out.

Around this time, I also had heard that Joe had become ill, possibly with AIDS. One day when I was driving back home, I saw Joe on the street, and indeed it looked like he had AIDS. I asked Buzz about him and according to Buzz, Joe was very, very ill and in and out of the hospital, and in and out of the Hamilton-Turner House. Finally, Joe's illness became so bad he moved to the Rose of Sharon, a high-rise apartment building just a block behind the Hamilton-Turner House. It was owned by the Catholic Church and rent was based on income. It was very nice with elevators and help—just what Joe needed. I went to see him a few times and it was so sad. I don't know where he got the AIDS, although I had seen him in bed with men. I don't know if he'd ever tried a needle, but I do know he'd do anything anybody would give him. I just don't know and I didn't want to know. I tried to talk with him.

"I don't want to lose you," I said.

"Honey, you won't. I'm bigger than all that stuff," he said.

It was the last time I'd see him alive.

In November of 1991 I received a phone call from one of Joe's friends and he was crying.

"Nancy, Joe's gone," he said. "I was with him, Anne was there, as was his mom."

I started crying and asked if his death had been easy.

"He kept a sense of humor to the end, Nancy," then we both cried. I just hated that this wonderful, talented, intellectual, charming human being, who was only 44, would no longer be in this world. I wondered if he had taken all that wonderful energy and applied it in the right direction, how different his life—and mine—might have been. He died of pneumonia from HIV complications at the Rose of Sharon. The paper listed that he died at the Hamilton-Turner House and I was glad.

Joe never got to see The Book as it came out in 1994; I think he would have loved it, though, and would have gotten a real kick out of it. He would've also made sure we played ourselves in the movie.

Time moved on and I proceeded with trying to buy the Hamilton-Turner House.

Chapter 22

Midnight Madness

Charles had promised me money to start a business as I had used some of my inheritance to send his boys to school, and he still owed me some child support. I also needed his "doctor credit" to purchase the House, so I called him. He didn't see how in the world it would ever work, but I told him I would work out all the details if he would just give me the money he'd promised. Once the House was purchased, after a few months he was to quick claim the property to me and I would own it—we trusted each other that this would be the deal. I told him I would somehow or other make payments after I was settled. He said OK, and I started going from one bank to another to try and work out a loan. I got turned down every time. Finally, an independent mortgage broker by the name of Lin Walsh, who with her husband, had started a company called Independent Mortgage in Savannah, said she could help and I should show her the house. (Lin and her husband were divorcing but she was willing help me.) I immediately liked her as she was a no-nonsense lady around my age, and she seemed to know what she was doing. She and her secretary really gave me some hope so I started calling her every day.

"Lin, I think we can do it this way. Why can't we do it that way?" I'd say.

Anyway, one thing led to another and finally she found a bank in New York who'd get us a mortgage deal. They were coming to do an appraisal but to get a 30-year loan, we could only have four kitchens. The house had eight, so we had to do something quickly. Three were galley kitchens, so I put bicycles, lamps, clothes and lots of things in the kitchens, put up bi-fold doors and covered it all with burlap. We forgot to unplug the refrigerator on the first kitchen, and you could hear the noise from it, so we had to take everything all back out and do it over again. For the fourth kitchen, we bought paneling, put it up and then brought 12 foot trees in to cover up the paneling. The appraisal was done, we secured the property, closed on it in March, and I was the proud owner of a 10,000 square foot Mansion with very little (of any value) in it. The next day, the front page of the newspaper said that we had bought the most expensive house ever to sell in the Historic District of Savannah. That was March of 1991, and Charles was listed as the buyer. The purchase price was $475,000.

My idea was to open it as an historic house with tours every half hour, and eventually have a bed and breakfast upstairs while I lived in part of it. Jacob was in the middle of seventh grade, and I didn't want to move him then, so I started going back and forth, as usual, from St. Simons to Savannah. Mike's mother, Jane, and her friend Fred stayed with Jacob in St. Simons when I needed help.

When I bought the building, it had a few undesirable tenants. As leases would expire, I would take over that apartment and start to redo it. One particular unit was painted all black. The local SCAD students were very artsy and they loved black, so they painted the floors, the walls, the ceiling—everything—black. I should own a piece of the Kiltz Company as they have a thick white covering that you buy, that is very smelly, but it covers up even black walls so you can paint over them. Anyway, I was gradually making the Mansion historic again.

I needed furniture for the house—big furniture to fill rooms with 16-foot ceilings. Buzz took some of my antiques that I had acquired over the years and traded up for me. People had a hard time selling the larger antiques so Buzz used that to his advantage. He would take my normal size things and sell them and then find the big ones, bargaining for a good price. Before long, I was furnishing right and left and getting it ready to open. Buzz helped me with everything.

I was having a difficult time getting approval for my business permit. The "Gods in the Marble House," as I called the Metropolitan Planning Commission, weren't crazy about a woman—who wasn't a Savannah native and who came from a partnership with Joe Odom—taking over a residential business and turning it into a tourist business. I pointed out that Lafayette Square had many tourist and business attractions already going on: The Low House, Flannery O'Connor's home, the Cathedral, a law office, and gift shops, and I produced letters from people who were thrilled that I was bringing back this fine Mansion. I had even talked with Mr. Adler, a local, respected preservationist, who said he didn't see anything wrong with the whole idea; but I just couldn't please them. All told, it took me almost a year, but finally they had to give me the permit because I met all of the city's criteria.

I had spent about six months in researching how tours in these houses were run. I also researched the family who had built the house (Samuel Pugh Hamilton), and put everything together to start a 20-minute tour. Ms. Bette Davis from Chattanooga, Tennessee, a descendant of the Hamilton family, came down for the grand opening. We had a wonderful reception and the paper wrote a story—*Southern Beauty Gets a Facelift*. I was off and running.

Besides being a mother, I did everything in the house by myself. I did all the cleaning, all the touring, all the business, all the repairs, everything. Mike was, at this point, getting a little fed up with how much time the business was taking; it was a whole lot more than anything I had ever done. He was into hunting, fishing, and going and doing, and I just wasn't being the girlfriend he wanted, so things on the romantic front were not very good (again) at this point in time. I have since learned that it is really hard to run a business of this nature and have any sort of romantic relationship with anybody, unless they love what you do, and they are willing to work beside you and do the work with you. Before long, Mike and I were not speaking anymore and it was over.

About the same time, my mother, who already had Alzheimer's, and my Grandmomma were living together in our house in LaFayette (Charles was kind enough to let them stay there even though we were divorced) when my grandmother got very ill. I had to go up and see about the situation, and I put her into a nursing home. I got someone to live with my mom at the house, but I was back and forth every two or three weeks to check on Grandmomma and mother. It was an eight-hour drive from Savannah to LaFayette, and it was brutal. Grandmomma had not been herself for the last two years; her mind was there but her body wasn't and it was hard. She finally did die, and it broke my heart. I still miss her deeply.

Finally, mother got to the point where I couldn't leave her at all, so I brought her to The Hamilton-Turner to live with me the year Grandmomma passed away. Home health care workers came by to help with her bath and medicine. Jane, my old boyfriend's mom, was selling her home and had nowhere to go. My friend, Kathleen, took Jane to my house (I was on a trip to Disney World), and put her in the room where mother was until they could figure out where Jane could go. Jane's kids wanted her to go to a high rise apartment where the residents were mostly older people. Jane was a pretty, still young Irish lass with a partner, Fred, and she didn't want to go there. At first I was a bit perturbed that Kathleen left Jane and Fred at my house. What was I going to be able to do for her, and where could she and Fred stay? But, as often happens, if you just let God work, and you just try and do the right thing, what you thought would be a problem ends up a blessing. After mother's turn for the worse, I don't know what I would've done without Jane and Fred. They ended up staying, helping me to care for mother, and for a while that worked out fine. They also helped with Jacob in St. Simons.

I had put mother on the Garden level of the house because she could look at the square in front, watch the people, and enjoy the action. The Cathedral's day school, which housed 300 children, was right next door and she could also watch the children as they lined up to go to class. Tour buses would stop at the Cathedral to let people in to see this beautiful building and she could observe all of that. One day, however, the local city bus driver came in for help. It seems he had a lady on the bus who would not get off, and she was insisting he take her to Chattanooga! It was mother, of course. I had a devil of a time convincing her that it wasn't the bus to Chattanooga, and she should come home. I moved her to the top floor of the house where there were lots of steps up and it helped contain this kind of "fun."

Mother then had a stroke and was in Memorial Hospital. She'd get up in the night and wander off. One night about three in the morning, I was staying in the room with her and all of a sudden I heard lots of noise. She had wandered off into the lobby and was stark naked. I said, "Mother, what are you doing?" She said she was leaving and didn't want to take someone else's clothes. (The nurse told me her flesh was just flapping in the wind.) She came home to the House and we continued her care.

One of the health care workers was Kathy Metts, and she helped me a lot. She was the wife of Dr. Jimmy Metts, the coroner for the Jim Williams shooting, and a person featured in The Book. One night Kathy, Jimmy and their daughter came to my house for dinner. Dr. Jimmy asked me how I made the Hamilton-Turner the success it was and I told him, saying that I could teach Kathy what to do. He thought he could pay his taxes doing tours, so I helped him get set up with furniture and tours.

Linda Odom called one time and said she had sold a tour for the American Orient Express and she didn't have anywhere to take them. What could she do? My house was being repaired, so I suggested the Metts house. She brought tour groups in and they'd get a Mint Julep drink and lunch, and I'd sing for them. That ended up being a partnership that would last some years, even after I sold my house.

There was always something breaking with eight bathrooms, eight kitchens, eight air conditioning systems, and eight heating systems. One day I needed a plumber. My friend, Lin, told me to call Buster Hodges (not his real name). He was the best plumber there was and when Buster came in, it was automatic electricity. He was sitting backwards on the toilet, trying to see what was wrong in the "water closet" tank. He was really impressed with the thirty-something year old toilet and he said it was top of the line when it was made in the late 60's and would have been very expensive. He wanted to show me that it had a special chain that the water ran down, thus making the toilet totally silent. When I leaned down to look at it, we were inches from each other's faces. Well, there you go. First kiss...yep! Right there on the unique toilet.

He was just wonderful and the next thing you know, he and I were an item. He had two children whom I became very close to, as I did to their mother (we are still great friends to this day).

I moved Jacob up from St. Simons, but I moved him from a little island with hardly any crime whatsoever into the historic district of Savannah where crime was high. There were homeless people everywhere and Jacob and I were not use to this. About three months after Buster and I started dating, Jacob asked Buster to move in with us. We were both a little afraid of our new area and, bless his heart, I think Jacob kept a big stick by his bed at all times. Looking back, I really did him an injustice moving him up here, but I thought it was a chance for us to have a better relationship and be together, so I thought I was doing the right thing.

Our house was growing slowly but surely, and I had a successful business. I hired a part-time tour guide after a year, and he and I were doing historical tours every 30 minutes. I had a bed and breakfast opened, and had weddings, receptions, luncheons and dinners at the House. It became a very popular place for people to have their events. I hired two more tour guides shortly thereafter, and served on several committees around town in connection with the Chamber of Commerce.

At this time, my son Wes had some problems. He had gotten a job right out of college at Georgia Southern University in Statesboro, Georgia as a recruiter for the school he had attended. He was in charge of the state of Florida as well as his alma mater, The Darlington School in Rome, Georgia because he had done so well there. He loved the job and had a credit card, car, and clothes all under the auspices of Georgia Southern. One day he was in Florida, talking to about a thousand young people about his college alma mater and how great it was, when he went down on one knee—he almost passed out and was physically ill. He went to the ER and they said that he had had an anxiety attack. Now, Wes had spoken in front of thousands of people, was a gifted speaker and a bit of an entertainer, and never had trouble with anxiety or stage fright, so we were suspect. At one point, a doctor thought he might have a brain tumor, so we were watching it closely.

Wes continued to have dizzy spells, saw floaters in his vision, was sick to his stomach, and generally was not well. In the meantime, people began getting sick at his office in the Rosenwald building, which had been built for the university in the late 1930s. First, one person got sick with lung problems, then another, and still another began having severe sinus problems. They decided to check the AC units. Bingo! There were terrible mold spores and nasty things that were making people sick, including Wes. He spent more than a week in the hospital, having tests and they decided the condition of the AC units caused the Sphenoid sinus cavity in the middle of his head to get infected. He had to have surgery to have it drained and repaired, and he needed daily care, so I brought him home to the House and gave him one of the suites. Every day, a nurse came to administer heavy duty antibiotics through an IV, and he finally recovered, but it took a month or more. He accrued a mountain of medical bills which the university refused to pay after a while. I wrote a letter to the President, urging him to pay attention to the building and to pay the medical bills, and it was all finally straightened out. About ten years later, the building was renovated. It was a very scary time, though, for my son and for my family.

Then John Berendt, who had been gone for a while, showed up again and started calling me. He said he had just completed a book and he wanted to know if he could talk to me. Knowing that he didn't really care for me, I wondered why he wanted to talk, so I avoided him and didn't return the calls.

One day he called again and said, "Look, Nancy, you know I loved Joe, but I could certainly see his faults. You know, I'm not a dummy, and there were a lot of people he hurt, and you were one of them. Now your character is one that I want to use in my book. Everybody loves your character and I want to include you."

"What does that mean?" I asked.

He explained that some of the things I said, and some of the things that went on with Sweet Georgia Browns he wanted to include in The Book. I said that I would rather he didn't, that a lot of that time was a growing experience for me, and it was just a place I really didn't want to revisit. He said he understood but would I please just meet him for lunch sometime. I never called him back. Then, one day, he showed up at my doorstep. He said he was in Savannah to get some last minute details done for his book, that he had a publisher which was Random House, and would I please have lunch with him at Clary's.

I agreed to meet and butter wouldn't melt in John Berendt's mouth. You would have thought that I was his long-lost sister. At lunch, he was all smiley and nice, and not nearly as pious and condescending as he had been on previous occasions—when he was just cutting. For example, one Easter I dressed in a white suit and attended church services at the Cathedral. When I returned home, I changed into Easter colors of yellow and orange. As I walked down the stairs, I heard John tell Joe, "She looked like the Virgin Mary this morning and now she looks like an Easter egg." He was just mean, at times, and I always felt like he thought I was a little redneck from Tennessee who was just blonde and female, and had the nerve to own a big historic Mansion in Savannah. As I said earlier, I also felt like he resented me for taking away precious time from his beloved friend and confidante, Joe Odom. Joe spent a lot of time with me—rehearsing, singing or whatever—and it took a lot of time away from John Berendt's time with Joe. And remember, I had always thought that John and Joe were something more than just friends, but it was never any of my business to ask Joe who his sexual partners were, and I didn't care to know; I just always suspected. John would take Joe off to trips to New York at times, and Joe would come back shaking his head and saying, "Whooo, those high-faluting queers. You know John knows them all, and he knows all those places." I just never asked any questions—but I had an inkling.

So here we are at lunch that day, and he read me the part of his book where Mandy (my character in The Book) is driving with her knees and doing her makeup, and he asked me to tell him that story again.

He said, "That's about all I'll be putting in it—just a few little things like that. The major part of The Book is about Jim Williams." I said I knew Jim, and John said, "When did you meet Jim?" And I told him about the night we all went out to dinner at 45 South, where Joe called me and said to dress and fluff up because we were going out with Buzz.

John said, "I know that you really didn't want to be in The Book, but I promise you will like it. Everyone loves your character, and we've just got to put you in."

In my opinion, I do think he needed my character in The Book, but not because he liked me. I think he realized he had to have a heterosexual relationship to keep The Book saleable to everyone. Without our story, The Book was just about a homosexual shooting, a homosexual trial that took eight years, and a story about a prominent black drag queen who had a friendship with John Berendt.

"OK, John, but there are a couple of things here," I said. "I want you to change my name and my place of residence, and you promise it won't be anything but just silly stuff like the makeup story. You know, they're going to think I'm a bimbo, driving with my knees and such, but that story is real."

"Well, that's OK, that's about it," he added.

He promised he would honor my stipulations and I met him later at an office to sign some papers. The papers spelled out that I would never draw anything from The Book, that I would have no rights to The Book,

I would never make any money from The Book, and I would never sue. That bothered me and I asked John why I would want to sue. "Oh, you won't, you won't. I have already told you what it's about and you don't need to worry."

He asked what name I wanted and I had always liked the name Mandy ever since Barry Manilow's song came out. I also thought about Nicky, as my dad's name was Nick and I hadn't known him until I was 16. Either one was nice but I combined them and Mandy Nichols was born.

John did publish and I received an advance copy in December of *Midnight in the Garden of Good and Evil.* My good friend, Lin Walsh, and I were on our way to Florida to spend a little time in the sunshine with my brother. I said I had The Book and we read through it briefly to see where I appeared and what he said. In the front, John had put the inscription, "To Nancy, December 1993, You're tops in my book." It hadn't hit the shelves yet but would be coming out in late January. As we drove along, I would read to Lin and then she'd read to me and we would laugh.

We loved a lot of the stories in The Book, but she said, "You know, Nancy, this is not the way it was at all."

"No, it's not," I said, "but I guess it doesn't matter. Nobody is going to read a book about Savannah and an obscure little killing. Who knows Savannah, an unknown city in the South? I really doubt that it is going to get anywhere, but it sure is funny. And most every funny story in this book came right out of Joe's mouth, and what Joe didn't say, Jerry Spence filled in (Jerry, you recall, was the hairdresser and Joe's friend who played himself in the movie). It also sounds just like Joe and Jerry—it's full of their stories." Lin noted that Berendt didn't even come until way after the murder—"but he's got their stories in there."

We were enjoying it, and then we forgot about it.

When I returned home, I got a phone call from the Chamber of Commerce. They said that a news team would be in Savannah to talk about The Book, and they wanted me to be available. I said OK, but I didn't go. I just didn't want to be a part of it. I called Lin to ask her advice and she said just to avoid it.

The next few reporters that called said, "Ms. Hillis, we realize you are Mandy in The Book. Will you talk with us?"

"What makes you think I am Mandy?" I said.

"Well, you are the only blonde, green-eyed, former Ms. BBW that was in business with Joe Odom."

I asked Lin, "What am I going to say? These reporters keep calling."

"Nancy, just bat those eyes and say you never lived in Waycross, and that should work."

It did work. It let them know that I wasn't going to talk to them. But what happened was that the reporters would be miffed that I wouldn't talk to them and they would write whatever they pleased. I was called the "big-haired, big-boobed, lounge singer" and "Joe Odom's moll," you know, like Bonnie was Clyde's moll—and I finally realized it would be better to talk to them and let them know that Mandy was Nancy Hillis and Nancy Hillis was a mother, a business owner, and a pretty normal person. I was not the empty-headed, good time girl who helped Joe Odom take advantage of folks.

The next time the Chamber called, it was to appear on *Good Morning America*. The show was going to be in Savannah on the River Queen on River Street. Emma was going to be there, John was going to be there and would I please be there. I fluffed up and went down to River Street. I stood there and watched the camera crews come in and then Ben Tucker walked up.

Ben Tucker was the black jazz musician who owned Hard Hearted Hannah's, the Dixieland Jazz bar where Emma Kelly played above the Pirate's House. Ben was also the entrepreneur who took over our club after City Market padlocked it, and he became the proud owner of the signed Steinway piano.

Ben came up to me after he unloaded his base. I assumed the Chamber had asked him to come and back up Emma. He said, "I've got to get this base on the ship. Tell me about this book business."

"Ben, it's just a book. Do you remember John Berendt?"

He said he didn't remember meeting him, but he knew he hung around with Joe. Ben said, "You know I didn't hang around those gay boys."

"I know, but he's written a book."

"Am I in it?" he asked.

"Ben, honestly I haven't read it all. I've only read bits and pieces. I haven't read it cover to cover."

"Well, I guess I've got to be in it somewhere and I guess I'll find it. Where's Emma?"

At about that time, here came Emma and as they were getting on the paddleboat, I stood back. I was still a little afraid, and, suddenly, John Berendt jumps out of a limo. He had on his denim shirt, khaki pants, and his Docksiders. "Well, Nancy, I am a little surprised to see you here," he said.

"John, how are you? The Chamber called me and asked me to come. I understand *Good Morning America* is here."

"That's right," he said. "The crew is over there getting set up. How did you like The Book?"

"I think I do. It seems to be pretty good. Congratulations on getting it published."

"Oh, yeah, now let me see. Why do you suppose I changed your name?"

"I guess it's because I asked you to, John."

"It seems to me it was that nasty abortion. That's why I thought you would not be at any of these."

My heart felt like someone drove a shovel through it. I had had an abortion many years ago and never told a soul. Was this what he was referring to? If so, how did he know?

With that, he walked away. I stood there for a minute and asked myself if I had heard him correctly. I looked at him, and all I saw was his back as he walked into the flurry of newspaper people and the *Good Morning America* crew and they all started talking. At that point, something in me said, "Run, Nancy, run," but I stayed in the background and a couple of people from the Chamber came up and said they would like to get an interview. I kept trying to avoid it and I was able to. I was only seen as part of the crowd on the show and didn't say anything. I needed to go home and read that book cover to cover to see what I missed. It was like a fury—my mind was racing and I scanned it looking for anything that had Mandy in it. I didn't find anything about an abortion in The Book and I thought, "What in this world is he talking about? Am I crazy? Did he really say that to me or have I lost my mind?"

Time went on and The Book became more and more popular. I had four tour guides by now and I was asked to sign more and more books.

One time we set up a book signing in the yard of the Hamilton-Turner House. It was Chablis, Emma Kelly and I, and special tours went by to meet us and sign books. Some would take a tour through the house. Charles had been coming over from where he lived in Alabama once a month to see Jacob, and he appeared during this signing.

"Dr. Hillis is here," said one of my guides. "Where should I put him?"

Well, Chablis heard the word "doctor" and her ears perked up.

"Oh, Nancy, did she say 'Doctor Hillis?'" asked Chablis. "Are you married to a DOCTOR? Not a dentist or foot doctor or chiropractor, but a reee-aaal doctor?"

"I was, Chablis," I said, "but we're divorced. He's an emergency room doctor."

"Oh, my my, do you think he'd give me my hormones?" and she patted her chest. "You know us girls feel better with some hormones."

I laughed at the situation and said, "Chablis, I'll introduce you to him but you are on your own, honey—just ask him."

"Oh, I can handle it," she replied. Only Lady Chablis could do that.

She sashayed up to him as he started up the stairs and introduced herself as only Chablis can do. She leaned over to get close enough to whisper. I watched absolutely delighted as Charles' eyes got bigger and he looked in my direction for help. But he put everything down and asked her what kind of pills she was used to taking. She spoke up, smiling and being oh so flirty saying, "Oh no, I takes injectables; that's the only thing that works." Charles got out his prescription pad and proceeded to write. Then he looked puzzled and asked her, "Whose name, uh, what name do I put on the prescription?" She told him some name to use and the deed was done. She kissed him on the cheek and he smiled a nervous smile and said thank you to her. The guide took him on to his room.

Later at dinner, I asked if the prescription could hurt Chablis and he said no, that it would just help diminish facial hair and other male qualities, and help to bring out the high voice and feminine characteristics Chablis wanted.

About a year before The Book came out, a young girl by the name of (we'll call her Delilah Smith) had approached me one day about a job. Her grandmother owned the oldest tour company in Savannah (author of the guide the city used to train guides) and Delilah said her grandmother was bankrupting the business. She was looking for a job and asked if I needed help. She had a city license and was quite good so she started helping me. We became friends and she and her husband helped me do lots of things. She, the husband, whom we'll call Bubba, the children and I went to Disney World two or three times together, and we had a nice relationship. One day Delilah approached me about opening a gift shop in the space downstairs at the Hamilton-Turner House where currently there was nothing. I agreed, but I told her I didn't have any money.

"Oh, that's OK," she said, "Charles will give you the money. We'll both put in $1,500 and you give me rent-free space for about a year. I'll run it, and then in six months we will look and see where our profits are and how much we can put back in the business." She had gone behind my back to Charles for the money and he agreed. I was a little miffed, but it sounded like a win-win situation to me so that's what we did.

After about six months, we had made no money. I kept asking her to see all the financial books, but she said she would get to it eventually, but there was no money to be made yet. I kind of figured she was right, so I didn't push it. I said we should keep it for six more months and if it didn't work by then, we'd close it and rent out the space. She agreed. Then The Book came out.

One day she came to me and said, "Nancy, my grandmother has read this book, and we are not going to sell it in the gift shop. It is full of homosexuality, black drag queens, voodooism, and things that we just don't believe in. You know, I sing in the choir at Ardsley Park and my father is the minister of music, and my husband is studying to be a deacon. This is against all of our Christian principles and we are not going to sell it."

"Delilah, I could care less whether you sell it or not," I said. "I am not interested in selling it either. I hope it will be done and gone before long. It covers a time in my life that I'm not proud of and I think it's going to be a flash in the pan and will be gone."

She responded by advising me not to admit being in it.

"I'm going to have a real hard time saying that," I replied. "I am not a good liar, and I don't think I can avoid that. It has been made too public, and John Berendt seems to have a big wheel behind him that is promoting The Book like I've never seen before. It is what it is."

My love life continued. My boyfriend, Buster lasted a couple of years. Then came (again, not his real name) Dudley Howard. I was out with my son Wes and his fraternity brothers one night and I went to get a round of drinks for them and all of a sudden a man's arms went around me from the back.

"Wait a minute, who are you?" said a gentleman.

"I'm the waitress and I need to go."

It was Dudley Howard. He came over to the table and told the boys he was sorry if I was one of their girlfriends but he thought I was cute and he just had to talk with me. He was ten years younger than me, but he asked me to go out with him.

"If you want to see me," I said. "You have to call and ask me to go out." I thought I'd never hear from him again.

We started dating and fell in love. He was a good, good man. We dated about seven years and he lived on Wilmington Island. He was an engineer and was on call a lot, and he also had custody of his two children so I took his children around and I became part of their lives. (We, of course, took our kids to Disney World several times together.) His kids slept at the house and he finally moved in and I slept on a trundle bed, and Dudley in a separate bedroom. He asked me to marry him, and I've asked myself a dozen times why I didn't marry him but I was just afraid to get married again. I told him that I did want to marry him someday, just not right now. He worked right beside me in the Hamilton-Turner Mansion, he went through some tough times with me and we had some great times. He did run around on me though, and it was a very dramatic break-up, but that came later.

I was known to go to Books-A-Million upon occasion to have a cup of coffee and get away from it all. I was there one day and the manager came up to me and said, "We know you're Mandy in The Book, and we would like to have a book signing. We had Mr. Berendt in, but we would like to have all the other characters here, including you. Do you know any of the other characters?" I said that I did and I wrote down what I knew and he contacted them and set it up. On the appointed day of the signing, Emma and I showed up first. We were supposed to sing an hour or so before we signed books, but the line of people waiting was wrapped clear around the building and the manager said, "Just get over there and start signing.

Some of these people have been here before we opened this morning." Dudley, who had brought me, looked at me and said, "I suppose I should read this book; I thought it would be nothing."

We started signing and we were joined by Wanda; little Miss Gloria, the wonderful black maid who worked with Joe and me; Johnny, Jim Williams' barber; Jerry Spence; and Lady Chablis, and lo and behold, who is in the line but Delilah Smith. Every time someone came up to take my picture she would be behind me, smiling, with four or five books in her arms.

"Delilah," I said. "I thought you didn't feel right about this book."

"Oh, well, I think because it is a local book and you know, it's gonna be historic someday. I decided I would get a few first editions for an investment."

I think Delilah's Christianity went out the window when the dollar came in because she ordered cases and cases of The Book from Random House. Then she came to me and asked if I would sign them, as she could sell them for more, so I did.

About this same time, Delilah also decided to pay me rent.

When she handed me a check for $475 and called it rent that month I said, "Delilah, what about my $1,500 and what about our partnership?"

"I think it would be better if we paid you rent as we are just now making a little money."

People who were coming on the historic tours began asking questions about The Book. It was getting to be a hassle so I had to quit being a tour guide because people wanted to know if I was Mandy. I couldn't give a history tour and then entertain questions about The Book. People who cared about the history didn't care about The Book and vice versa and it was becoming a conflict. So we started one book tour a day at three o'clock. I was staying out of sight until my employee came upstairs one day.

"Nancy, these ladies have been here from Hilton Head three times to see you and you are going to have to come downstairs and at least meet them. They know you are here. They've researched it and they know that's your car out front. Will you just come down and meet them!"

"You've got to be kidding."

"No, ma'am, now they've paid three times for a tour and they've driven over here three times just to meet you."

So I went down to the parlor and as I entered the room they all jumped up, "There she is. There she is. Oh, Mandy, thank you for coming down. We were wondering what kind of makeup you use and where you get your hair done. Someone said you have your hair done in Atlanta—who does it?" It was one question after another. They reminded me of hysterical groupies, but these ladies were in their 50s!

One day my employee said, "By the way, have you opened your bills today?" She was very good about taking care of my mail. She would put the junk mail in the trash and have the bills ready and in a pile.

"OK, tell me about the mail."

She proceeded to tell me I had the electric bill to pay, and the water bill to pay, and this bill and that bill "and you got three marriage proposals but I threw them in the trash because none sent in their financial statements."

"Whoa! What did you say?"

All of a sudden I realized that this thing was on a roll. Lots of tour groups and reporters from all over the world began appearing at my front door. I didn't think I was a major character in The Book, but people loved Mandy Nichols, and as far as they were concerned, I was Mandy—it sure made a difference in my business.

I quit signing books at night for Delilah as it was just taking too much of my time. In the next month or so, I kept seeing books from people who would walk in the house and ask me to write something special in them. I'd open their copy and it had a signature that said "Best Wishes and God bless, Mandy, AKA Nancy Hillis," which is how I always signed the books, but I looked and realized it wasn't my writing. Finally one time I went downstairs and confronted Delilah.

"Are you signing my name to these books?"

"Well, they'll never know the difference."

I asked her to stop doing it, that it wasn't right.

"Well, I can sell them for more, and they sell faster," she said. "Won't you sign them for me?"

I told her that I couldn't and she put such a guilt trip on me, but then one day I overheard her talking to a tourist. I was in my office which was in the gift shop area. Delilah did not know it because I came in the back door.

"I've heard so much about this book," said the tourist. "What's it about?"

"Oh, it's about a killing, but it's got all kinds of awful stuff in it. I'm a Christian and go to the Ardsley Park Baptist Church, and my husband is studying to be a deacon, and this whole book is against our Christian witness, but we have to sell it because the lady who owns this house is in it."

I was so mad and hurt, I wanted to go right in there and confront her, but I decided that wasn't the best time or place. I went outside and walked around the square some to calm down. Here she was calling herself a Christian, implying that I wasn't. I had thought we were friends and that she was caring and loving and I was just crushed. And how dare she become little Miss Pious when she's made money off this book while insinuating that I was a low-class heathen. I was upset and tossed and turned all night; I had been betrayed by a friend whom I loved. But then an idea came to me and the next day I went to her.

"I know it's been a problem for you selling this book—that it's hurting your Christian witness, so I'll lift this burden off you. I haven't been able to sleep over it, and I asked God to help me. I'll sell the books upstairs so you don't have to deal with it." I knew I was using God to get my point across and I asked him to forgive me but I was fed up with the situation.

"Oh, I don't mind." She was steaming, and I could see the panic on her face.

"Oh, but I heard you do, so I'll sell them upstairs from now on." There was nothing she could do.

Chapter 23

Mansion Madness

In 1994 we had a horrible wind and rainstorm. The water broke through the roof and came down all four floors. The insurance company came out and so did the J.T. Turner Construction Co. and we got started fixing the damage. They brought in machines that sucked the water out of the plaster and sheetrock, and there was no way I could have any business so I had to shut down for about three months. During that time, it kept raining and raining. The insurance company, who wanted to patch the roof, was negotiating with the construction company who wanted to put a whole new roof on the house, as did I. (I did say I would take a patched roof if it was guaranteed, but the construction company would not guarantee a patched roof.) In the meantime, it kept raining, and the roof kept leaking. By the time I would get all the pans upstairs emptied of water, it was time to go back down the four floors and empty the ones there. I called and called the insurance company and said, "If you all don't decide on something, the whole ceiling on the top floor is going to fall." Sure enough, one day, kaboom, it fell. I called the construction company and told them that whatever they had to do to come out now and do it as the whole ceiling was falling. Finally, the insurance company approved the new roof, which was going to cost $12,000, and they began putting it on.

All of a sudden the work halted because the insurance company was balking over the rest of the damages.

The roof came down again, twice as bad as before, breaking furniture, lamps, scratching floors and ruining the walls and woodwork. A year and a half later—in December of 1995—they were still negotiating the wind and water damage.

On December 13th, I returned to my house at noon. I always parked my car next to a school on East Macon St. under the third grade window, so kids were in school that day. A black man jumped out of a yellow Nissan truck, looked at me and said, "Give me your fucking bank bag."

I said, "What bank bag?" and then he stuck a big, long, silver gun in my stomach where I could *really* feel it, so I held up my hands and said, "Oh, that bank bag," and I told him it was in the car. I had put it under the seat.

"I want the damn keys to your fucking car," he then said, so I gave them to him and he motioned with the gun for me to come with him. He bent into the car and grabbed my purse, and for a moment I backed up, thinking I'd haul off and shove him with my foot and then run. But I saw a second man on the other side of the car, looking straight at me, so I froze. I had all of my staff Christmas presents in the car, and he grabbed them all, along with my bank deposit and purse and put them in the truck and he and his friend took off. I dialed the police right away and just kept yelling the car tag number and saying, "They're in a yellow Nissan truck, headed East on Macon St. and they are in plaid shirts, blue jeans and are wearing baseball caps," over and over so he'd get it. The dispatcher kept saying, "Ma'am calm down. We need a little bit more information." I shouted, "Like what!!?? I'm giving you information; they are now going south on Habersham. Please write down the tag number!"

"I need your name, address…" and I cut in, "My name is Nancy Hillis and do you not realize that I have my eyes on the robbers' truck and they are leaving the scene? You can get that stuff later after you dispatch a car and go after them. They are getting away!"

"Ma'am," he started. I said bullshit to myself and hung up.

It happened that that afternoon, I was going to lunch with my friend, Michael. Now Michael was known as 007, James Bond. He wore James Bond clothes, had "007" on his license plate, and his phone number had 007 in it. He was waiting for me in front of the house and I told him that I'd just been robbed.

"Get in the car, we're going to get them," he said. "Call the police."

So I called again and told the dispatcher we were in pursuit of the robbers and were now at 60th and Habersham and to send someone quickly. This time the dispatcher said, "You can't do that ma'am." My reply was, "Then you come do it and we will stop."

There were now two vehicles as they had split up and the yellow Nissan turned and went the wrong way on a one way street to get away from us as he recognized me. We followed the other car and he pulled over and jumped out of the car—with my $2,500 Chanel purse in his hand—while his car kept going and ran into a tree. That purse had been a gift from Charles and was very expensive. I would have NEVER spent that much money on a purse and I knew I'd never have another one, so I was determined to do my best to get it back.

Michael put the car in reverse, pulled a gun that just fit in the palm of his hand, and told me to lean back. "Is that the only gun you've got?" I said as it was not a very big gun. He gave me one of those "I-can't-believe-you-said-that looks," and shouted sternly, "lean back and roll down the window; this gun will still kill him." I turned my head and shut my eyes. He put his arm across my chest, fixin' to shoot, but the guy disappeared into some bushes.

The police finally arrived and later that day we were asked to identify the men from a lineup. We did and two weeks later a detective came by to tell me that these were drug dealers who had 20 witnesses who said they were having communion at mass that day at the time of the robbery. He said, "You are single, at the house alone, with 20 witnesses backing their story, and I think you should just let it go. They will eventually be caught and will go to prison, but it's not worth your life over $100 in cash, the purse and the presents because they will threaten and maybe hurt you." I never saw my Chanel purse or the presents again.

We filed another insurance claim for the robbery and the company had to settle the claim.

Around that time, Delilah and I were failing to communicate because she continued signing my name in her books. She kept doing things I asked her not to do and I was about at the end of my rope with her. I decided to present her with a lease for a lot more rent and I knew she wouldn't sign it, but I thought our relationship would end somewhat peacefully and she would move on.

On January 8, 1996, we were sleeping when Jacob came over from the other side of the house and said, "Mom, there is a real fire and I am not kidding." I knew he meant business and I got up and couldn't breathe. The smoke was so thick you couldn't see your hand in front of your face.

Dudley was spending the night and he jumped up, ran to get the fire extinguisher, and he and Jacob ran downstairs. He hollered to get my mom and Jane (along with our guests) out from upstairs. I could hear Fred, our resident handyman, coughing. He already had bad lungs from smoking and I yelled at him to crawl out the window. I started up the steps and got overcome with smoke, passed out, and rolled down the steps, hitting my head on the carrousel horse I kept from Sweet Georgia Browns (it saved my life). The blow brought me to my senses, and I crawled to the window, got my breath and realized just how bad the fire was. I grabbed the phone, called 911, grabbed my Yorkie, Elliott, jumped in the shower and wet us both down. I wrapped him in a wet towel, covered my face, and yelled to mother and Jane, who were standing at the top of the stairs, to go out the back and not try the stairs. Dudley went up and took them to the fire escape where he led them to safety. Later Dudley came through the downstairs fire escape with my parrot, Nonee Bird, and I could hear him saying, "Stop biting me you stupid bird, I'm trying to save your life." We were able to get the whole entourage out, and we checked into the Hilton at 5:30 am, all covered in soot. The house was damaged extensively. The parlor floor was burned and the fire went downward, so Delilah's gift shop was burned, too. After being treated for smoke inhalation the first thing I thought of was that Delilah would be gone.

I couldn't go back to the house for a week or two as I was so upset. Dudley had told me it was really bad and so did the fire department. Then two days after the fire, guess who showed up? Delilah, hugging me, loving me, holding me and telling me that God would take care of us and every-thing was going to be OK and when could she move back in.

"Delilah, I'm still being treated for smoke inhalation, the house is inhabitable and I don't know what we're going to do."

"The place on the other side of the garden level wasn't touched. Can I move my stuff over to the other side and open up the shop?"

I couldn't believe it. "You think you can do that with the house not open?" I said.

"Oh, yeah," she said. "I can't afford to be down." At this point, I told her that as soon as I could, I would move mother, who had Alzheimer's, and her caretakers, Jane and Fred, back in that part of the house, so all was up in the air at the moment.

One Sunday, while we were having Sunday brunch at the Hilton, a gentleman recognized me and asked if I'd sing. "I'd love to do it if the piano player wouldn't mind," I said. Mark Cartwright was playing the piano, and he said he didn't mind at all, but he mostly knew only country songs. We came up with a song, and I performed. Afterward, the General Manager asked if I would be interested in singing in the bar in exchange for some of my room charges (it was getting expensive at this point as we had two adjoining rooms for me, Dudley, Jacob, Jane, Fred, two parrots and one dog). I said yes so I worked with Mark and we were able to get a duo going. I started singing for my supper, so to speak.

As I got stronger, I started to do tours at the Hilton as the hotel was kind enough to let me use it for that purpose while the house was being fixed. People really wanted to meet Mandy, and The Book tours were so popular we went to two a day. I also made arrangements with the tour companies to bring their groups by the hotel's bar that was closed during the day, and the hotel served drinks and were able to make a little money while I was telling stories and signing books. Thanks to the Hilton I was able to keep things going.

We were at the Hilton for two months when we finally decided that mother, Jane, Fred and Jacob could move back to the part of the house where Delilah wanted to open the gift shop back up. She thought that she could still have her little gift shop in the front and the rest of us could move in the back, but, I needed an office and a place to sleep so I told Delilah she could not move back in. She was not happy with me at all!

I had learned that Delilah had taken all of the gift shop inventory that was not damaged by the fire to her home. The inspector did not want anything moved, but she took it anyway as she had big plans. Michael, my attorney friend, had noticed that in the paper she had asked for a business license in the name of "Hamilton's Fancy Goods." This was the name Mr. Samuel Pugh gave his four-story, 15,000 square foot shop on the north west corner of Bull and Broughton in 1873 after building the Hamilton-Turner House. Michael got an injunction against the name of her new shop because it was attached to our historic House. This, of course, added fuel to the fire.

"When do I get my money?" she said.

"What money?"

"I want my space finished in back and I want my contents money."

"Wait a minute, what contents money. What are you talking about?"

Delilah had begun talking to people about how she was going to sue me for negligence and for not covering the gift shop inventory; the insurance company got wind of it. This threw a kink in the whole thing because remember, I had three claims with this company: wind and rain loss, a robbery, and now a fire. They cancelled me. When I asked why, they said it was because they didn't realize I had several businesses all under the same roof: the bed and breakfast, the gift shop, the tours, and so on.

By this time, I had to get an attorney to help me try and unravel this mess. And Delilah finally opened a store in Savannah, and most of the things in the store were about *Midnight* and it did sell Chablis' book, *Hiding My Candy*. Delilah had pins, pictures, books, maps, coffee cups, anything pertaining to The Book, and John Berendt sanctioned the only *Midnight* Fan Club at her store. The lady that was so offended by The Book, and wanted me to have nothing to do with it at first now had a shop with a Bird Girl statue out in front, celebrating *Midnight in the Garden of Good and Evil*!

Chapter 24

Trouble With the Press

One time a young reporter from Washington D.C., who wrote for *George* magazine and the *Washington Weekly Standard*, came to the house and asked me questions about The Book and my life. I gave him the regular song and dance and answered all of his questions.

"I've done some research on you, Nancy, and you weren't even in Savannah when John Berendt said you were, is that correct?"

I told him that was correct. I had come to Savannah in 1987 and the shooting occurred in 1982. John had not been here either.

"So you didn't meet John Berendt walking down Jones Street to borrow ice, did you?"

I said that was true.

"Why did you let him write that?"

"I had no control over what he wrote."

"Did you know that that was what he was writing?"

"Of course I didn't."

Then he laid Joe's death certificate on the desk and said, "What do you think about that?"

This set me back a minute, but I said, "AIDS is a horrible disease and a lot of my friends have died from it. I wish they'd find a cure for it, don't you?"

"Well, John says you had sexual relations with Joe. Do you have AIDS?"

I got up from my chair and said, "Sir, this interview is over."

"Well, what do you have to say about this?"

"I did not write The Book and it's just a book," and I walked out.

Later, the reporter called on the phone.

"Doesn't it bother you what John said in The Book?"

"No, this is a book. It is not the Bible. It is a piece of entertainment and it has done a lot of good things for Savannah. It is well written. It is funny, and why should I be such sour grapes?"

"You should because it is a nonfiction book and you can't sell a nonfiction book that is totally full of fiction."

I mentioned that some of it was based on facts.

"That is what he should have said—a fiction book based on facts. He shouldn't have sold it…."

I interrupted him. "Well, I'm not a literary expert; I just know that it was just a good piece of entertainment and I laughed a lot."

"I'm going to confront John Berendt with this because it is important now that it is such a successful book. It will be important that the facts are straight."

"OK, but he will get mad at me and blame me for not sticking to his story. He already doesn't like me."

"What do you mean he doesn't like you?"

"He's been ugly to me on several occasions," I said. I told him the story about the Heritage of Golf Tournament in South Carolina. MCI, who was the sponsor, asked if I would speak to their group at the Pirate's House. Emma and John were also to appear. They came by the Hamilton-Turner House where we chatted, and then I went to lunch with them at the Pirate's House and we listened to Emma play and John speak. I signed books in the back while he spoke. When I walked into the room, he flipped around, obviously angry and said to the tour director, "What in the hell is she doing here?" The director said, "You mean Nancy? People love her. She's in your book and she has a right to be here. She is being paid just like you are."

The reporter asked me for Jeannie's number and said he'd verify the information. "Why does he treat you that way?"

"I've reflected on it over and over and I simply think it's because if you take the heterosexual relationship of Joe and me out of The Book, then it's mostly a gay book, so I think it was a business decision. I definitely don't think he intended to make me a star, but for some strange reason, I received some notice, and now I think he's afraid I'll speak up about how it really was. I also think he thought that I would be so aggravated and angry at the way he placed my character with Joe and other things, that I wouldn't have anything to do with The Book, but I've been forced to have something to do with it, and he knows not all of what he says about me is true.

The facts are: number one, I have a sense of humor; two, I don't take life so seriously or I would never have made it this far; and three, it is just a book. The only book with which I carry much credence is the Bible, and there are few things in there that I wonder how in the world it happened. Not that I don't trust God, but I just wonder. For example, I wish He'd explain to me how the Red Sea parted, but I guess it doesn't matter because I love God and believe in His Book one hundred percent. I guess if He made the Red Sea, then He can part it if He wants to! There is not another book in this life I feel that way about. That's the only important book I know of."

"I appreciate the way you feel, but I am going to have to investigate this," the reporter said. I knew this was not good news, but I had no idea just how bad it would be.

Top: The boat Granddaddy piloted on the Tennessee River. He'd blow the whistle, Grandmomma would hop on her horse and ride to meet him.
Bottom Left: Papa Lee Brown, 1930s.
Bottom Right: Myrtle Exum Brown.

Top: Brown's BBQ Restaurant on Broad Street,
Chattanooga, Tennessee; Grandmother and waitress.
Bottom Left: The pink sign that I lived below and loved.
Bottom Right: Mother at age 16.

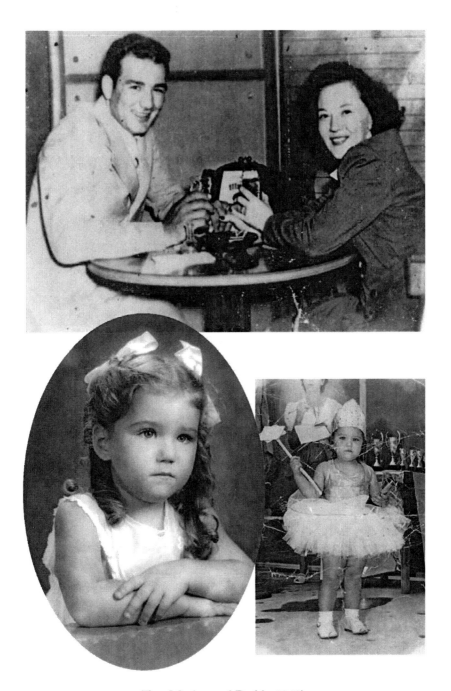

Top: Mother and Daddy, 1940's.
Bottom Left: Me at age 4.
Bottom Right: Little Miss Miami, 1949.

Wes' daddy, Charles Wesley Bonner.

Top: Grandmomma and me.
Bottom: Granddaddy and me.

Top: Superior Rating, Chattanooga Band Festival, 1964 (Nancy, far left).
Bottom Left: Drum Major, Chattanooga Valley High School, 1966.
Bottom Right: Miss Majorette of America Pageant, 1966.

Homecoming 1966.

Top Left: Graduation 1966.
Top Right: Solo twirler, University of Tennessee at Chattanooga, 1967.
Bottom: The band I sang with in 1967.

Top: Charles Hillis and me on our wedding day, December 26, 1973.
Bottom Left: Mamie Hillis, Uncle Raymond,
Mother and Grandmomma on our wedding day.
Bottom Right: Jacob and me, 1978.

Me with (left to right) Eleanor Jackson, Charles and Aunt Evelyn.

"If you can't hide it, just decorate it." Ruth Crews,
"The Last of the Red Hot Mamas."

Top: Litus Real Estate Team, St. Simons.
Bottom: The cover of *Big Beautiful Woman*, after I won the pageant, 1986.

Me as the model for Hanes Just My Size panty hose.

Modeling Hanes Isotoner slippers.

The invitation to the grand opening of Sweet Georgia Browns.

Sweet Georgia Browns poster, 1988. Joe at the piano, Gary
Strickland (trumpet), Ron Morris, waitress, me and Val Davis.

Top: Joe Odom at the piano, 1989.
Bottom: Left to right: a friend, Mary Mopper, Joe Odom and Wanda Brooks.

Top: Me and Joe at the Cloister Resort on Sea Island, Georgia.
Bottom: Me and Aunt Evelyn.

The Hamilton-Turner House on Lafayette Square, Savannah, Georgia.

The great Emma Kelly and friends.

Jerry Spence and I.

Top: Jeffery Hall, me and Lady Chablis.
Bottom: Me and my good friend, Linda Odom.

Top: My great friend Kathleen Yeckley.
Bottom: My bird, Elvis, and Coach Yeckley.

Wes (in college) and Jacob, a senior in High School.

EPIDEMIC!

Adolescent drug abuse has exploded into epidemic proportions. Parents and professionals alike have been challenged to react positively to change their own awareness and attitudes about this problem.

by Nancy Hillis

A MINISTER from South Georgia was frequently challenged by a parishioner, "Hey, preacher, what do ya know fer sho?" The minister finally found the perfect answer: "One thing I know for sure is that a rattlesnake can't straddle a rail fence."

What can we be sure of? Change. Nothing stays the same. The way we react to change can certainly vary — we can ignore it, resist it, or commit to making it a positive force.

The Epidemic

Drug and alcohol abuse has changed from a personal, adult problem to a medical, social, economic, and political issue. It is startling to see how rapid this change has occurred. Ten years ago, would you have expected to visit a third grade class in your community and find little boys in Cub Scout uniforms and little girls in jumpers learning about drugs that even adults cannot handle? This scene is both terrifying and encouraging —

Nancy Hillis (Mrs. Charles L.), from Lafayette, is a member of the Wayne County Auxiliary and chairman of Health Projects and Substance Abuse for the Auxiliary to MAG. Send reprint requests to her at P.O. Box 846, Lafayette, GA 30728.

Nancy Hillis displays some of the materials she uses in her talks on substance abuse. Photo courtesy of Bob Nichols, Chattanooga News Free Press.

terrifying in that drugs are such a problem even third graders must be prepared to deal with them, and encouraging in that we finally are fighting back to prevent drugs from taking any more of our children.

The unbridled greed of the drug culture has reached down to tap the youth market. We watched it saturate our colleges, then seep into high schools, then junior high, and finally grammar schools. It is easy for the older child to influence and sell to the younger.

Parent Involvement

Parents were the first to react with imagination and energy. The grassroots parents' movement began in small, isolated, neighborhood groups who came together because their children were smoking marijuana and experimenting with alcohol and other drugs. These parents were not indifferently ignoring nor bull-headedly resisting the change; they were intelligently involved by taking positive action. They embarked on a project that had nationwide ramifications. Out of one of these parents' groups in Georgia, in 1977, two Atlanta parents started the first resource center in the country to focus on the education and mobilization of parents for the prevention of adolescent drug abuse. Two caring parents, Keith Schuchard, Ph.D., and Thomas Gleaton, Ed.D., co-founded the now international organization known as Parent Resources Institute for Drug Education (PRIDE).

My article from the April 1985 issue of the Journal of the Medical Association of Georgia.

Nancy L. Hillis
Nancy L. Hillis, a graduate of the University of Tennessee, served as Chairman of the Adolescent Drug and Alcohol Abuse Committee for the Medical Association of Georgia Auxiliary and as a delegate to the American Medical Association Auxiliary in Chicago where she testified at the house of delegates hearing on drug abuse. Ms. Hillis acted as a Consultant on Alcohol and Drug Abuse for the U.S. Army Base at Fort Stewart in Hinesville, Georgia and Southeast Coordinator for Governor George Busbee's Task Force on Drug and Alcohol Abuse. She is a certified speaker for PRIDE and is an advisor for Senator Culver Kidd's "Stop Drugs at the Source" campaign in North Georgia.

Top: My bio.
Bottom Left: Charles and his friend, right before his death.
Bottom Right: Me and Jeffery Hall.

Nancy Hillis, otherwise known as "Mandy" from the book and the movie Midnight in the Garden of Good and Evil loves Vidalia® Onions and is our celebrity spokesperson. She's famous from Savannah, GA to Hollywood, CA, but our Vidalia Onions are the "star" of every meal. They're available to appear on your table from late April through the Holidays.

Top Right: Wes and Sheila.
Bottom Right: Spokesperson for Vidalia Onions.

Wes, Jacob and me at the ALS Walk-a-thon, 2013.

Top: Jacob, Jeffery and me.
Bottom: Lin Walsh and Jerry Spence.

Singing with the Good Ole Boys in St. Simons at Blanche's Courtyard.

What I call the Holy Five: left to right: John Brown, Bruce Kelly, Joe Odom, Jim Williams, and John Berendt, seated at the Hamilton-Turner Mansion.

From left to right: Jacob, Nancy, Mickey, Wes and Sheila at Disney World.

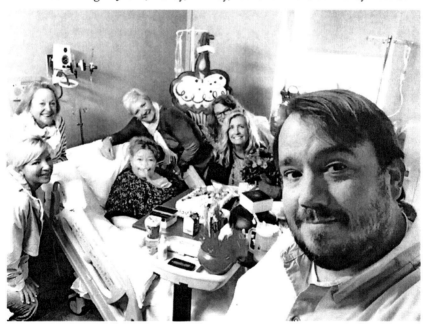

My birthday this year at the nursing home: left to right Sheila, Linda Odom, me, Mary Anne, Kathlenn Yeckley, Valerie Beaudreau and Wes.

Me and my son Wes right before my illness.

Chapter 25

The Movie

I heard rumors that *Midnight* was going to be a movie, so Dudley and I went to LA to stay with a friend who was a photographer, and to visit the producer and writer of the film. We wanted to drive to MGM and talk to Nita Zuckerman, the producer we had already met in Savannah, and John Lee Hancock, the writer of the screen play, whom we also had already met. They told us to come by at two in the afternoon, so our friend said he'd take us to Paramount first and then we'd eat in the commissary as it would be fun. That's what we did and it was a hoot. They were filming one of the *Star Wars* movies and all the people were in costume, having their lunch and that was so wild; there were all of these characters with their weird make-up and costumes; one guy was breathing through "gills" on his cheeks and it looked so odd; you couldn't keep your eyes off them, the make-up was astounding—so cool and so much fun. Then we went to Beverly Hills to see the Beverly Hills Hotel. We saw where the stars would sit in the lobby and around the pool, and where staff would bring phones to them for their calls; I bought souvenirs and we got our picture taken in the Polo Lounge—it was great. Then we went to MGM.

The MGM people were so sweet to us, and my map (called The *Map of Good and Evil According to Mandy*) which was a map of Savannah that listed all the locations of the places involved in The Book, was on their wall and they were using it. They held up the copy of *Variety* that said Clint Eastwood was to direct the movie. It had just come out that day. We chatted and chatted, and they had some questions, and we had a great conversation. I said that I was wondering, if the Mandy character was in the movie, "You know I sing and dance, and I'd maybe like to play myself." They said right away that Mandy was in the movie a lot, but the two of them said that it would take a female lead and they needed a big name movie star to play the part. I asked if I could make a suggestion, and I suggested Dolly Parton—long fingernails, make-up, big hair, a singer from Tennessee, bubbly—someone who looked and acted like me. They laughed and said they'd think about it. I said that I also had a song that a guy, Rick Burris, had written called *Midnight in the Garden of Good and Evil.* His sister brought it to me and it was a cool song; it would be perfect for the movie. They ended up using all Johnny Mercer songs (which I love), and they weren't interested in the song. It's a shame because it was just great (see the lyrics at the beginning of this book).

We left and everyone was proud that I asked to appear in the movie as myself. You never know until you ask, and I asked.

I was doing a tour, standing at the front of the parlor in the Hamilton-Turner House, and somebody snuck in the parlor door and it was the producer, Ms. Nita Zuckerman, and a good looking, dark headed guy. I introduced Nita to my tour group, though I didn't know the guy, and he finally said, "Miss Mandy, I'm your Joe." It was Paul Hipp, a Tony award winner who won the part of Joe Odom in the movie. He hugged me and it was just great. They hadn't started filming yet, and they came by to say hello. Once filming began, I did go to the set some days, but I was just too busy to go very often.

Another time, I was painting the little gift shop area where I had tried to open a breakfast place (more about this later), to make it a *Midnight* museum. We had a life sized cardboard cutout of Joe where people loved to have their picture taken; all kinds of memorabilia from the places featured in *Midnight*; a painting of the Bird Girl (a statue that was featured on the cover of The Book, and very famous in its own right) on the wall; just everything you could imagine and the people could look at it while they were waiting for the tour. My main tour guide announced that someone was there, wanting to meet me. I turned around and there was Allison, Clint Eastwood's daughter who played Mandy in the movie. She had a hat on and no make-up, and I was a mess from painting, but we went and chatted about lots of things. She had tattoos; one on her wrist and one on her ankle and I asked her how they were going to hide those, as I didn't have any. She said she had this magic stuff in a can that would cover them right up. I told her I'd like to have a case of it for my whole body—it sounded like good stuff. She was about to have her 21st birthday, so young and very sweet, and long, tall and lanky like her father.

She did ask me what John Berendt had against me as she had been at dinner with him, her dad and other main characters, and he insisted that Mandy was not Nancy Hillis, but a "combination of all the women in Joe's life."

"What's up with that?" she asked. "None of us at the table could figure out what he meant, especially after all this time." I told her that John just didn't like me, and he did "mess with my character;" that Joe had been gay and we were never lovers, but it made for a good story.

She and I had a great time together.

Ever since our Oprah appearance, John Berendt had his people looking into my background to find out anything they could that was negative about me. I kept hearing from my friends that people were coming around asking questions. Someone from LaFayette called to say there were people there, asking about me, and then Georgia State, where I did my internship to learn about adolescent addiction, said someone had been asking around there, too. Someone was trying to find out if the things I was saying were true.

When I put together my maps for *Midnight* fans to see the places connected with The Book, my publisher had put in my bio that I had been a former Miss Tennessee. When it came time to put out the maps, I said that wasn't true, but a member of the publishing company said it was too late to change. The barcodes had already been put on and some had already gone out, and no one would recognize it or care anyway, and they didn't change it. The thing is, it was not true; I had given them three pages of information, that I had been in *many* pageants, and I was from Tennessee, and somehow it got in that I was Miss Tennessee and they didn't think it important enough to change. I let it slide; I thought, "Who would care? It was thirty years ago," and that was a mistake—my mistake. The error had started many years before when it was printed in a local magazine. I had respected the feature writer who wrote the article about my being Miss BBW of America and she listed myriad pageants I had been in and won. It was mistakenly written that I had been Miss Tennessee and I let it go. I should not have. I own it—it was my mistake.

Berendt's people now called the Miss Tennessee headquarters to talk to the President of the Miss Tennessee Corporation and head of the pageant to say that I had said I was a former Miss Tennessee and was that true. The President confirmed that I had not been Miss Tennessee. They said that I put the lie in writing, and I was making all kinds of money off of portraying myself as Miss Tennessee. The money was for the maps, and I only made, I think, about $1,200 selling them. I was in pageants, always in the top five finalists, and I was in the Miss Chattanooga pageant where I won Miss Congeniality. I have the trophy to prove it, but I was not Miss Tennessee.

The President sent a cease and desist letter, saying that I should withdraw all the maps, and that if I didn't cease and desist, they would be forced to sue. "Call us if you have concerns," so I did.

I asked the President, whom I had met at the pageant, what was going on, and he wondered what was going on in Savannah, as he had been contacted by people, and was sent a copy of the infamous map. He said that the man who had called made it sound as if I was using the title to sell maps. Later when he saw the map, he realized it was really nothing and I wasn't using the title at all to sell maps. I explained that I had made the author of a bestselling book mad, meaning John Berendt. He laughed and asked me to tell him about it. I explained everything, and he said, "Well honey, just don't do it again." I told him when the maps sold out, I would not reorder any more. I apologized to him and he was very nice. "Don't worry," he said, "things happen."

The next day I opened the Savannah newspaper and a headline jumped out at me that said something like: *Nancy Hillis Sued By Miss Tennessee Corporation for Lying About Being Miss Tennessee.* I called the President back and asked why he told the newspaper this. He said he hadn't told them; "We don't do that," he said. I told him that it was in the paper. He apologized, and I later found out that Mr. Berendt or one of his people made an in-way with the President's secretary, and obtained the information and took it to the newspaper. That discredited me more than anything else I've ever done. It made me look like a liar; and I would hear people in elevators say, "Is that woman still operating that house over there?" Oh, you mean Miss Tennessee?" and they'd laugh. It was so humiliating, but it was my fault—I inadvertently gave them the ammunition.

John Berendt had been on numerous television shows and when the question came up about his fabricating some of the parts about my life in his book, he'd say, "What do you have to say about anyone who lies and portrays themselves as Miss Tennessee; what do you think I think about that?" and then he would laugh like I was a nobody with no integrity.

After some time, the movie was finally finished, and there was a rap party at the Lucas Theater, supposedly just for the crew and actors, but they sold tickets to raise money for the restoration of the theater. I wasn't invited to this one but I bought a ticket. Clint Eastwood and his wife were there, as was Kevin Spacey. I had heard that they asked anyone who had a talent to go ahead and perform at this party. Kevin did a drama piece and gave $150,000 for the restoration of the best box seat in the Lucas, and it was to be named in honor of Jim Williams. (The Lucas is what it is today because of *Midnight in the Garden of Good and Evil*.) I decided I could sing *Hard Hearted Hannah*, and Ben Tucker and his band were the house musicians, so I felt comfortable. I just got back stage with everybody, wasn't asked or anything, and just got out and sang my song. I received a long standing ovation (because there were no seats in the theater anyway), and Sonny Seiler, the lawyer for Jim Williams, but also the person who played the judge in the movie, came up and said, "Nancy, I was really entertained by you," "I didn't know you had all that in you, and that voice!" I thanked him.

I had on my signature boa and they were auctioning items from the movie and/or characters (again for the restoration funding), so I gave them my boa. It went for $850 and I had worn it for years; it had had beer and wine spilled on but I'd sprayed it and kept a Bounce sheet in with it to keep it as nice as I could. Later, the lady that got it called and asked if I'd stand with her and get a picture. I did. She said she'd put the boa on to go out and feel like she was somebody. That was great. I also had my picture made with Mr. Eastwood.

Savannah had the premier of the movie in 1998; Jacob and Wes wanted to go, and I was caught up in the whole scene. Several of my friends came down from Atlanta, and I purchased tickets for them and my employees (they were $250 per ticket and some of the money, again, was going towards the restoration of the Lucas theater and some was going to a downtown charity). I got three carriages full of people and we pulled up to the red carpet, and we walked down. Chablis had an entourage, and I had an entourage—the people who helped me. I had on a black St. John long skirt, split on the side, and a matching black jacket with white lace, rhinestones, beads and buttons and bows on it. It was long sleeved and just gorgeous. I stepped off the carriage into one of my employee's hands, and I sauntered down the carpet. It was wonderful. Everyone was cheering, yelling my name, and there were so many lights it looked like daytime. There must have been reporters from all over the world because I heard different languages and it was a mad house with them yelling, "come here, come here." This was my 15 minutes of fame; then all of a sudden the crowd got really loud. I looked around and there came UGA, the University of Georgia bulldog, also featured in the movie, in his tuxedo, and he was getting all the screams. My moment was over and I said, "let's go." We went in and watched the movie.

I didn't like the movie. To me, (I had already told John Hancock) they missed the point—he missed the characters—he didn't expand on them enough. Yes, the killing happened, but *Midnight* was about the characters and the feel of Savannah. He said that if he had done that, it would've been three hours long. "So," I said, "so was *Gone with the Wind.*" He said they weren't funded for a movie that long and they did all they could. Also, I thought Cusack had his mouth open too much, that he needed another expression to stick on that gorgeous face.

After the movie was over, everyone was asked to get up and speak, except me—I wasn't asked.

Chapter 26

Youse Gots ta Steal It

The former bar manager at Sweet Georgia Browns, Kathleen (McNamara) Yeckley, our Irish lass with the bright red hair and long fingernails, had married Coach Yeckley, a Notre Dame graduate and a highly respected coach and teacher at Benedictine, a Catholic military school for boys in Savannah. They had built a new house on the Isle of Hope and it had a lagoon in the back. She wanted to get Ken something for Christmas and she said she'd love to get him some ducks for that lagoon. I told her it could be done and how to do it. "You can get one for him and I'll get one for him," I said, "and then he'll have a pair." "We can get them in Jesup because I know a guy who'll sell them to us."

I called and talked to the man in Jesup and he said he'd get me a pair. We agreed on a male and female, and I told Kathleen I'd bring the ducks to her annual Christmas party. Our plan was to get ducks, put red Christmas bows on their necks and take them to the house after the traditional church service (at the Methodist Church at the Landings) was over, and then have them waddle on to meet their new daddy.

The day came to get the ducks, and I called and got the man's wife to tell her we were coming.

"Honey, he's done broke his leg and won't be able to get the ducks for you."

"Can I catch them?" I asked.

"No, the insurance won't allow it."

"Could I help you chase them?" I was pleading.

"No, baby, we'll have to turn you down. Call us in six weeks."

I was distraught, but as I was driving home, I drove by Lake Mayer, a lake in a Savannah park, and saw these ducks and geese—hundreds of them. I called Kathleen and told her that I couldn't get the ducks from Jesup, but I had driven by Lake Mayer and they had lots of ducks we could get.

"Nancy, those belong to the city and Lake Mayer. We can't take those ducks."

"Yes, we can. We need to thin them out and relocate them. We're going to give them a better life."

I told her to get a blanket and a box and meet me at 11:00 pm.

"What will I tell Ken? He'll wonder what I'm doing meeting you at 11:00 pm?"

"Tell him anything—you figure it out. It's Christmas and there are lots of secrets at Christmas. Tell him you're helping me do something. He thinks I'm a strange friend, anyway. Just meet me at the Huddle House and we'll get our plan of action."

When we had our plan together we set out for Lake Mayer. There was a big, new Cadillac and big, black Lincoln there—and they were not there for ducks. I felt as if it was a drug deal going down, so we left, went back to the Huddle House and waited a bit. We returned to the Lake and the cars were gone.

"You got bread?" I said.

"Yes; you got the blanket?" she answered. I said yes and off we went.

Just as our legs go over the fence, they all came a running toward us, making a racket, quackin' and honkin', screaming and flying, and she throws the bread. They swarmed all over us and we were scared to death. We both screamed and jumped back over the fence. It seemed as if there were thousands of them coming after us.

"All right, calm down," I said. "Let's try it again. They can't bite hard and we can do this."

"What are those big things?" Kathleen asked.

"Those are geese."

"How are you going to get one with thousands of them coming in your face?"

"I'm just going to do it. We've got to do it. You want to give up? Don't throw the bread until we get over and I have a duck."

So we went over again and they started coming in droves. (I felt like we were in the Hitchcock movie, "The Birds.") I landed on one, wrapped the blanket around him, went back over the fence, trying not to scream, and shoved him and me in my Mercedes. I sat there with Kathleen, and held Mr. Duck in my arms like a baby. I was rubbing him and telling him it was OK. I kept his head covered to keep him calm and Kathleen and I looked at each other and burst out laughing. We had done it! We had duck and goose bites all over, but we had survived. Now what?!

"Let's go to the House and I'll put him in the bathtub," I said, "then we can come back and get another one." Kathleen drove the Mercedes while I sat with our prize duck in the passenger seat. We took him (her?) to the Hamilton-Turner House and put him in the bathtub with some crackers. We sat there just looking at him. He pooped, of course, but we thought he was just beautiful.

"Look how cute he is," Kathleen said. "But we don't know if it's a male or female."

I said we weren't going to worry about that now and we just had to go now to get another one. Back we went. We did the same thing and this time I got two right together. We went back to the house, dumped them in the tub, and found out we now had two ducks and a goose.

"The goose is good, but he's ugly," said Kathleen.

"We're not taking him back," I said. "So this is it."

They were just a-quackin' and Dudley got up to see about the ruckus.

"What is that noise?" he said, and then he saw the critters. "Oh my God, where did you get those?"

"You don't want to know."

"Nancy, that's stealing," he said.

"No it's not. We're relocating them. They're moving on up to a fine neighborhood; they were starving out there."

Dudley asked, "How long will they be in the bathtub?"

"Until tomorrow night."

Dudley and I had been together five years and he was used to my weird ideas and stunts so he just shook his head and laughed.

Those critters quacked and quacked all night but none of my tenants or guests said a word.

We did all the traditional Christmas Eve events with family and friends including the midnight candlelight service at the church. We had gotten the big, red bows on the critters' necks and they looked so festive. We put the animals in the foyer and then herded them into the family room where they waddled and quacked away. We shouted "Merry Christmas, Ken," and he was surprised. They finally made it to Ken's lagoon and he loved them. It was worth all the trouble just to see Ken's face that Christmas, to see the many smiles the ducks brought to the families' faces for years to come, as well as the laughs that came when friends heard the story of the relocation of the ducks. The ducks were happy, too.

Another great story involved Minerva, the Voodoo Priestess that supposedly helped Jim Williams finally get acquitted of the murder charges.

We had a guest named Debbie from Texas that would come periodically to the House and stay for a while. We were the exact same age and discovered that we were both at the University of Tennessee at the same time. I felt like I had known her all my life—we were that good of friends and still are close friends to this day. It wasn't cheap to stay that long in Savannah, and I asked her how she could do everything she did here.

"I've been real lucky. My family owned a little bakery for over 100 years."

I thought it was a little family bakery, well off, but quaint. Well, one time she invited me to Dallas to see her. I got off the plane and saw a tractor trailer full of bread and the sign said, "Mrs. Baird's Bread." I was dumbfounded—"little family bakery!"—they were the only bread company in Texas for a long time.

Anyway, my friend, Linda Odom, who owns a tour company called Tales of the South, did a *Midnight* evening for a bunch of physicians that included a performance of a play Gary Strickland and I had written. Her daughter, Monica, and her friends did the dance parts to the song written by Rick Burris; Gary did the music; Mark Cartwright played the piano; we got a drag queen to perform; and we put together a whole play that was just great. It was cute, funny, and had good music. I invited Debbie and her friend to go and she was just in heaven. She met Jerry Spence, and, of course, he could be so charming, and she just loved him. He would end up going places with her when I couldn't go because of work, as he was always up for a road trip and a good time.

One day she went out with Jerry and her sister-in-law, and they came home and said they wanted me to go with them tomorrow, that they had found where Minerva, the Voodoo Priestess character from *Midnight*, lived.

"We found her, we found her," they yelled. They were so excited. They told me that she lived behind a tennis court, across from a cemetery, in this modest, tiny raised wood frame home, built on a concrete foundation. (You could see the concrete through the floor planks.) They had gone to the door and met her, and she invited them right in.

After a bit, as they were leaving, Minerva said to Debbie, "Youse got a friend, a pretty friend wid blonde hair, she and you both have snakes around your feet."

Debbie said she knew Minerva was talking about me as I was the only blonde friend she knew in Savannah.

"She told us to come back tomorrow and bring you," Debbie said. At first I said no; I was scared of it all, but they convinced me to go.

So, we went. Minerva (whose real name was Valerie Fennel Aiken Boles) was short and round, about four feet tall and two feet wide, with one little gray braid, and she looked like she was ancient but she was in her 70s. She had oxygen in the room, walked with a walker and also had a cane. She had huge eyes that got bigger as she talked. Sometimes she talked in a whisper, and sometimes she'd go down to a deep, southern growl, saying things like, "Youse gots ta steal it." She was kind of creepy and I knew we better do what she said.

She began, "Youse girls got three enemies. Dey hate you, and youse need ta git the snakes around your feet off you. Now you knows who dey is. (I wasn't sure, but if I had to guess, I think they were John Berendt, Charles' new wife whom we'll call Hattie, and Delilah Smith.) Think about it and write what dere names is on this piece of paper wid da red pen. Don't cross any T's or dot any I's, and don't lift da red pen off da paper. Fold it up and go out and git some twigs and bring it all back ta me."

Then she handed us a Ball jar.

"Put this right under where youse sleep, under you, and when youse gets up in the morning, the first time you goes to pee, pee in dat jar. Keep da bottle right under where youse sleep. Do this and after three days, bring it back ta me."

"Now, let me take care of dis baby."

Debbie's sister-in-law was trying to get pregnant and she was having a hard time with it.

"Here's what youse gots to do. Go buy some fresh sheets, white only, only white sheets on de bed. Only white towels and don't shower. Take a bath and make sure he takes a bath and takes it wid this." She produced some kind of dried herb that looked like basil. "Then youse gots ta git you a diaper from a baby that's used it before, and youse gots to bring it back ta me. Just a cloth diaper—a clean one—but already used.

We thought this would be a piece of cake—we'd just find someone who used cloth diapers. But just as we were walking out the door and saying goodbye, she held us captive with her scariest, low, Voodoo voice as she said, "One thing about da diaper—youse gots to steal it. I'll do my work now; you do your work now. Don't you forget—all white towels and sheets. You make him take a bath in my stuff and tell 'em it's some kind of aphrodisiac or somethin'."

Now the woman's husband had no idea what we were up to. He would've never understood because he was about as manly as you could get—a sure, long, tall Texas gentleman who loved to be on his boat anywhere. I often wonder how she ever got him to do all those things.

On the way home I asked how in the world we were going to steal a cloth diaper. Women didn't use those any more, they used disposables. We drove by the projects, thinking there might be some on the line. There weren't any. Jerry suggested another area, and we drove and drove—no diapers. I thought of church. Kathleen went to a kind of primitive church, and they had a nursery there with supplies, so I called Kathleen to ask her about going there. She said that the window in the kitchen was always open, that that's how she got in when she locked herself out (she cleaned the church once a month), and we should go there and crawl in through that side window. We had brought a package of Pampers because I felt so bad about stealing a diaper from the church. I was elected to go in the window first, and I went in head first and got about half-way in and couldn't throw myself in all the way. Jerry got behind me and pushed and I flopped down on the floor and he flopped right after me. We searched, but didn't find a cloth diaper; we left the Pampers though, and we were at a loss.

Every morning, I would go to have a coffee and then walk to City Market to paint pottery. That very day my potter called and said, "Your pot's ready for pick up. It's fired and done." She had recently had a baby and I asked her if she had the baby with her. She said no, but that he was with her mom. I asked her if she was using cloth diapers and she said she was. She was an Earth Mother and she thought that was the best.

"I've got some girlfriends here visiting and I want them to meet your momma and I want us to see the baby. Can we go by and see the baby?"

I don't know how I did it with a straight face. I was thinking, "I'm a thief, I'm a thief," and she said fine, go right ahead. I think she thought it was a little weird, but she said OK. We went there, and Debbie and I played with the baby and talked with the grandmother, who was a beautiful Italian lady with a heavy accent, while the sister-in-law and Jerry slipped upstairs to the baby's room to make the heist. They were quick and soon stood at the living room door with "Cheshire cat smiles" on their faces. We thanked the grandmother and went out to the get-away car.

The sister-in-law and Jerry proceeded to show us the trophies—three diapers. They stole one because it was straight, another because it was shaped to fit a baby's bottom, and a third because it had an unusual shape—they weren't sure which one Minerva might want, so they took all three.

The sister-in-law had to go back home to Texas, but we had her three diapers plus our jars of urine and we went back to see Minerva and she was tickled.

She gave us some red felt and a quarter that looked brand new, and some kind of spice.

"Youse take dis out dere," and she motioned to the kitchen. "I'm putting da quarter in and da spice, and it's already sewed up on two sides. You take it out dere and sew up the third side and den sew around da quarter that's in dat felt. By dat time I'll be finished with dis and you'll be finished with dat."

So we went to the table in the kitchen and there were bugs and old food and it was creepy, but we sewed. We couldn't believe we were doing this. When we finished we went back in and our urine was purple, and it had our pieces of paper with the names of our three enemies down in it with sticks and a coin or two. She handed us an envelope and in it were several pieces of chalk.

She then says, "Youse gots ta go down ta da water, down ta da ocean somewhere where a bridge is and when youse gits down dere, you take this chalk and write on a rock, 'Evil evil go away, evil evil go away,' three times. If the chalk breaks don't pick it up. Don't dot no I's, don't cross no T's—just all of it needs ta connect. Understand?"

Debbie asked her what happened if all the chalk broke.

"Youse just quits writin'. It's full of evil. Don't pick up da chalk. If it breaks, leave it dare, leave it dare. And what chalk you don't use, leave it dare by da rock. Then, when da tide is goin' out, take your jars, look over your left shoulder and say, 'Evil, evil go away' and throw dat water (our treated jars of urine) over your left shoulder, bottle and all, and don't look back. Git outta dere, and if you ever go by dat place again, don't look at it." We paid her what she asked and left.

We were spooked, wondering how we ever got ourselves caught up in this, but we were determined.

Do you know how hard it is to find a place that you can get to close to the water by a bridge without being in mud up to your nose? It's practically impossible. We went all over downtown Savannah, all over South Carolina, all over Tybee, until we were passing Ft. Pulaski and right there was a place. Debbie mentioned that it was government property and I said it'd be all right. We had to sleep over the jars again to get to three days, then we headed to the spot. We sat in the car deciding who should go first. I was the more adventuresome one, so I said I'd go first to find a good way.

"No, if you get caught then I won't get to go," she said. "I'll go first."

When she came back she was saying, "Oh no, I don't know if I did it right cause I heard the glass hit something and break."

"That's OK. It went in the water didn't it?"

"I guess. I didn't turn around. I wasn't supposed to turn around."

"Well, you did everything you were supposed to do, didn't you?"

"I guess. I did my three sentences and my chalks all broke."

I said it was OK and that things were fine. So I went down and did the same thing and then said, "Let's get outta here."

We called Minerva and told her everything ."It's all right; youse done throwd it in da water, didn't you? It be all right. Y'all come see me when youse can," she said.

I did see her again when I went back with Linda Odom and her daughter Monica, who was doing her thesis on Gullah culture, the culture that developed when the South had slaves. (Slaves spoke all kinds of languages and dialects and had to develop a language and culture so they could communicate. It became known as Gullah.) I told Linda that Monica needed to meet Minerva and have that in her paper—that it was sure to get an A. I didn't want to go back, but I did and she was quite helpful to Monica, although we could tell she was getting older. We could also tell she was upset because she had a grandchild that had been arrested. But then all of a sudden she started talking about Jim Williams. She called him James, and said that James Williams was in love with her.

"Yes, sir. He bought me silk panties. He bought me suits ta wear ta da court. He brought a tailor up here ta make me beautiful suits. Ise did go ta da trial and put white powder in da DA's pocket, and dat writer, he don't know. He just lied. James wanted to marry me. I could've live in dat big house. I helped him with da dead boy's spirit. The jury had all white powder around dere feet."

We stayed about 45 minutes and Linda handed her some money and off we went. She was such a major part of the Book and movie, and we wished there was a way to get her some money from it. Tour guides would occasionally take folks over and have short sessions with her and she was able to have a little money, but she never, to my knowledge, saw money from the Book or movie.

She died in 2009.

By the way, the sister-in-law did get pregnant. Whether the spells worked for us or not, I can't really say.

Chapter 27

Something Wicked Comes This Way

The worst thing that can happen to anyone is to lose a child, and you can lose a child without them actually physically dying. They get sick, or get a disease, or have an accident that impairs them to the point where they don't know you; well, it happened to my youngest son, Jacob.

At four years old, toe-headed Jacob, with the freckles on his nose, had so much personality he was stopped by Neiman Marcus' head model who then asked me if I would consider allowing him to model. From age four to seven he modeled and earned enough money to pay for one year of college. He excelled in baseball and made the Little League All Stars team. In high school, he was well rounded, had lots of friends and played every sport Savannah Christian had to offer. The cheerleaders at school helped me to give Jacob a surprise 16th birthday party and about 150 kids came in spite of the fact we served no alcohol—he was that well liked.

At the end of his junior year, Jacob signed up to go to Europe with the French class. Lots of his friends were going, and after discussing it with Charles, we decided we'd split the cost and let him go. I put down the first payment and when it was time to pay the rest, Charles balked. He had married Hattie (not her real name) and she didn't want to pay. I pawned my diamond and emerald Rolex for $1,000 and pawned a few more items to get the money and he went.

About six days into the trip, one of Jacob's friend's father, phoned me to say Jacob might be calling and he'd be upset. Evidently in one city in Sweden, the boys had bought some beer and the only way they could figure out how to cool it was to put it in the shower. They did that and then went off for dinner. When they got back, water was all over the room because the labels had come off the beer and stopped up the drain. All the guys freaked out and left, leaving Jacob to clean it up. He got mad and picked up a chair and threw it into the window. Jacob's friend had called his dad, who was an attorney and judge, for legal advice, and dad talked to the hotel and the chaperones, and then called Charles to ask for the money to fix the window and room. I had given Jacob plenty of spending money but he had to use it, plus the money Charles sent, to pay for the damages.

This was the first incident that made me know something was wrong with my son. I had talked with Charles about Jacob's mental state before, and he always pushed if off saying that I just didn't understand how to handle an adolescent. My gut told me otherwise and now I knew I was right.

Charles had been married before to a female barber, and I liked her very much. He brought her to the Hamilton-Turner House to show her around, and I felt sorry for her because everybody that walked up to us asked if we were sisters—she looked so much like me. She even said to me, "I did not realize how much we looked alike!" Trying to make her feel better, I quietly said, "Yeah, but you're a lot younger."

She was like a replacement and I felt bad for her. She was smart and sweet, and good to my boys. But, then Charles stopped bringing her and started playing around with someone else—Hattie. He started changing the minute he let Hattie into his life and then he married her. He brought her to the House one time and we all tried to be nice to her, but she was mad, and obviously didn't want to be there. Charles gave her a tour and a guide went with them to explain the rooms. He joked and tried to keep things light, but she didn't find anything funny. I tried to have a conversation with her and she hated the fact that I had that House. She was 5'8", a big woman, who wore a lot of makeup, had blonde hair, and was rough looking—it was like if you said anything wrong to her, she'd whip your butt. When they left, my tour guide said to me, "Double double, toil and trouble, this is not going to be good."

One time Wes and his future wife, Sheila, went over to Alabama to see Charles and Hattie, and when they came back Wes said, "Mother, she's trashy." Sheila agreed and said that over her bed she had a picture of herself, scantily clad in red lingerie, and just about everything was showing.

"Over their bed?" I said. "Doesn't she have a daughter about 12 or 13? That can't be good for her daughter!"

I asked Wes how she acted around Jacob.

"Mother, it isn't good. She rubs all over him."

One day, Jacob brought home a video that was taken out by the pool at Charles' house and Hattie was saying, "Jacob you're hot. Girls will be after you. Boy, you got a body." I didn't think Charles would ever let anyone hurt his children, so I just couldn't imagine that anything bad was happening; he always was protective of his boys—they came first. However, I later learned that the situation was a rolling monster.

Jacob would visit Hattie and his father often. I told Dudley I wanted Jacob home, that I thought something bad was happening over there. He said there wasn't anything we could do because if Jacob wanted to be there, he could choose to be there. He was getting a car, his dad was paying for school, and he liked it there and didn't want to leave, so I had to let it go.

For his freshman year in college, Jacob went to Georgia Southern and stayed with his best friend in a dorm. Things went well for a while, but Jacob was acting up and his best friend and he were drifting apart. Wes got him (and his friend) a job as waiters at a sorority—an ideal job for a young man, but the supervisor said Jacob was so sad all the time and Wes had to tell Jacob to leave. For the summer, I brought him home and he got a job as a bagger at Kroger. He hated it and quit. He went to St. Simons and stayed with his good friend and his parents. About three weeks into it I called to talk to him, but the dad said that they didn't know where he was. He said Jacob had left the job one day and just disappeared. They hadn't seen him in about four days. They said they had heard he was sleeping in his car.

"Where are his clothes?" I asked.

"They are here, but we haven't seen him."

"Can you send your son to look for him?"

The son found him, but Jacob wouldn't talk to him; he said he'd only talk to Wes. Wes called and asked him what he was doing. "Nobody can find you. What happened to your job?"

"I quit."

"Did you quit or get fired?"

"Both."

"Where are you sleeping?

"In the car."

"Why don't you go home to mother?"

Jacob said no and went to Alabama. He and Hattie, who was closer in age to Jacob than to Charles, had already gotten involved and he didn't want to leave her—he was having sex with Charles' new wife which I didn't know for a fact, yet. I kept asking him to come home, but, of course, he wouldn't.

It was time for school and his sophomore year and I set him up in an apartment as that was what he wanted.

After about three months he called me to say that he needed to see somebody; something was wrong with him and would I come to get him. I called my friend, Kathleen, and she got halfway to my house when Jacob calls again to say he is on his way. He came home and we stayed up all night, talking and talking in circles, and all I got out of it was that he was disillusioned with God.

"He's like the Mafia, mom; he gives you all these rules knowing you are going to break one or two or more, and then he zaps you into hell."

I was flabbergasted. I said, "Jacob, who told you that? If someone told you that, they are wrong. We go to heaven by the grace of God no matter our sins. If you ask for forgiveness, he forgives."

Jacob asked me what if a person kept doing it.

I said that you tried your best, and asked forgiveness, that that was the way it worked. God didn't zap you into hell. Jacob kept rambling and that was the one thing that kept coming up, that he thought he was going to hell.

There was a day program at Charter Psychiatric Hospital in Savannah, and Anne, his therapist, said we should send him because he needed more help than what she could give him. He should go to the program and not worry about school. That was the plan. He went 8-5 everyday and for the time being, that was the best I could do.

A few days later, the premier for the movie, *Midnight in the Garden of Good and Evil*, was taking place. The night of the premier event, a friend of mine and her husband asked if they could take Jacob out for a little while. I told Jacob he had to be home at a certain time so he could go to his therapy session the next day. Everyone else, including my good friend

Evie and her friend, had gone to bed (as did I). I got up the next morning and took Jacob to Charter and when I came back, Evie, who had known Jacob since second grade, and her girlfriend were sitting in my apartment and Evie was crying.

"What's wrong," I said.

"I don't know how to tell you this."

"What is it?" and she told me.

The night before, Jacob came to Evie's friend's room, saying he couldn't find a place to sleep, and she told him he wasn't supposed to be in there, and she told him to leave and shut the door. Then he came to Evie's room, and she asked him what was the matter with him—had he been drinking? He couldn't come in—he didn't need to be there, and she shut the door. The next morning, she was shocked and horrified to be awakened by Jacob sitting by her bed putting his hand between her legs. When she told me this, I just grabbed her and hugged her and we cried together. She said she had been like his mother, and she couldn't believe he'd do this. I told her I was so sorry and that I now knew that he was a lot sicker than I thought. I told her I would call and have him put in the hospital, that he needed to be there, and I didn't want him home any longer. I just cried and cried.

I called Charter, telling them that Jacob had tried to molest one of my friends and he needed to be put in the hospital as an in-patient. They asked if I was his guardian, and I said no, I was his mother. They told me he was 20 and they couldn't keep him if he didn't want to be there.

"He's really sick and needs help," I said, "I'm coming out there and want to talk to a nurse, therapist, psychiatrist, just somebody—I want to tell y'all what he did and you have to hear what I have to say. I want to know why he did such a thing."

I went out to Charter with Jacob, and I confronted him with what Evie had said and asked him what on earth he was thinking. He put his head down and started to cry. He said he was drinking and I said that wasn't an excuse as that had nothing to do with it. "I want you to stay here until we straighten this out. You need help." He just kept saying he was sorry.

I called my therapist, Anne, and told her what was happening. She asked me if he had ever been molested by someone. "No," I said, "Surely to God, Charles wouldn't let that happen." I knew Charles was a little odd, but I also knew that he'd never let that happen to one of his children.

Later I got a phone call from Charter, asking about insurance. They had talked to Charles for insurance information, and Charles had dropped the insurance. There was none. Charles then talked to Jacob and brow beat him into coming to Alabama to go to the hospital where Charles worked as there would be a discount. He said he couldn't afford the big expensive hospital in Savannah—come to Alabama.

They were coming to get him, and I said to the person who called me, "Over my dead body." I waited in the parking lot for Charles and Hattie, and when they arrived, I jumped out and ran toward the car. Charles kept going but I went behind them and started bumping the car—in fact, I bumped the crap out of it. She started to get out of the car and I got scared because she was twice as big as I was, but Charles got out then and I said, "You are not going to do this to Jacob."

They ran into Charter and told the desk I was crazy, and they wanted to call the police, because I rammed into their car. The police came and I said they weren't taking my son to Alabama, that I was his mother and had custody of him, but the Charter people said that he was 20 and could do what he wanted to do. The officers then asked me if I'd abide by what Jacob wanted to do, and I said yes. Jacob said that his dad couldn't afford Charter and he should go. I asked Charles where they were taking Jacob, and if they had a psychiatric program.

"They have a psychiatric floor," Charles said.

"A floor? A floor—are you crazy? He needs help—a real place that will help him. What kind of program will they have? Will they just give him medicine and send him home?"

Charles said he would see that things would be done for Jacob and all would be OK.

I said I'd take him.

"Nancy, are you going to drive 12 hours to Alabama when we're right here?"

"That's right; I'm taking him and I want to see where you are putting him, what the program is, and you're not talking to somebody that doesn't know something about this. I've studied this kind of stuff long enough. I want to know."

"All right," he said.

I called the hospital where he was to go and asked if they had a program. "Well, no; we have a psych floor, but no program." That was it—I was determined to go.

God was looking after us, because I knew it would be tough for me to drive that whole way, and I dreaded it. We went to the airport and one of Jacob's former coaches was an attendant and he got me a special fare to Chattanooga where my brother lived. He picked us up in Chattanooga, we spent the night with him, I borrowed his car, and Jacob and I went on the three hour drive to Alabama. We arrived and a nurse came down and said they'd take it from there.

"No. I want to see what program he's going into; I want to see where he is going!"

"We don't really have a program."

"I want to see where you are putting him. I'm his mother."

We went upstairs and they put him in a regular room and I was not happy. (It was also Thanksgiving and I had never had Thanksgiving without my boys.) I told Jacob that this wasn't a good thing for him, that this was just a crisis center, but he wouldn't budge. The nurse said he'd see a psychologist, and if needed, a psychiatrist. I said I didn't like it, and I made a fuss, and shortly after, here came two Alabama state patrolmen and a couple of real important looking nurses and they said that Jacob was an adult and there was nothing I could do. I said I had to go get his clothes which were still in the car, and they said I could get them, but I should give the clothes to the administrators. Two State Patrol officers and the head nurse walked me down to the lobby; Dr. Hillis hung the moon there, and everyone was at his beck and call. I found out later that Jacob spent Thanksgiving alone and then went home to Charles' house after three days and that the hospital had done nothing for him but continue his medication for depression.

I focused on living at this point, trying to call Jacob, but Hattie would answer and just set the phone down, and I knew if I showed up, I'd be arrested. I couldn't talk to my son.

I was desperate to get Jacob home and he always loved going to football games, so I bought four tickets to the Orange Bowl game in Florida. Dudley, my brother and I went and Jacob drove his new car and met us in Ft. Lauderdale, and my son immediately began talking disrespectfully to me. My brother said, "Hey, bud, watch your mouth. When did you start talking like this to your mom?" He had never talked like that to me before. Dudley told him to stop and Jacob smarted back, "You want to stop me, let's see what you've got; you're not my father and I don't have to listen to you." Dudley pulled over, slammed on the brakes, and out they went: Dudley, Jacob and my brother. I didn't know what to do. My brother got in between them and stopped the fight and after about 30 minutes of yelling and talking we went on to the game. When we got home, all I could do was cry. Both Dudley and Jacob apologized, but I knew right then that Jacob was still in need of help. But he went back to Alabama and wouldn't come home. I found out later that he had enrolled in a community college and had a job at the hospital where Charles worked. He evidently was fired when he fell asleep under a patient's bed.

Charles arranged to have Jacob come back to college in Statesboro and had him move in with Wes's roommate, whom we'd known for years. The roommate's father owned a four bedroom house and that's where Jacob stayed. Soon they called me to say I needed to come up and see about Jacob. He had dropped all his classes, was staying up all night and sleeping all day. He hardly ever came out of his room and there was a smell coming from it from old pizza boxes, fast food wrappers and such. I knew Jacob was sick and my psychiatrist friend said that it sounded like schizophrenia. She asked me if I had insurance, which I didn't, and I knew Charles didn't have it either, but I called Charles to ask for help. He barely spoke to me. I asked the psychiatrist what to do and he said the choices were Georgia Regional for a diagnosis, or "you'll have to get a whole lot of money." He said I could get him on disability but that would take some years and that psychotropic drugs were very expensive.

I called Wes and told him he needed to help me go to the probate judge and have Jacob committed, that he needed help. We went to the judge in Statesboro who happened to have a brother in the same condition as Jacob, and he granted our request and signed the papers. The police came to get Jacob and he didn't want to go so they had to handcuff him and it was very sad. He went to the emergency room to get a doctor to declare that he needed to be admitted (that was the process), and they then took him to Georgia Regional and it was awful. When I was finally able to see him, I realized they had given him something that affected him severely; his head would just droop and seemed stuck on his shoulder and he was staring into space and drooling. I asked what they gave him and they wouldn't tell me. I asked to see the head nurse, someone I could talk to and I was told he was an adult and I had no say whatsoever in what was given to him. Eventually, they put him in a halfway house without telling me where he was going. Their attitude was that he was an adult and they didn't have to tell me—I was like the enemy. He didn't do well at the halfway house, so he went back to Georgia Regional.

Someone said that I needed to become guardian for him, that then I could have some say in what they did, so I went to do it. The staff was telling Jacob that this would be a bad thing for him, as he'd lose control over his life, that he'd never own land, have a car, get married, and so forth, without my OK. That time, I failed to win guardianship. Later, I talked with him and was able to convince him to let this happen, and we got in line to try again; this time it was granted. He stayed at Georgia Regional for two months and when I went to get his medicines, the pharmacist said that the bill for them was $5,400. "I'll have to wait," I said. (Who in this world could afford $5,400 a month in medications?) I went down to the bankruptcy court to explain and they gave me about $2,000 to help me. I went and got his medicines and I started to devote my life to taking care of Jacob. He was schizophrenic and that is like pushing a chain down a dirt road.

I knew I didn't have a lot of money, but I had a house I could sell.

That was my first thought of selling the house, but I just really didn't want to give up yet. I thought I would just have to find a way to make more money. I thought I could do it if I took the garden level that opened on the street (where Delilah and I had the gift shop) and made a restaurant out of it—just bagels, coffee cake, fruit, yogurt and coffee. I'd have people ask me in the morning if I had breakfast, and I'd have to send them to Clary's, just around the corner, so I knew this would be a good idea. My little place would just be very small, only seating 18. There would be no fryer; just a breakfast casserole, biscuits, bagels, and fruit for breakfast, and sandwiches, salads and soups for lunch, but it might work. I went to get a license to do it.

In the meantime, a prominent Savannah man and his wife and child moved into the neighborhood and I took a baked good over to welcome them. All seemed well until I held my yearly charity "Haunted Mansion" event and scared their daughter. I had her come over and showed her all the tricks, music and sound effects we used to scare folks and she laughed once she knew the secrets. But it didn't sit well with her parents. On top of that, the man was the son of well respected people, and was voted or was appointed as chairman of the Metropolitan Planning Commission, or as I called them, "The Gods in the Marble House." When I was called to go before them for my restaurant license, his guns were loaded. He said (and was quoted in the paper) that he lived on Lafayette Square and just couldn't imagine the trucks, garbage, smell and such that my restaurant would create in his neighborhood. Then the priest from the church said there was no place to put a dumpster for the garbage that would come out of this restaurant (there would not have been that much garbage to merit a dumpster) and they were balking on giving me a license.

About the same time, the "Gods in the Marble House" (really my neighbor) were fearful that the front porch was falling off my Mansion and presented a danger to my guests. It had moved a few inches in a hundred and something years, and they were going to shut me down if I didn't rebuild it. I got a city engineer to look at it, and he advised me to take the roof down from the porch, screw some cables to the house which would hold the porch, and that would fix the problem. It also would not cost $20,000; only a few thousand. I had it done and the whole thing took about six months.

There was some flack over my Christmas decorations. The Historic Savannah Foundation always held a contest over whose business was decorated best. They liked fruit and greenery and that was fine for small houses/businesses, but if you had anything over 5,000 sq. feet, that would have looked lost. The larger places had porticos and the front door was almost hidden, so you had to go more dramatic to make an impact. For example, Marsha and Ronnie Thompson of Ms. Wilkes fame, lived in an historic house just up the street from the Hamilton-Turner House and they decorated their home with whimsical pieces of hard wrapped Christmas candy. It was delightful.

I researched what an 1800's period house's Christmas was like in its heyday and had my friend help me with decorating. She had been a decorator for the malls and had more talent in her little finger than most had in their whole body. Carousel horses were the rage in the 1800's so she created them using wood, some kind of plaster and Styrofoam. She painted them beautifully, and made a canopy to go around every porch on the house, hanging Christmas balls on them in every color painted on those horses. The horses were placed on the porches and though the decorations were extremely labor intensive, they were amazing, unique, and our guests adored them. I know my friend did it out of love and friendship and I will never forget it. But, of course, the Foundation and the neighbors found fault with the decorations, and it added to the difficulty in trying to get my license.

Meanwhile, the chef I hired to do the garden restaurant had to move on for another job, and combined with all of the trouble from the MPC, I just gave up on the restaurant idea. By the way, the chef did manage to steal two checks from me and wrote himself a hefty amount on each. He also stole most of my sentimental jewelry: my Grandmomma's two caret diamond, my antique watch fob from Charles' father's watch, and several diamonds and emeralds. I had them stored in a jar in the cabinet and he just took the whole thing.

Life rolled on and one day Charles called me and said that finally he was going to take the House out of his name and put it in mine. "I know you and Hattie don't get along, and I know how hard you've worked for it and it's yours. I owed you the money I put in it, so I'm going to turn it over to you." It was obvious that Charles was going behind Hattie's back, putting the House in my name so she couldn't take it from me. I thanked him and breathed a sigh of relief.

Shortly thereafter, a realtor friend called me to say that Hattie called and asked how much she could sell the Hamilton-Turner House for. Hattie then found out what Charles had done, and all hell broke loose because I received notice that I was being sued by Dr. Charles Hillis for the contents of the House. She probably pitched a fit and he was scared of her, so he compromised by going after the contents.

I asked him what was going on and he tried to tell me that a lot of those things were his.

"My goodness Charles, we divided the furniture five years ago when we divorced."

"Well," he said, "maybe just give us that bed that was mother's."

"You mean the iron one you put out at the road and I picked up out of the trash and had it redone, and now it's gorgeous and you want it back?"

He admitted he had to satisfy Hattie. I told him how dare he do this, and I also mentioned that I had been letting him get by two years without paying child support. I told him to tell Ms. Hattie if they went and sued me, watch out; they were pushing me in a corner, and if they hauled out the lawyers, so would I.

Chapter 28

For Sale

I was out of money, still had lawsuits going, and knew Jacob needed help; so I finally put the House up for sale. The realtor said she'd do the advertising to sell it by creating ads saying the House would bring in so much a year in profit with tours, breakfast, weddings, and so forth. It was what you'd call a "fluff" piece to build the property up for prospective buyers.

After a while, the realtor's contract ran out and about a week later someone said my ad was still running. I said I wasn't going to list it again, and if somebody wanted it, they could bring me an offer. A little while later, the realtor called to say she had an offer on the House.

"What's the lowest you'll take on it?" she asked.

"Just bricks and sticks?" I said. (Every realtor knows exactly what this means.) "No furniture or anything not attached? No rugs, no shutters, no chandeliers, no floor to ceiling bed, no mantle (it was leaning against the wall)? I'll take $900,000 with no negotiating (I'm not sure that was the exact price I said, but I know it was over $800,000 and under one million)."

She brought a young couple through and they wanted the chandeliers, all drapes, all rugs and the floor to ceiling bed.

The bed was special and it was located on the parlor floor. I couldn't afford a full tester bed, so my brother took some mahogany crown molding taken from a 150-year-old bank building in Miami, and he made a frame for a bed which he nailed to the 18 foot high ceiling. I then "dressed" the bed and its fake canopy with 20 yards of beautiful fabric. The floor to ceiling bed looked spectacular in the house. The best compliment I ever had was when Mr. Harper came in and looked at the bed and said, "Did you buy a full tester?" I said no, that my brother had made it. "Well honey, you have outdone me. You have done more than "buzzed" it," which was what people said about Buzz's decorating—it was "buzzed." I was thrilled.

I didn't even counter the offer. I told her that there was no negotiating.

"At least give her that bed; she's carried away with the bed."

I told her the bed wasn't real and it wasn't permanently attached, and I could use it again. I told her there was $20,000 in fabric in the bed. If she wanted to buy it, that's what it would cost. I had already lowered the price much lower than I wanted, and I was NOT going to get into a back and forth battle with them trying to get more out of me. I told the realtor that as far as I was concerned, the original contract was dead and she could take or leave this offer. I was not giving anything else. The couple didn't buy it and I thought that was over, but the next thing I knew, the realtor was suing me for non-performance on a contract.

Then the IRS contacted me and wanted to go over my finances. When they came to talk to me they brought up the fluff piece which said "a million dollars can be made from this house." I explained that it was a fluff piece to sell the house—that what it said wasn't real. He asked me how they could print such a piece.

"They are realtors; Barnum and Bailey; they fluff up a property to sell it. It's income producing but I'm not producing that much—you've got my forms."

"But you've been in a book and a movie," he said. "How much did you receive from that?"

I told him I had received nothing except a thousand dollars because they wanted to use my carrousel horse in the movie so I rented it to them. That was it.

"But people get paid for being in movies," he argued.

"No they don't. I was an extra in one scene, but didn't fill out any paperwork, so I never received my $75. Had I had a line, I would've gotten residuals, but I didn't have a line. I had no idea it would all roll over me like a steamroller."

Now I had trouble with the IRS; Charles and Hattie had sued me for the contents of the house; and the realtor was suing for non-performance of a contract. Then I received notice that Random House was suing me for books that I thought Delilah had ordered, and Delilah was making noises about suing me over her loss of property. I went to Swainsboro to get a bankruptcy lawyer to fight these people and he agreed to take his proceeds out of the sale of the house. At this point, all my bills were caught up except for a $4,282.52 per month house payment, but I had all these people suing me and I had to fight in court, so we both felt that I could file Chapter 11 and be OK once I sold the house and satisfied the judgments—I could then take care of Jacob.

One day a man named Chris came by to look at the House. He'd come from Key West to start a trolley tour company in Savannah (now Old Town Trolley) with his partner, and needed property to get established so people wouldn't complain that they paid no property taxes and therefore were not vested in Savannah. He loved the House and everything I'd done, and I made the suggestion that maybe all three of us could be partners in it. He said he'd have to talk with his partner back in Key West and he'd let me know. After he left, I was saying thank you, Jesus, because it would be a way to work everything out. So I told my attorney we needed a meeting and told him to come down with me to Key West to talk to the boys.

I found out that these young guys, right out of college, had moved a house from somewhere to Key West, started a tour business with a "Conch Train," and made a fortune, and they decided to do it some more. After we talked, Brett went back to Savannah and I stayed to have supper. We had a great time (best conch I ever had) and I thought things were good. I got back home and in about a week Chris called to say they'd run this thing every which way to try and make it work, but there wouldn't be enough money, and that his partner didn't want to take on a third partner. "Right now we're going with something else," he said, so that was that.

My lawyer said we'd have to file bankruptcy after all with this deal falling through. The suits were still going and the wheels of justice, as you know, are exceedingly slow, so I was in limbo. Mother was now in a nursing home on Tybee because she needed a feeding tube and I couldn't care for her properly in my home. Dudley was still around, but our relationship was looking dim, and I was working myself to death.

Mother went into hospice and I was there back and forth, every day. One time I came back to the House and the little insurance guy wanted to talk about the mirror that was hanging in the parlor. It had gotten burned by the fire in the left hand corner, and one guy said he could redo it for something like $12,000, (I had an antique dealer say it was worth $25,000) and the insurance company said their guy said it was worth $1,200. (I knew it was worth more than that.) He said we had a problem. I was so upset about my mother and Jacob, and just had had it with everything, and I started in on him. He kept on trying to stop me, saying he wouldn't pay to let my guy fix it.

"My estimate might be high, but yours is way too low," I argued. "I'm so tired of y'all arguing about every little thing. The ceiling fell in because you wouldn't fix it; the roof fell in, then we had to deal with the pigeons that came in because you hadn't fixed the roof; I was out of work because you closed my doors; I have no money coming in; my son is very sick; and now my mother's dying; just leave me alone," and I walked away from him. It was rare that I lost my cool but I did that day. I went to my mother and had to arrange for her to go to the hospital as she was so bad. There were mounds of paperwork to do and it was taxing, but she went, I stayed with her, and she died a couple of days later.

Dudley took me to a place near Albany where his parents lived so I could grieve, and then I got a phone call.

Latrece, the girl who helped run the Mansion when I wasn't there, called to say that a reporter was trying to reach me and would it be OK to give him this number. I said fine.

"I'm getting ready to write the article," he said, "and I have spoken to John Berendt and he really doesn't like you. He told me something and I have to verify it with you. You can either deny it or verify it and give me your side of it. John said he could prove that you and Joe had a sexual relationship—that he left it out of The Book—but it happened. According to him you and Joe had a sexual relationship because you got pregnant with Joe's illegitimate baby, and you went to Joe begging him to marry you, and he wouldn't marry you, but said he would pay for an abortion. He did, but the check bounced, and John said he'd prove it."

These are the exact words the reporter said to me. I was flabbergasted and didn't know what to say. My thoughts flashed back to our conversations and this was a repeat of the statement he made to me before at our appearance on the riverboat. I couldn't say much as Dudley and his family were all ears as to why a reporter was calling me.

"I'm busy now; my mother just died, my son is very sick, and I can't talk about this now. Please call me next week."

A week later he called to continue the discussion.

"So you are denying it?" he said.

"Implicitly! My question to you is that are you going to print this on one man's word?"

"No, he says he has two people who can verify it."

"Really? Who?"

"One is Jerry Spence, the hairdresser who lived with Joe."

"Oh really, is he out of jail yet? Last time I heard from him he called me collect from the jail where he was arrested for beating on a car because he got thrown out of Club One, the gay bar, because he was drunk. He beat up the car and tried to beat up the policeman, and he had seven counts against him. I didn't know he'd gotten out of jail as I recently took him underwear and socks to the jail."

"Well, then the other one is a lady you were in business with, who says she found a letter you wrote concerning all of this and she is going to fax that to me."

"Who's that?"

"I can't say, she has asked me not to reveal her name."

For a moment I couldn't fathom that Delilah Smith, who leased my gift shop, would be that much of a liar, and would say such a thing. She didn't even know me when Joe and I knew each other, so I couldn't think it would be her. But later, my former boyfriend Buster, called me to warn me of Delilah calling and looking for dirt. I asked him what he said to her and he said, "I said, 'Delilah, shame on you, shame on you. As much as that woman has done for you, shame on you.'" I thanked Buster for saying that. I'm sure Delilah wrote the letter and tried to say it was me.

We hung up and I decided that I'd better tell the boys in case he did print the article. I didn't want them hearing it on the street. I told Wes, who was 27, first and he asked me not to tell Jacob because he was sick, and he thought Jacob wouldn't see or hear about it anyway.

I said OK, and then he said, "Mom, you know, I liked Mr. Joe but he didn't even like girls; is that John Berendt gay, too?"

I said that I wasn't sure and added, "If you see me in the tabloids having Michael Jackson's alien baby, just kind of laugh, OK?"

The day before the article was to hit publication the reporter called again.

"Nancy, I didn't get the letter, and I don't mind telling you who it was from now because I think she is probably not a good source. It was Delilah Smith, but I did get three letters: one from Mr. Berendt, one from Mr. Berendt's lawyer, and one from Random House lawyers, and they are all denying the allegation; they are retracting it and saying they had a bad source, and if I print anything about the alleged abortion, that it will be my butt and not theirs."

I asked him what he was going to do and he said, "I'm submitting the story the way it was told to me, and my editor will do what he sees fit." I thanked him for telling me and asked him to send me a copy of the story.

The story came out and the article danced all around the abortion issue, that Mr. Berendt said that the truth wasn't in me, that I had had trouble with the law, and just on and on with bad stuff. The local newspaper in Savannah ran an editorial about it saying, "He said, she said." Then, a letter came to the editor from Delilah's husband, saying something to the effect that I was not very truthful, that I did have a relationship with Joe Odom, and how could I bite the hand that fed me. The Book kept the Hamilton-Turner House going and put expensive clothes on my back, and how in the world could I write anything negative when this man had done nothing but good for Savannah and had created excitement for our town.

Thinking back, I believe it was Jerry Spence who spread the rumor about an abortion. Jerry came to the house one time drunk and I was doing a tour in the parlor. I had a SCAD student working as a guide who also protected me, and I asked him to go and get Jerry out. He got another guy and the two of them went, one on each side, and took Jerry and headed him out the door. But Jerry knew the Hamilton-Turner House well because he lived there at one time, so he came back through the fire escape, into my dressing room and down the stairs.

He ran into the parlor and said loudly, "Well, hello, and welcome to Savannah. This is Jerry Spence."

I said that we were about ready to move on and here came the guys back to get him out.

"Oh, no you don't," Jerry said, "Do you ladies have any questions for me? You know I lived with Joe for years and we were less than lovers and more than friends—figure that one out!"

My guys tried to get him and I was wondering what in the world I could do as it was so embarrassing.

"Ah, ah, no, I'm not going out again," said Jerry. "How dare you throw me out of my house. I lived here first. You threw poor Joe out when he was sick. Do you know she threw him out when he was dying?"

My guys finally got hold of Jerry to take him out. He was screaming and hollering, "Here I go again, just like a bad cat," and I took my group in the next room and said, "Welcome to Savannah!" I explained that I didn't throw Joe out when he was dying; that Joe had lived here in the garden level because he was friends with cousin Buzz, the former owner, but he got very ill and couldn't live alone any more, and he moved to the Rose of Sharon. When I bought the house, he'd been gone about a month.

Jerry was vicious that day. I loved him to death and I wish I could've helped him, but when he was drunk there was nothing you could do. He's the funniest, quickest, most precious thing when he's not drinking, but when he's drinking that bad Jerry comes out and it's a nightmare. He's been slapped to the floor so many times because he insulted people. He gets angry and says, "I always get the fuzzy end of the lollipop—give Jerry the fuzzy end of the lollipop cause that's all I ever get." That's one of his sayings; he's full of them. He's in his 50s now and they say you could make a calendar of all his mug shots because he's been in jail so many times; and they get better and better because now he sees it as an opportunity to have his picture made. I'm surprised he's not dead.

Later, Jerry got even madder at me because when the reporter called him to talk, he said, "I understand your stage name was Judy Delight."

"Who told you that?" Jerry asked.

Of course, it was me, so then Jerry hated me more; but when Jerry needs me for something, it's all different.

Chapter 29

Sold!

After a while, when we went returned from Albany, in walked a gentleman I'll call Spencer Lafayette. He was very nice and said he and his wife Bertha wanted to buy the property. In the meantime the house had made the front cover of *Sky Magazine*, the airline publication. It had appeared on thousands of planes around the world, and my business got better, because people wanted to come see the House; they didn't care what condition it was in—they just wanted to see it. The upper floors had not been damaged by the fire, and they wanted to stay there, so I had a thrust of interest but didn't know what to do about it—I had Jacob, the IRS, momma dying, the suits, and it was all happening at once. I'm sure I was hard to live with, and Dudley had just lost his children (he had had them since they were babies when their mother left them, and now that they were teens, they thought the grass looked greener on their mother's side), and we were really having troubles.

Spencer said he was thinking that I might work for him and his wife. "Suppose you come in for duty at 6:00 pm and work until 11:00 pm or midnight and live here," he said, "and we know you sing, so you could do that. We'll let you off on Friday and Saturday." So they offered me a contract and we negotiated; I wanted $100 more a week, and I wanted a one and a half percentage of the gross because I knew what the House could do. I also needed an apartment that was large enough for me and my son; and I wanted a three year contract. They agreed.

The sale was $875,000 I think, and they weren't supposed to get the stuff that wasn't attached. They said they didn't want it, as they were going to gut the house, but when we settled, all of a sudden they wanted some of it. I sold them the mantel for $5,000 even though I paid $10,000 for it. They also wanted the chandelier; but they didn't want the fancy bed.

They were interested in some of the furniture and I said I'd get an appraisal from an expert on all the pieces except the few that I wanted, and then they could get their expert to appraise them, as well, and we'd see where we'd end up and decide on a price. They used Jere Myers of Jere's Antiques and I used another lady. Both estimates came back and they were only $200 apart, so they were both close, good honest appraisals. It was something like $180,000. They wanted some of the things I wanted and that was sticky. Then they offered to pay forty percent of what it was worth, and I suggested that whatever they wanted, they could have it for the price appraised by their dealer. I had 10,000 square feet of furniture, and four storage buildings full of holiday decorations for the house. You get the picture.

I said I needed a chance to sell the things they didn't want so would they give me a little time to get those things out of the house. I knew a company in Florida that would take the pieces I wanted and put them in a warehouse, stage some of the other pieces in the House (sales were best done in the House), advertise to generate interest, do a two-day event (one day for a preview and one for the sale), and handle everything. Everyone agreed and I asked also if I could stay in the House for a month before they took possession to give me time to get everything taken care of. They agreed to everything and we settled and closed on the sale.

We're rolling along, and the third day after I signed the contract, they called to have a meeting. They had a contractor with them. The contractor said that the first thing he needed to do was a demolition and that I couldn't be there, and I needed to be out in about a week instead of a month. I was floored. I said even if I didn't have a sale, I needed more than a week, that we had talked and agreed on this, but they ignored me and went from sweet to awful. Spencer was embarrassed, I think, and I told them they'd have to talk to my attorney. The contractor said there was nowhere in the contract that said I could have a month, so he could proceed. I called my lawyer and complained that he hadn't put it in the contract.

"Nancy, we talked this to death and agreed; I didn't think I'd have to put it in the contract." I wanted to strangle him through the phone!

We had a big problem. I called the moving person and he reiterated that the items needed to sell where they sat for the best price, that people wanted to say that they bought their item from the actual Hamilton-Turner House. He said we'd need at least two weeks. We got lawyers back and forth and in the meantime, the contractor had a guy knocking down the walls in the lower level. I told the guy to get out but he said the boss had a schedule and timeline and he needed to get started. "That's their timeline and they'll lose money if we don't go now," he said. Why didn't they tell me this before?

A couple of months before all of this I had committed to a singing engagement in Knoxville, Tennessee. The Tennessee Shriners had asked if I would come to a party for their poster child, a twelve-year old girl who was born with all of her limbs totally connected to her body. She had already had several operations on her legs and arms, but she needed more. The officials asked her what she wanted for Christmas and she said that she wanted to meet Mandy from *Midnight in the Garden of Good and Evil.* Even though I was in a personal and business mess, I was determined to fulfill this little girl's wish. It was November, my new employers were trying to evict me, and when I got off the plane in Knoxville I got a call from Bertha Lafayette saying, "You get this damn mirror out of my parlor." I hung up on her; I just couldn't deal with her right then.

God really does know how to help us get through things because this engagement put everything in perspective. I went ahead and sang for that little girl, and she came running up to me to "hug" me as best she could with her little body. She said, "I love you Miss Mandy/Nancy." We talked for a long time and I had a chance to speak with her mother and learn about their lives. The girl had had so many operations and was going to have another one to try and correct her arms so she could use them. Her mother said, "I just want them to help her to be able to wipe her own bottom." She was only 12 years old. Before I left she picked up a pencil with her mouth and wrote, "Thank you and I love you Miss Mandy," and she signed her name.

Even with Bertha Lafayette calling and yelling at me for leaving town when I was supposed to be moving my stuff out, and for yelling to get my mirror out of the parlor, I knew I didn't have any problems compared to this little girl.

While I was in Knoxville, Dudley, Wes, and some friends went to put things in boxes and get them out of the house and my employees helped, but we weren't sure where we were going to go. Then my friend, Lin Walsh steps up and says she is buying a condo down the street from her present one, and I could live in the present one after she moved into the new one. The Lafayettes couldn't tell me when I was going to get back in the House, and I needed a place to rent month to month so this sounded perfect. Lin also needed some items for her new place so I said I would sell her what she needed from my "extras" for half of the price listed on the appraisals. Between the two of us, we furnished both houses and still had stuff in storage.

The next day Dudley called me and asked if I was sitting down.

"We were moving until about 2:00 am and I guess we slept in this morning and when we got up, ready to move more, there were four tractor trailers pulling away with your stuff."

Evidently, the Lafayettes had just called these transfer trucks to haul it all off, and Dudley didn't know the name of the company. He went to find out where the stuff was headed, and to insist that we weren't responsible for the expenses involved in moving it.

If it wasn't for the little girl, I would've lost it—maybe just given up. I just would try and remember this little girl. "It's just stuff," I'd say over and over. I tried calling but no one would talk to me; they avoided me, but Dudley somehow found out where the stuff was. We went out to the large warehouse that covered several acres, and they had already put it in crates and stored it, putting some things way up high in this big warehouse. When the man heard the story, he couldn't believe it was my stuff, but he helped us get it all open to see just what we had. He had thought he was moving the Lafayettes' stuff, and now he was really upset because he had it picked up and he didn't know who would pay him. (If I hadn't been suing my employer and landlord, I would've paid him.)

Some months later, they brought my things to a warehouse I had rented for storage. There was me, four black guys, five tractor trailers, and one yellow dog. There was some garbage that they had stored and that I had to pay for, and some of my stuff was gone, including the beds. The Lafayettes had just made a mess of it all. I cried and cried and the yellow dog, who really liked me, brought me stuff to throw and made me smile, and if it weren't for him I'd given up.

After the sale of the house went through, I submitted a plan to the bankruptcy court as to how I was going to settle all the suits. I was going to pay off the mortgage, and when all was said and done, I'd pay whatever else needed paying as best I could. We went ahead and started on the suits and the first one we tackled was the real estate suit.

The realtors who were suing me were Cici and Elias Cain (not their real names), big time brokers in Savannah; and he had served as City Councilman for 15 years, the last eight of which he was mayor pro tem. Cici was also a community leader in many areas, and was what we called "old Savannah." They were a very popular, good looking, highly respected couple of old Savannah society, with lots and lots of friends all over the city including judges and attorneys. They were suing for breach of con-tract, or non-performance of a contract, or something like that.

My lawyer got halfway through and the judge told the attorneys in a private meeting in his office that it was very clear the proceeding was going to hurt someone really badly, so our lawyers should get together and try and work something out. He gave us until Monday and my lawyer asked what I could give. I said I'd give them $5,000 for their trouble, as they ran ads in the paper—I would give them that much. They laughed at it but I dug in—they didn't deserve more. The lawyer told me he thought I was making a mistake. "I have dealt with this judge before," he said, "and he is trying to tell us that it is *really* going to hurt one of the parties, probably you because of the Cains' political clout. You're not being 'old Savannah' is not in your favor," he added. "I think the judge is telling us we are going to lose!" I asked him about right and wrong and he reminded me that sometimes right and wrong has nothing to do with the legal process. He said, "How about we give them $30,000—half of what they were asking for?"

"Absolutely not," I retorted. "I would rather lose it all than offer them a penny more and I know it's right. I'm a realtor and I know. I had said, bricks and sticks, and that's what I meant."

We went back to court and I won. The judge said there was not to be a penny paid, that Cici, with her husband right beside her, had done some really wrong things. I was so upset that they had tried to "bulldoze" me into buckling, and that it had cost me $20,000 to fight them, so I notified the Real Estate Commission in Atlanta, showed them all the paperwork, and they pulled her license. According to my friends, it became the case at every realtor meeting to illustrate what not to do.

I now tackled the suit with Charles over the furniture. The judge said it should've been settled at our divorce years ago and he was sending it back to civil court. Charles wasn't listening to this, so we were delayed some more. My lawyer said this wasn't his thing so I had to get a civil lawyer and we went to court. Charles came with a seedy-looking lawyer from Alabama. He proceeded to tell the judge about how I owed $100,000 to Charles for various things. But Charles hadn't paid child support or alimony in years, and it came to over a $100,000 and we proved that. After weeks and weeks, and lies, and lots of wasted paper, the judge finally said that the facts were that Charles was in arrears in child support, and though he might have given money to me for various things, she considered those gifts, as nowhere was it in writing that the money was in lieu of child support, and he wouldn't be allowed to do that anyway. She said it seemed like we had been in business together, that it was in my name because he had given it to me; and now Johnny-come-lately, he wants everything because I was going to bankrupt. He got nothing, but the lawyer bills were up to about $80,000. It was just sad and wasteful.

Delilah never went through with her suit, so it disappeared, but the bad thing was that everything I did or didn't do became front page news in the paper and the headlines made me look terrible. My integrity was questioned at every turn, and the news was always slanted against me. I wasn't "old Savannah" and, by God, I was going to pay. I won every case, but at what price?

It was heartbreaking, because all of that wasted money in lawsuits and lawyers could've been used to help Jacob.

Chapter 30

Jail House Rock

Two or three days before I left the House, my ears started hurting and one started to bleed. I drove to the doctor and had to pay a $160 fee so I wrote a check out on the Hamilton-Turner account for the amount because it was all I had with me. I lived out at Lin's condo but my mail was still coming to the Hamilton-Turner House. I hadn't done an address transfer because I was at the House every day, and they were saving my mail for me. I knew I'd be back eventually, so I'd just pick it up when there. I never received notice that the check cleared but I called the bank to ask and they said it had cleared (banks, too, make occasional mistakes). I closed the account from the Hamilton-Turner as the Lafayettes now owned it; then the $160 check presented itself, but the account was closed and unbeknownst to me I had a bounced check.

One day a police car pulls up and puts a notice on my door telling me I had to appear on a bad check charge.

The next day I went down there to explain and to pay the bad check charges. I had on a jump suit, some nice jewelry, a jacket and big belt. The officer told me to sit down, and then another officer comes and handcuffs me.

"Wait, I'm here to pay," I said, "I want to explain," and he says to tell it to the judge. Nobody would listen to me, and I asked for my phone call, and they said only when I was through processing. They put me in a holding cell where there was a toilet in the middle of the room, and lots of big mean ladies. They had taken my jacket and shoes, but not the beautiful big belt nor my jewelry. Those women taunted and taunted me; "yeah, look at those diamonds on that girl," they said. I was scared to death.

One said, "That girl looks like she needs to be fisted, and I bet she don't know what that is."

I wasn't sure what that was, but I knew it was bad. I asked if I could be moved and this big female policewoman hears me and says, "I need to search her." They did a strip search; she put on a glove and put her finger where I didn't want it to go. I wanted to die. I've never felt so humiliated and scared; I didn't know what to do; I couldn't say anything. Then I ended up back in the cell with those women, and they started up again. I began kicking the door as hard as I could and hollering and finally some guy asked who was making all that noise. The women hollered, "She is, it ain't us." The man said, "I'm putting your ass in solitaire." I just whispered thank you Jesus. They all screamed, "I don't want to go to solitary," and I said, "I do!" He pulled my arm way up behind me so I had to walk on my tiptoes, and he threw me in a room by myself. It was so cold, but I was so grateful.

I finally got to make my phone call and I called the lawyer in Swainsboro, and he was out of town, but I got his partner and he started working on getting me out. He called me back.

"What have you done to piss somebody off? That judge is not letting you out. I'm trying to get something going but it's not working."

I asked what judge, and it was the same magistrate judge that I had had a run in with a year or so back concerning a painting never paid for. According to this judge, I had "insulted an officer of the court."

The story was that we had had a *Midnight* party at the Hamilton-Turner House and the ticket allowed the holder to meet Mandy, Emma, Chablis and see the beautiful art of *Midnight*. A young man who had just graduated from college was at my house and he was painting the Hamilton-Turner House in pastels, and they were beautiful. I felt that his career could take off given an opportunity to show his art at the party so I told him to bring some of his art over to sell. A lawyer bought a beautiful painting of Conrad Aiken's grave for $250 and took it home. (Aiken was Poet Laureate of Georgia and won a Pulitzer Prize. His grave and bench is in Bonaventure Cemetery and it is said a tour guide took John Berendt there to have a martini and talk about the history of Savannah. The painting showed the bench at the gravesite with one single martini glass sitting on it.) He was supposed to send a check, but a month later, he still hadn't sent the check. The boy came down, went to the guy's office, and picked up a check but it bounced, and the young artist called me to help and we took it to court in Savannah, with me testifying for the artist. Well, the lawyer happened to be good friends with this judge. The lawyer insisted he had sent a check and why was the kid acting like this. I spoke up and told him the check bounced, and we would be suspicious about another as it might not be good. The judge said (and boy was he mad), "Ms. Hillis, I'll have you know this attorney is a trusted member of the bar, and an officer of this court and his check will be good." We took the check over to the bank, and they said the lawyer would need to release some funds; we went over to the office and told the secretary, and she released the funds, and the kid finally got his money.

That was the judge who was now holding everything up. I had insulted him and the whole legal system and he was going to show me. About 11:30 pm I was still there after all day, sitting on the floor, wrapped in layers and layers of toilet paper to try and keep warm, and finally, this nice man opens the cell door and says, "Who are you?"

I told him.

"Lord, I think you were supposed to go at 3:00 pm."

Nobody had told me; I could've gone at three, but I was so quiet and thankful that I wasn't in the room with those women, and didn't want to ask any questions that might cause trouble, so I just sat. I was feeling raped, humiliated, and I wondered where Dudley was all this time. I finally got out and called him.

"Where have you been?"

"I'm at Doc's bar having a drink with some friends and I'll be home in a bit," he said.

"That's what you've been doing while I've been in jail all day?"

"Well, I tried to call and get something done; I called the lawyer but our hands were tied."

I couldn't accept that and when I saw him I jumped all over him, I was so mad and hurt. He was supposed to have my back! Be my knight in shining armor!

"Having a drink? Is that how you handle it? If it were you in jail I would've been down there, in person." He caught all my pain. "As far as I'm concerned you can just leave."

I was so angry at Dudley. I got in the shower and stood there until all the hot water was gone; I just couldn't shower enough to get the awfulness off of me. I couldn't even tell Dudley all that had happened; I was too shook up, hurt and shocked. I scrubbed and scrubbed—to wash it all away. It was like the time my mother's fiancé, Buster, stuck his tongue in my mouth, and I put that ole white soap in my mouth to wash it out. I just couldn't get clean enough.

As I said, Dudley and I had been having trouble and unbeknownst to me, he was already seeing a bartender whom he later married. One day my friend Debbie from Texas and a couple of her friends wanted to see Lady Chablis and they got in a cab and there was a cell phone in the back seat. She saw the name, and it was Dudley's girlfriend's phone. Debbie came over to show me and I said, "Oh, let's go give it back to her!" So we did, and she didn't say a word because she had seen my pictures and knew who I was.

I had lawsuits going on all over the place. A tour guide was looking into suing because she had an office in my house when we had the fire, and she wanted money for her losses. (She was another person who sold my books when I asked her not to. Guests would bring books to me to sign and when I asked where they got them, they'd say, "Oh, we're not supposed to tell you. We bought them from our tour guide." I confronted her one time, saying she'd be paying me for the book I just signed, and she pitched a fit. I never did receive papers from her.) Delilah Smith was suing for loss of income. I had cut her out of the gift shop, but she felt she was owed money for her contents. (She never followed through with the suit.) Random House was suing, as well, because Delilah had ordered books, and money was due for them. I did not order them, nor did I make any money off of them, but she saw it differently. Come to find out, one of my employees, my manager, had ordered the books. I just hope they were paid for in the bankruptcy but I really don't know what happened. And on top of it all, I couldn't talk to Jacob.

Chapter 31

"You've Outrun the Cops"

While I was waiting to move back to the Hamilton-Turner House, I had been living in Lin Walsh's condo at Tybee Island and she wanted it back for bigger rent. She could make $1,500 a week instead of $1,500 a month and she needed the money. I was so fed up with everybody and everything and she wanted her place NOW and I was miffed—I didn't know where I was going to go. We were friends and I had let her use the House for clients and guests to impress them, using it for parties (at no charge), or for St. Patrick's Day. I felt she could have waited an extra month until I could find somewhere to stay.

She was also mad at me because I had charged her for the furniture left behind, although I had given her some great deals. At this point I was so worried about Jacob, and where I was going to go I couldn't think straight. No one wanted to rent by the month, especially if you had pets, so it was really tough finding something and it wasn't happening for me.

I had a friend who lived with his partner on Victory Drive in a big house with spare bedrooms and a beautiful pool. They gave me a bedroom there and I brought my seven parakeets, my parrot, Elvis, and my little Yorkie dog, Elliott. (My other parrot, Nonie Bird, was with friends at St. Simons.) They let me rent month to month, and were just so nice about it. The Lafayettes were giving me $1,000 a month to live somewhere until the house was finished and I gave that money to my friend. Well, he turned it right back over to me, bless his heart. These two men were really kind to me.

St. Patrick's Day arrived in Savannah, and one of the best places to watch the parade was the front porch of the Hamilton-Turner House, as the parade marches right by the House. I was just going to quietly sit on the porch and here came the house's construction foreman, and his entourage. I thought he better not tell me I can't be here. We didn't like each other at this point. His right hand man, who had helped me with my reconstruction, was not honest; they charged my insurance company for port-a-potties that they never put out there; they charged for disposal bins that they never put out there; he just wasn't honest. So we sat there and my friend, Bobby Register from Nashville, Tennessee, came to be with me for my 50th birthday, which was two days after St. Patrick's Day. I told him he could spend the night with me as the boys on Victory Drive had another bedroom. We went down to McDonough's Pub, and Billy, the owner, needed help so I went behind the bar and was a waitress for a while. It was chaotic. (I made $400 in tips!) I just worked from 4:00 to 8:00 pm and he asked if I'd come in the next day. Work had always been a kind of therapy for me so I was glad to do it.

The next morning I went down there and started bartending. Bobby wanted to take me back to Tennessee to see friends, because I was so down and I said OK, we'd go after I finished helping Billy, and that was our plan.

I was thinking that I wished I could leave on a better note with Dudley, as we had been together for six or more years and went through a lot together. I felt really terrible about how we left the relationship. That fact in itself deserved a better ending, so I called to find him. (We hadn't been broken up but a couple of weeks.)

I paged him and he called back. I said it was me and that I just wanted to talk. "I'm going tonight to Tennessee with Bobby," I said, "and I'm turning 50 tomorrow and I don't want us to be mad at each other. Could you come down and talk?"

He said he couldn't come and asked if I was drinking because I was at McDonough's.

"No, I'm working for Billy for a while," I said. "Where are you?"

"It doesn't matter where I am," and he hung up on me.

I decided to call back and noticed that the call back number was my friend Lin Walsh's number. Lin's boyfriend, answered the phone. "I know who this is, what do you want?" he said really nastily. I asked why he was talking to me like that.

"You left Lin's place in a mess."

"I got all my stuff out; the rest is Dudley's. He has to get that. I moved all I could."

"And we want the damn key; where's the damn key?"

"I guess it's still on my ring; Is Dudley there?"

"Yeah, and he's got a right to be here."

"OK, he's got a key, can I speak to him?"

"He shouldn't have to give us the key, you should; you rented the condo!"

He was just trying to pick an argument. I said, "What in the world is going on?"

"We want the damn key right now, you understand?" and he hung up.

The longer I thought about the situation, the madder I got. They were out there, all drinking or something, being nasty, and I had called in good faith; it made me mad.

I called Billy and told him I needed to run an errand, could he fill in for just a while. He said yes, that he was just ready to tell me to go home, so I left and headed out to Tybee. I was going to give them the key and see why they were ganging up on me.

I went up to the door and knocked. First, I hear them all running towards the door (it sounded like a "herd" of people). Lin opened the door and lunged for me. I think they were high on something, but they were mad and for sure, they had been drinking. Dudley and the boyfriend grabbed Lin and pulled her back. Dudley kept saying that I needed to leave, but I wanted to know what was going on. They accused me of drinking down at Billy's and I said I wasn't; I had been working.

Lin then says, "You're a fat bitch." All the while the boyfriend was holding her back so she couldn't get to me.

"You want a piece of me?" I can't believe I said that, and I further said, "Let her go, let's see what she's got."

That's not me but I was so mad; if she wanted to try and beat me up, come on woman. They slammed the door in my face.

I was so mad I yelled, "OK, I gave you this planter out here, with these sea oats and everything, I'm taking it back. You can't have it." It was like a comedy.

She opened the door and said, "You're so fat," and slammed the door.

I yelled out, "You're right, I'm fat, but I can do something about it. That silicone came up from your breasts and went to your head. You're ugly and you can't do anything about it. Those fake boobs are the only thing you got that's pretty." I didn't know if she'd had a boob job or not; it was the only thing I could think of at the moment to get back at her.

The whole scene was so awful! We were like two kids.

"I don't know what y'all have been doing but you are crazy as hell," I added, and I turned, kicked the metal door with my tennis shoes and went downstairs with that planter and put it in the trashcan. I started off the island, and got to the Lazaretto Creek bridge and realized that I still had the key in my hand. I went back, put the key on the elevator, and yelled that there was their damn key. Lin must have notified the police, because as I turned onto the Strand (the only street to her condo), there were four police cars there. I crept right by, trying not to get noticed. I went to the stop sign and in the rearview mirror I saw two cars behind me with lights on. I looked and saw them get out with handcuffs and such, and said to myself that this wasn't going to happen—I was never going back to jail again. As one of them tapped on the window, I shoved that pedal down and took off like a shot. When I got down to Butler Ave., there were two cars sitting there making a road block. I went up on the sidewalk and went around them and over the Lazaretto Creek bridge, then the Bull River bridge. I could see at least three of them chasing me but I kept going. It was pouring down rain, and a couple of times I hydroplaned; I prayed with the lyrics to a famous country song I liked, "Dear Jesus, take the wheel." I thought I was going to die.

I was determined that I wouldn't go to jail after the experience I had had some time back. It was late, Lin was a resident, and I would've gone to jail. I thought they had probably radioed the Savannah police, so I pulled over in the woods and hid for about 30 minutes, then I crept back to Victory Drive. I went to the back of the house in the alley to hide the car, and yelled to Bobby that I was running from the cops.

"Go get your stuff and let's go," I yelled.

"What's the matter," and I told him that the police were after me and we had to go NOW.

"What for? WHAT? What did you say?"

"I got in an argument with Lin and her boyfriend and Dudley, and they called the police on me and I ran,"

"What? You ran from the cops? Nancy Lee, you did not!"

"Yes, and I'm not going to jail; come on, please come on."

We started loading stuff; I said to get Elvis. "I'm going to take my little birds, too," I said. He gets them and the door opens and they started flying out. I was able to save two so he put the two left back in the house. We grabbed my dog, Elliott; left a note for the boys and pulled out. Bobby told me to lie down in the car so I couldn't be seen and I was so scared. He asked where we were going and I suggested we go to Atlanta and stop at Evie's (my good friend from St. Simons). Evie had her own real estate license and was working for one of the largest home builders in the fastest growing county in America. We had been friends for over thirty years and I needed a safe haven to figure out what to do. She also was using a lot of my furniture and storing some in her garage and I had to see about getting that out of the way, so I called her. I didn't tell her about my plight; I thought I'd wait until we were face to face. We got there in the early morning, put Elvis up, and we went to sleep. Of course, Evie was wondering what was going on, but I just gave her the highlights and said we were too tired to tell everything now—I'd fill her in after we rested.

In the early afternoon she woke me up and said, "I just read the Savannah paper; what the hell is going on? You are on the front page of the paper!"

Sure enough, there was a picture (not a very good one) of me on the front page with the headline reading something like *Nancy Hillis, aka Mandy Nichols, Outruns Tybee Cops.*

"I'm harboring a criminal," Evie said.

"Yeah, but it's OK, they won't come looking for me here." She said they had listed me as 49 years old and she was going to text them and tell them that today was my birthday and I was actually 50. We laughed. What are good friends for?

Bobby said he was going to take me out for my birthday that night; and if I wanted to go to Nashville with him the next day, that's where we'd go. I didn't know what to do. I needed to call my attorney, Tammy Bowen, but I knew she would be mad at me. Tammy was one of the most wonderful people I have ever known in my life. She was a true, "talk-the-talk" as well as a "walk-the-walk" Christian, but I knew she would fuss at me and rightly so. Anyway, Bobby and I went out that night to my favorite restaurant, Van Gos, and he said, "Honey, I just think you ought to come on to Nashville with me. Come back home to Tennessee."

"Savannah's my home now, Bobby;" I said, "and it's where I became me. I was a majorette, Mr. Brown's granddaughter, Dr. Hillis' wife, and I'm finally just me. Savannah is the first place I was able to be the real me—my own woman, so I want to stay. Besides that, there is a lesson I am supposed to learn going through all of this, and even though I don't know what it is, I have to see it through."

He reminded me that it always got me in trouble. "You are the sweetest person who ever walked and YOU'VE OUTRUN THE COPS and they are going to get you for that."

I told him I knew that, but I'd do it a thousand more times because of what happened to me in the past, and then and I proceeded to tell him what happened to me in jail the time before. He then understood.

The next day I called Tammy.

"Tammy, it's me."

"Honey, where the hell are you?"

I told her where I was.

"What were you thinking?"

I told her the story.

"Lin and her boyfriend are talking like you were drinking."

"I guarantee you they were drinking." It was known that Lin and her friends often went to the bars on Tybee and "tipped the cups," as they say. Let's just say everyone knew who they were in the local Tybee hangouts.

Tammy said she didn't know how she'd get me out of this one, and I apologized. She said we could sue the city for what went on last time when I was in jail for check bouncing. "Who hurt your arm that time," she asked. I told her about the jailer who pulled my arm way up behind my back when he escorted me from the holding cell to solitary. I had to walk on my toes to keep him from breaking the arm. "We'll get them for that," she said.

I told her I didn't want to sue anybody any more; I was living in a courtroom now, and I was tired of it. I told her I'd been inside a courthouse more than in church here lately. She said that they should not have been allowed to treat me that way in jail, and if I had called her...."

"I couldn't call you," I cried, and I explained that they only let me have that one call and I had called my other lawyer, because he knew about the bad check and he was supposed to be taking care of it.

"OK, well let's move on. Billy will testify that you were working and not drinking, won't he?" she asked. I said I was sure he would. She repeated, "Bobby will say you hadn't been drinking, too, right?" Yes, I assured her. "Well, I can get a list of the bars Lin and her boyfriend were in, too, but now I have to think how to proceed. You are going to have to come down here and be booked, but I promise you, I'll be with you; we'll do the fingerprints and the picture, we'll walk in and then walk right back out. You will not see the inside of any kind of cell; I promise."

I was so thankful to have Tammy as a friend and lawyer.

I spent the night at Evie's; Bobby went on to Nashville; and I decided to go back to Savannah with the understanding that I would come back up and stay with Evie in Atlanta for a while until things were settled.

Tammy told me to buy a wig, and I bought a red one (always wanted to be a redhead).

On the way back, we went to Swainsboro, and stopped for breakfast. We're sitting there and all the cops came into this restaurant to have their breakfast. One of them had a hometown newspaper and I could see the article about me (and that awful picture) as he read what was on the other side of the front page. I had the wig on, and Evie told me to quietly go on ahead and get on out, she'd take care of the bill. I put on my sunglasses and sauntered out to the truck. They didn't recognize me or else they didn't care.

Tammy said she was going to call the Tybee police and tell them she had me and we were going to come quietly one night without anyone knowing it. She called me back and said that the press had word I was going to appear at the Tybee police station the day before and hoards of reporters showed up. Tybee didn't want that any more than I did so they'd be thrilled to have me sneak in some night and do this quickly and that's what we did. We went late one night, did the fingerprints, picture, and we walked out—that was done.

Now we had to talk about the trial. Tammy had a brain tumor—wasn't supposed to live beyond a year after they found it, but here she was, still alive, some 15 years later. But it was beginning to bother her again, and some days she couldn't go to work. She said, "God is keeping me alive to help you," and I believed it, because she was the best, "but you are really running me in a circle," and then she laughed and said, "God knows I like a challenge."

After living with Evie for about a month, I came back to live at the Hamilton-Turner House as planned. The Lafayettes questioned me, and said if I got a felony charge from this they'd have to let me go, but I was back at the house, living on the garden level which was partially underground. You entered from the street level and walked five or six steps down to the door. The walls were old Savannah grey brick from the 1800's, and the area had included former servants quarters; it had been a storage area for food, canned goods, laundry supplies and so forth and now, this was the space Jacob and I were living in. I loved it as I wanted to hide for a while.

I had moved Jacob in with me when he was released from Georgia Regional and I was determined to get him better. We were trying one treatment after another, and I had a plan to keep him busy. We'd start out in the morning, going to the Y. He didn't want to go, and it was tough getting him up and out, but I made him. I would do a workout and he'd find a place to go to sleep. They'd come and tell me he was in the back stairwell, sleeping, and I said to tell him to get up—help me out. He wouldn't walk or work out, but I made him go. Then we'd go to a nice lunch somewhere, I'd get ready to go to work just upstairs on the parlor floor, and he'd watch TV, and have dinner—we did that every day. Jacob wanted to go back to school, but he never passed English, so I went to Armstrong University and talked with them, and they said they could tape the lectures and we could go over them again and again, take the test alone in a quiet area, and pass. He and I took English 101 and 102 and we passed with a B! Jacob wasn't doing great, but he was doing something and that was good. But expenses were going up.

In the meantime, the relationship with the Lafayettes, especially Bertha, had not been good since three days after I signed the contract. She'd embarrass me in front of guests; she'd yell about everything; and I think they thought that after the Tybee incident, they could dissolve our contract, but I hung in there. My hours were officially 6:00-11:00 pm but often I'd work until 1:00 am or so, as guests would still be out. I would wait until all the guests were "put to bed."

One day when I was at the House, I woke up and water was pouring in my bedroom and was up to my knees. I called upstairs and they got some people in to clean it up and check it out. I had never had a leak there, but it was leaking in the wall. They had several people try and fix it, but it just went on and on and I began to get sick, and my furniture was getting damaged. They didn't seem to care. My rugs were ruined and it just wasn't getting fixed. Finally, I cut a piece of carpet out and took it to a lab and found out it was growing spores and mold, and I went down to the city to tell them, and the city went in to say if they didn't get it fixed in 24 hours, they would shut them down.

Talk about mad! They were really mad and Spencer said I had really done it this time; and from that point on they pushed to get rid of me.

One day Bertha called me to come upstairs right now. I pulled on some pants and a T-shirt. It was 7:00 am and I was asleep. We had some late guests so I had stayed upstairs until 1:30 am.

"Do you see this? This front door was wide open this morning when we got here at 6:00 am."

We had a guest in our place who smoked, and I knew he went out at least three times an hour, so I assumed that he'd gone out to smoke after I went to bed, and he didn't lock the door. I certainly had locked it at 1:30.

"Don't you know how to lock it?" she said.

We had all these guests eating breakfast, and she's just a yellin'. They were trying not to watch. They all knew who I was because of *Midnight* and I had spent hours chatting with them, making reservations for them and giving them a tour and history of the House.

"Bertha, I put the lock in; I know very well how to lock it. Would you like for me to show you?"

She continued to yell and yell, and I just walked away. She jumped on me for every little thing, continuing to try to embarrass me in front of all our guests. Spencer wouldn't do that—he'd call me in the office to speak with me—but she would do it out in the open.

One time she saw me give a basket (which was mine) of sample soaps and lotions with our name on them to a guest. She accused me of stealing them. I told her I had given them to a guest that was most unhappy over a dirty room, and I figured this would go a long way in appeasing her.

"You can call her, if you like; I was trying to make amends and that didn't cost you much. I don't want soaps—why would I want them?" I knew they wanted me to quit but I just couldn't; it was the only stable thing I had going in my life, so I just hung in there. I had a contract and I wasn't going to quit.

There was a bright spot in this time of trouble. We had a guest come into the House to meet Mandy. We talked and she learned I was once a star twirler.

"How would you like to be a celebrity judge for the national twirling competition taking place at Disney World?" she asked.

"Wow," I said, "Disney is just about my favorite spot in the whole world; I'd love to do it." I went down to Disney and was told that as a celebrity judge, I'd need to lead the parade down Main Street when the park opened and again at 4:30 pm. I, of course, said yes and was just thrilled.

I wore leggings, a tank top, black shorts, and a red blazer that I had spent weeks decorating with a huge picture of Mickey Mouse on the back in jewels, and a small picture of his face on the front pocket. It was gorgeous and just sparkled—everyone loved it. I marched down the street and up to the castle and when I looked around I could see hundreds of these girls, with hundreds of batons (they were in the parade, too) sparkling in the sun, and I just thought, "Thank you, Dear God," I had finally arrived. It was so awesome: I was a part of the magic of Disney! It is a memory that will be etched in my mind forever.

I did judge the contest, and I never saw anything like the twirling that took place that day. The girls were doing seemingly impossible moves, doing splits in the air while flipping and throwing the baton. It was just amazing and I was so honored.

With the success of the movie, people started flocking to see the House and Mandy, and after a while, the Lafayettes realized that I was the reason the place was doing well, so in spite of everything, once my three year contract was up, they asked me to stay another year. They didn't want me to live there though—they'd pay me to live somewhere within 15 minutes of the place. I was happy about that and I found a loft on the River which had a beautiful view and a balcony. I signed a year's lease and they paid for it. I used my screens to make two bedrooms and Jacob stayed there with me. If anyone came by that was hungry or needed something, I noticed that Jacob would go get them food, or give them money, or help them any way he could; he was easy to be taken advantage of.

The condo didn't allow pets, but I had brought my two birds in and, of course, someone found out so I was going to have to move. In the meantime, I was trying to get Jacob on disability as it was obvious he wasn't able to work. Finally, one psychologist got it and Jacob finally got on disability. For four years I had paid for everything myself, and that took most of my money, but finally, the disability came along and helped out tremendously. The profit on the house wasn't that much by the time I paid everything, and then the medicines, the doctors, therapists and hospitals for Jacob took the rest. I was going on my fourth year with the Lafayettes, but I was still concerned about Jacob.

One weekend we went to St. Simons for a visit and things began to unfold. I realized he'd been happy there, and I had a new opportunity on the horizon, so I thought if we moved back, Jacob might be better off. It was small and you could ride a bike, so we came back to St. Simons to our condo.

Chapter 32

Jekyll and Hyde

I thought things would be better in St. Simons; but within two weeks, I had to put Jacob in treatment again at Gateway because he had what I had begun to call "a come-apart" episode. He was there a month and the doctor said that given Jacob's history of the last six years, and given where he was now, I should take hold of being his legal guardian again in earnest, so I took control. After a bit, I was able to take him out for day trips and one day I picked him up to take him to the Georgia Southern football game where we were to meet his brother, Wes and his wife Sheila. I was always very careful about what we talked about—making it light and fun—to keep his fragile mental state steady. The trip from St. Simons to Georgia Southern took three hours, so we left early.

We were on our way and he said, "Mom, why did you have sex with Brodie (not his real name)?" Brodie was Charles' middle child who was in Darlington when we got married. He was his mother's child, taking her side, so he didn't come to the wedding and hardly spent time with us. Anyway, he asked the question and I thought I didn't hear him right. I asked him what he said and, again, he repeated the question. I was floored.

"Jacob, did you take your medicine this morning?" I thought he was hallucinating.

"Mom I've upset you, haven't I."

"No, but I can't imagine where you got such an idea."

"I shouldn't have said anything."

"Say anything you want to say, but who told you that?"

"Never mind, I don't want to talk about it."

I pulled over and he said, "Mom, we are going to be late."

"We are not going anywhere until I find out where this came from, because this is nothing I would ever do, and I don't understand. I know they might try and discredit me, but you should know better."

"That was part of the reason why it was alright for me to have sex with Hattie."

I was hardly breathing.

"You had sex with Hattie, and she and your dad told you it was OK because I had sex with Brodie?"

"Well, she told me you did and that there wasn't anything to it. She said she and I weren't related and you and Brodie weren't related so it was OK."

"That's one of the biggest baddest lies I ever heard. That never, ever, ever happened and it never would and it makes me sick to think someone would tell you that."

Here he finally admitted that he had been having sex with Hattie, and a fire ignited in my stomach. We were almost there, and I kept trying to keep myself calm, not overreact. "Dear God," I thought, "don't let me overreact. Let me stay calm and cool, get him to his brother and then make some phone calls."

I changed the subject and I got him to Wes and went to the bathroom and just cried because I now knew it had happened and I had to confront it. Then I got mad, I kicked the door so hard I bent the lock. Some lady asked me if I was OK.

I went "I'm fine," and I sat there for 30 minutes and paged Anne.

I told Anne what happened and she told me not to overreact; let him have fun with the game, and be nonchalant.

"Call me when you leave Statesboro," she said, "and bring him to my office. I want to talk with him to see if this is a delusion."

"I don't think it is, Anne."

"Oh my God. Just bring him by the office."

I don't know how I made it through that game, but I did and we went to Anne's afterward.

She talked to Jacob, and when she came out of the office she said, "Oh, yeah, it happened, but I'm not sure what to do as I'm not skilled in this area, and Charles and Hattie will put Jacob in all kinds of hell over this because he told you and that is not good." She called Todd Stanley, a specialist in adolescent sexual abuse, and he came on board. We found out that the seduction had been going on since Jacob was 14 or 15.

I called Kathleen, my dear friend, and she couldn't believe it. She knew Charles and she just couldn't believe he'd allow this. I told her I was going to kill him;"

"You can't do that," she said.

Finally, the therapist confronted Charles and it all came out. He admitted that Hattie had been having sex with Jacob and she had been doing it awhile, but that Jacob was 19 and an adult so it wasn't wrong, "and it was in my private home, and was my private business." I realized then that Charles was a Jekyll and Hyde.

More stuff came out. When he was younger, Charles would come down to see him (before Hattie) and they'd get a hotel and he'd have him for the weekend, and he'd bring magazines to share with Jacob (girlie) and he'd show Jacob "what to do" – masturbate. Jacob was a little boy in 3rd, 4th and 5th grade—that was so sick. Charles was sick and adult or not, Jacob's mental state was such that he couldn't handle the whole scenario.

Anne was speechless; "He's an MD and a minister; what the hell was wrong with him—I can't believe it; their business in their home? God."

The next few months were a nightmare of different care facilities. Some would let him out after just ten days, saying he was finished. I knew better.

One day, he got into a crisis situation and I took him to a treatment center connected to Memorial Hospital and he stayed a week. They wouldn't let him smoke (they gave him a nicotine patch and he chewed it) and he was mad. After a week, they wanted him out as they said they couldn't help him. A great treatment center in Savannah could not help him? What was I supposed to do next?

He was in a group home in Brunswick where he tried to kill himself. Thank goodness he took the wrong pills and didn't succeed. He went to a facility on the other side of the state in Moultrie, Georgia, which didn't work. I took him to a place in St. Augustine, Florida where they put him in a trailer in the woods. He had meetings every day, all day, and one time he asked to get a dog. The director said, "You can't take care of yourself, what makes you think you can care for a dog?" Jacob was humiliated and banged the door—that was it for that place.

Without my knowledge they put him on a bus in St. Augustine with $20 in his pocket to go to another place in Miami that the same group owned; they thought it would be a "better fit." I got a collect call from him at 1:30 am saying he was at the bus station but no one was there to pick him up. He had eaten and bought some cigarettes and only had about $4 in his pocket and he was scared. I told him to call back in 20 minutes, that I'd try to get some answers. I called the Miami police and they couldn't help because I did not know the address or phone number of where he was going. I started calling the emergency number of the treatment center in St. Augustine and got a recording. I called the St. Augustine police and they let me know that they didn't care for the treatment center. "They just turn people out in the streets with no place to go." Jacob called back and I told him I was working on helping him and he said he was really scared; I was scared too, but I tried to remain calm. I told him to call again in 20 minutes. (He was at one of those phones that call collect to someone and charge $39.00 per call.)

I called the emergency number again and told them I was on my way and I would get the police when I got there and report them to the authorities. How in the world could they send a mentally ill person on a bus with no one to meet him at the station (IN MIAMI); and how could they do that without telling his legal guardian? "If something happens to Jacob, your company will never know the end of it—they'll be lawsuits, newspapers and television," I warned. "It's 3:00 am and he is in a bad area of Miami with $4.00 in his pocket, and I don't have a number or name of this place."

That did it. I got a call from the administrator of the place who said he had gone to the bus station, and Jacob wasn't there. "I figured he had gone off to a bar somewhere to drink," he said and he wasn't very nice. I didn't believe that he had gone to the bus station at all, but I just told him to go now—Jacob was at the all night restaurant down the street and waiting. Someone came for him right away and they took him to the next facility. When I drove down the next day I found that the place was in a run down, former Holiday Inn; it was just horrible. I wanted to take him home but Todd told me to leave him there, that he needed to learn to be on his own. He also said, "If the last three treatment centers couldn't keep him, what makes you think you can?" I knew he was right, but these were street-wise people and Jacob immediately had trouble.

One day he caught his roommate stealing some of his things. He got in a fight with him, kicked him out and locked the door. Someone called the police, and the police told him he had to let the kid back in because he lived there. The manager wasn't the best, as he should've gotten involved, but to make a long story short, Jacob went to jail. He called me and I borrowed money and started to go down to bail him out (I was already in Jacksonville headed to Miami). I called his therapist who told me to pull over and talk first.

"He's in jail with the BIG MIAMI crooks, and I've got to get him out." I was panicked.

"Jacob is in the real world, and you've always shielded him from it, so he doesn't know how to cope. I understand he did nothing particularly wrong, but there are consequences for not following orders. Let me talk to someone and by bedtime tonight he'll be in a hospital or at least a part of the jail for the mentally ill, and he'll receive his medicine." Todd asked me to trust him; he loved Jacob and I knew he was telling me the right thing.

I decided to go back home, so with a heavy heart and lots of tears and prayers, I turned around.

I started calling this doctor and that doctor in Miami, Florida to get help, and finally reached one who understood. He contacted a woman who placed mentally ill people who had been arrested, in programs that would help them. She put Jacob in a place in Miami operated by a doctor from Cuba. It cost $600 a month and it was for mentally impaired people. It was in Little Cuba, which was like Savannah in the earlier years: a beautiful lady with a dirty face, and they had three gorgeous houses that they had re-done. One was for the offices and low functioning patients; one for middle functioning patients, and one for high functioning patients, and Jacob was put in the high functioning house. To a lot of people, the high functioning individuals look normal, but they are not; high functioning people are resentful they have the disease and it's really hard for them. Jacob remembers high school, college, all his friends as a child, his stints at modeling, and so forth, so he doesn't really believe he has a problem. But schizophrenia and delayed traumatic stress, which was his duel diagnosis, is not caused by something; it comes from a chemical imbalance in the brain and certain things will bring on an episode. His therapist and I were of the opinion that the molestation was a trigger for the schizophrenia; and when Jacob thought about having a girl friend, the first thing he thought of was the molestation and he flipped out. They played with his mind, and on top of it all, Charles watched. It is just sickening.

Anyway, the place was just wonderful, and a doctor watched over him and they took such good care of Jacob. My friend, we'll call her Betty, who was a nurse, drove down with me to visit and I was so impressed. I called Jacob just about every day and went to see him three times while he was in Miami.

I went to a lawyer to take Charles and Hattie to court over the molestation. Remember, this is Alabama, Charles' home, a small town, and it's the deep South. One police officer told me, "What a lucky kid; she's hot! This is a teenager's dream." These kinds of incidents happened a lot and men thought they were "training" opportunities, and women just turned their heads (or in this case, performed the training). I'm in Georgia; they are in Alabama, and I've got lots of strikes against me. Jacob's therapist also said he wanted to wait as Jacob couldn't handle any kind of courtroom experience now and he would've had to testify.

Jacob, at this point, was ridden with guilt over the whole ordeal. Think about it: a gorgeous big blonde, only nine years older than him, who wanted to have lots of sex with him; and he's 16, so he begins to enjoy it. But now as he was getting help, he realized how sick it was and he became ridden with guilt. He had stuffed all the emotions way down because, after all, his father was right there in the middle of it. I can't imagine how his mind was handling all of this.

I waited several years until six months before the statute of limitations ran out and approached the therapist again. He thought it might be helpful to Jacob if an outsider (the court) said that what Charles and Hattie had done was wrong, but he wanted to be assured that Jacob would not have to testify in open court, as that would be detrimental. We took it to court and the judgment was against them. This was a civil suit, so there'd be no jail time, but they'd have to pay. I had no dreams of ever getting any money—it was all just done to help Jacob and relieve some of his guilt that was making him delusional.

When the verdict was handed down, my lawyer, Tammy, wheeled around, held up Jacob's basketball and football pictures and said, "Justice at last. Thank you, Lord," and she did a little dance. The audience clapped and the judge rapped her gavel for order in the court.

Jacob was in the Miami facility for a year as mandated by the court, but he finally had to come out.

Jacob came home to St. Simons and we went on a Christmas cruise with the family and it was great. He was like himself; he had a smile; he was happy and fun to be around. He had a heck of a lot of medicine, about nine different prescriptions, but he was good. His meds cost about $6,000 per month, but disability paid it. For the next four and a half years it was wonderful. He went to work; he went to AA; and all was well.

Chapter 33

Life Goes On

During all this time, I was still working part time for the Lafayettes when The Good Old Boys from St. Simons called and asked if I'd sing with them for a special event so I went and stayed with Jenny, the piano player. She said that her nephew was there from Atlanta, and she made a side remark that she "didn't think he was quite right," but she wanted me to meet him. I met him and said hi and later when I went out to get in my car, he was there, and my car was all washed and polished.

"Who did this?"

"That would be me. A pretty girl like you shouldn't drive around in a dirty BMW (the car I had then), so I cleaned it for you."

I'll call him Joe; we chatted a bit. I didn't think he was quite right, but he had been in the audience that night at the special event, and he handed me a $20 tip (little did he know I had gotten a $300 tip before), and asked if he could take me back to Jennie's house. I said yes and he was all over me, and coming on to me. I was standoffish, because my emotions were at their peak, and I began crying and couldn't stop. He held me and that felt good, as he didn't try to get fresh, he just made a connection—someone who cared and listened. So he "sort of" became my boyfriend. He asked me what I was doing for money, and I said that I wasn't doing much, just working for the Lafayettes at the house I used to own. I wasn't singing much, either, as I just didn't have the heart for it these days.

Joe asked me if I'd like to be a car dealer. I laughed and said I knew absolutely nothing about cars; just how to drive them. He took me to an auction in Georgia and I thought it was fascinating.

"First, you have to go to the lot and pick out the cars you want to bid on," he said. "Then, you look on the computer to find out when they are going to be presented, and on what lane, then you bid; so you want to try it?"

He told me I could bid on a Mercedes we had looked at, to not go over a certain amount, and I tried it. They rolled those cars in, 12 lanes at a time, and it was so fun. We won and put the car on a carrier, and it went to the car dealership. He got about $250 for each car he bought. He thought we could buy some ourselves and resell them down on a lot on Fredericka Road in St. Simons. He told me the rent was $35 a week, and you let the car sit on the lot, in the shopping center where there were lots of people, and that this kind of thing was happening all over. He said if I wanted to do this, I had to go to Macon and take a class, then pass a state exam. He said he had passed the exam, but he couldn't sell cars right now. I mentioned that he just did, and he mumbled that it was on someone else's ticket.

"I can't have my own ticket because I had some problems with one place I worked," he said.

I asked him what kind of problems.

"Well, I was rolling the money and this guy thought I was embezzling, so I had to spend a year in jail."

That should've been a big clue. I felt like such an underdog and knew how much I'd been railroaded, but I believed him. Gullible me. I didn't know he was an alcoholic and bi-polar, I found that out later. Tammy, my attorney and friend, seemed to like him and she went to the same kind of church he did, and he could spout off Bible verses (chapter and verse) so I thought he might be all right. His Aunt Ginny was also like my own grandmother.

I went to Macon and took the class, and we became Mandy's Motor Cars. We rented a warehouse, and stored two or three cars in it just to see how we would do. I wrote the checks to pay bills, and he took care of the books. I told him to make sure he turned the sales tax in, and he swore he did.

Tammy was trying to help the minister at one of the churches who had gotten into financial trouble. She gave Joe the minister's Lexus, asking him to sell it for as much as he could to help out the minister. Joe said the car needed air conditioning and some other things, and Tammy said she'd pay for it—"just do what you have to to help the minister; I'll get my money back when it sells," and she gave Joe the money. He took it and he spent it on other things and Tammy lost her money.

He was a real wheeler dealer.

When I confronted Joe about this, he admitted he had a problem, and wanted to go to a therapist so I took him to Anne; she told me he loved me to death, and she thought he was trying, but he was bi-polar and an alcoholic. I had never seen him drink, but he evidently hid it well. She said he wasn't right. I got rid of him and closed Mandy's Motors Cars.

One day in 2008 I was riding my bike on St. Simons with my two dogs in my front basket and saw that they were working around an old beach house across from the Dairy Queen. It was a 1930s St. Simons beach house and I stopped and talked to the person there.

"I hope you aren't tearing this down," I said.

"It's ridden with roaches and we're tearing it down."

"Oh, no, you should build onto it, fix it up, name each room and have an historic place to have people stay. It would be a great place."

She asked if I had a card, and a week later I got a call from the owner of the building saying he was interested in my ideas. I brought my resume and talked about my experience with historic places. I suggested he keep the old building, do some research about it and present it as an Historic Inn. He liked the idea, and he gave me a job as his innkeeper and general manager. We put in a pub instead of a bar and he called it "The Village Inn and Suites" and "The Village Pub."

He said he needed furniture and, of course, I had a whole lot of it. "You want antiques," I said, "to keep the integrity of the historic look" and I told him about my stuff and about Jere's Antiques in Savannah. I had two gold sofas with a medallion in the middle, hand painted, and tufted but they had to be reupholstered to match his décor. We spent a couple of thousand dollars fixing them all up, and he rented my furniture.

The owner of the Inn had been a car dealer in another city and the business had bankrupted. He never had owned a hotel in his life and the woman who was his right hand person got intimidated by me and didn't like me. She had no experience, either, but everything I tried to do was wrong. She felt things were going too slowly, but there was so much to find out about the history of the house and people, and the research took a while. On top of that, the computer wasn't my forte so I was doing it the old fashioned way—by hand. Anyway, he ended up letting me go and I asked to be fired because I could get unemployment. He wanted to give me my furniture back, but he wanted money for the reupholstering. I told him he had the furniture for three months and he should subtract the rent from that and we got in a fuss, and he wouldn't give me my furniture. I had an antique dealer call from Savannah to tell him that I didn't have any money, and she would pick up a contract to do a big sale to pay him. I had the sale, and the sofas brought $2,000 so I gave him that money and asked for the furniture back. He refused and said he wanted it all. I just couldn't fight him. He was a big time developer in Glynn County, with big time lawyers and I probably would have lost. It would just have cost too much—more than he owed me. I sold some chairs and such, but I decided to just let it all go. I told the antique dealer to keep the chairs and other things for her trouble; that I'd rather she get them than him and I never called her back again, it just wasn't worth the hassle. I did not want any more lawyers and courts; I'd had enough and besides, I didn't have the money to fight any more. I'm sure he knew that.

There was another hotel opening up called the Ocean Inn and Suites and I applied for a job and was hired for the front desk. They had a wonderful view of the ocean and Lighthouse, and I saw so many things that could've been done to improve it. But the owner was foreign, from a country that didn't listen to women, and you know how that went over. I was there about a year. But what he couldn't ignore was I was the only person who gave him good ideas. They ended up sending me to the visitor's center at the Georgia-Florida line to talk about them. I did some weddings for him, too, and he made money, but he just couldn't take me seriously, so I quit. (The owner, a millionaire, fought me over unemployment!)

Before this time, I had become friends with Jeffery Hall—now one of my best friends. I had seen him at Club One as he was Lady Chablis' manager, and I noticed that her act got better when Jeffrey was there. I finally met him and talked with him at length about everything. He was doing theater and was so talented; I just loved him right off the bat. He was the Vice President of Corporate Administration for Goodwill, and I had clothes that he could use so I invited him out to the warehouse to show him what I had for sale. He said he could take all the clothes I could give him, so he filled up two trucks with clothes and gave me a receipt for about $3,000—one dollar per hanging garment, that's how many clothes I had. He asked me how I lost everything, and at that point, I hadn't told many people about my troubles or about Jacob, but I told Jeffery. I talked to Jeffery for hours, telling him my story, and he told me about his wife leaving him with a little boy. She had post-partum depression and later when she was better, she wanted her son back. Jeff was a great father and it killed him to give his boy up.

One job Jeffery had was working for the Vidalia Onion committee in Vidalia, Georgia and he asked me if I'd be a spokesperson for them and make a commercial. I needed the money and so I became the international spokesperson for Vidalia Onions. Vidalias are Georgia's number one cash crop and are only grown in a few counties in the state. Some are so sweet you can just bit into them like an apple and Jeffery and I joined some others in doing just that in Times Square in New York. Many thought we were crazy, but we let people know about these great onions. In commercials, we made meals using nothing but Vidalia onions—soup, pot roast, soufflé and dessert, and at the end of the spots I'd say, "So always go for the wonderful sweet Georgia browns," and I'd sing the first line of *Sweet Georgia Brown*. I appeared on their brochures, starred in their information video called "Nancy's Kitchen," and went to their food shows as the spokesperson; I did that for about three years and it was too much fun!

Chapter 34

Wedding Business

Not long after I left The Hamilton-Turner Mansion, the Lafayettes decided to sell it, and as I had always loved it, I put the word out to let people know that I'd be interested in partnering to buy it again. Charles had been making the payments on our condo in St. Simons for some kind of tax break, and I lived in it with the understanding that it would be mine eventually—this was all in the divorce contract. Well, unknown to me, he began missing mortgage payments, which I didn't know until I was served an eviction notice. Because he was in trouble financially, he had filed for bankruptcy, and the condo was in danger of being taken. Tammy, my lawyer, started back pedaling as fast as she could. She caught up the mortgage payments and had Charles deed the mortgage to me. We then sold it and made about $350,000. This was the money that I now had to try and buy back the Hamilton-Turner House, but, of course, I couldn't do it without a partner because we needed about $600,000 to purchase it.

One day, the contractor, whom I had called to see what kind of repairs might be needed at the House, called and said he had someone that might want to go into business with me to buy it. She lived at Tybee.

I called the woman and went out to meet her. She owned a bed and breakfast called the Savannah Beach Inn and the house was beautiful; a Victorian, done well, with a phenomenal kitchen. As I called out, around the corner came her son, Greg Bar (not his real name). He was so friendly. "Mom couldn't be here and I'm the one that would be doing a lot of the work, so let's chat," he said. He asked to take me to dinner and we went to AJ's and we had the best time. He was so interesting: he had written a book; he had a wolf-dog he had brought back from when he lived seven years in Alaska; he lived on a sailboat and could sail anything; he could fly a plane since he was a kid and he had a license to do so now; he'd run restaurants; and I thought he was fascinating.

That night I stayed at Linda Odom's house and she knew I met someone because I was just grinning. He called at 7:30 that next morning and he said he was fascinated with me. He thought I was his same age but I was 55 and he was 45. Anyway, he said, "I'd really like to see you again." I was really wondering about the Hamilton-Turner House and asked him about it. "I told mother, and we're interested," he said.

We went to dinner at the North Beach Grill, his mother came, we talked, and I liked her at first. She was a dynamic, older woman, a go-getter who had five children. She worked, had lots of creativity, and I really liked that plus she had owned a phenomenal place in Key Largo. She wanted a Polynesian theme and she went to Tahiti and got 21 Polynesians, including a cook, and built a hotel and restaurant around that theme. They had two or three shows a night, one on a boat, and it was a huge success until it burned. It must have been very cool. She said she and her family had also been out West for a while, serving customers who owned Lear Jets. Only a few people had Lear Jets at the time, and they needed to fuel up somewhere. The woman's family had a place that would guarantee a fuel up in minutes or it was free. They'd roll out the red carpet, coming out dressed in western wear (kids and all) with cookies, drinks and so on. They became quite the concierge company. For example, Mr. Walt Disney was one of their customers and he'd ask for special food and drinks when he stopped and they'd supply them.

I was impressed with everything they did. She had looked at the Hamilton-Turner House years earlier, but they just couldn't swing it then. I was hopeful it would work this time, but it took about six months before she said no.

I was disappointed, but I began dating Greg so I was around the Inn a lot. I started working for Kelly Services and they sent me to work for a lady who managed weddings on St. Simons. When she realized that I was good at event planning, she bought out my contract so I could work exclusively for her.

Around the same time, the wedding planner at the Savannah Beach Inn wasn't working out well, and Greg's mother asked if I would help with a particular wedding. I went there and took over and made the wedding beautiful. She just didn't know how to arrange weddings, and I did. She asked me to go to work for her, but I told her I'd have to ask my other employer, and that I made $400 a week plus a percentage of the money made on receptions. I was honest with my St. Simon's contact, telling her about it. She knew I was singing and that I was the Vidalia onion spokesperson, but she said she didn't care what I did on my own time as long as I did my work for her. She also knew that people who wanted Savannah, wouldn't be interested in St. Simons, so all should be well. I went to her office everyday from 10:00 am to whenever, and I also began helping Greg's mom so we were not in competition.

Greg's mom thought I was great and she wanted to hire other people, working under me, and expand the wedding business. She hired two people, and I wondered how she would pay everyone, but it was her decision so I didn't question it. I was paid a salary and also got ten percent of every wedding I sold and completed.

One day I had a wedding booked, and the mom happened to talk to the couple and she messed things up, telling them something other than what was on the contract. They got suspicious, upset, and she called me saying that I needed to help her out of the mess—they wanted their money back. I told her I couldn't do it, I was working for the St. Simon's woman at that moment, and wouldn't be able to help until later. She asked if I would call them on my lunch hour and I called the couple and made everything OK.

I had created a Word document with the title *Coastal Georgia Weddings* for the St. Simons woman. It was the information letter to the couples, outlining the details of their event, and it was my document so I used it for Greg's mom's weddings, too, just renaming it *Romantic Weddings of Savannah*. It was the same document for both companies. One day the St. Simons woman came in and she was cold and unfriendly then up drove the judge that did most of our weddings. They asked to speak to me. She handed me the Word document and asked if I had done it there and I said yes, that I had created it, but used it for Savannah weddings, too. The judge spouted up and said it was plagiarism.

"A woman almost went to jail for 25 years for doing that," he said.

Evidently this woman had gotten mad because I had generated this document at her place but was using it somewhere else; she wanted the keys and asked me to get out. She fired me and he scared me to death—he said he could have me arrested right now, that this was corporate espionage and I could go to jail. You know how I felt about jail, so I got scared. I went to see my friend, a lawyer, and he said she couldn't do such a thing. He assured me that this couldn't happen and I shouldn't worry. I had signed a non-compete clause though, and I couldn't do weddings on St. Simons any longer.

I was Greg's mom's employee all the time now and I worked for her until 2010. She was great at first, but then she became impossible. She would do things that were underhanded and unethical. I had sold an event at Bryson Hall, Linda Odom's reception hall, for a wedding, and Linda gave me a break on the rent. Greg's mom kept fussing that I could make more money. I told her that computers made it easy for people to compare prices, and we had to stick with the prices listed. She said if Linda charges $3,000 we should charge $6,000. I told her I couldn't do that; it was too much money, but she was having money problems and was becoming desperate. (She had been using The Fresh Aire Home on Tybee Island because it was cheap, and she could hike the price up to the moon.) She said she had charged $6,000 to rent Bryson Hall for another wedding.

"Good for you," I said, "but I hope you don't get caught. Those people can check up on prices."

Then she proceeded to tell me that it was the same date as the wedding I had already booked in Bryson.

"You need to change your wedding," she said.

"I can't do that, the invitations have already gone out."

"Well, I can."

"What are you going to tell this bride?"

"I'll tell her there was a big rainstorm and the ceiling fell down."

And that's what she did. The girl called me crying, and she said she had talked to Ms. Odom, Bryson Hall's manager, and that the roof was fine. I said that I knew, and that this was not me, it was the woman who owned the company and this was not the thing to do. I told her to call Greg's mom, and I apologized.

The girl's mother was smart and said she had a contract, and threatened to sue. That did it. I ended up doing the wedding for the girl and she told me that Greg's mom was getting no money; that they'd found out that she was getting the hall for $2,000 and not $6,000; and she was not going to pay it (the other wedding went by the wayside). She lost and looked terrible, and I told Greg I couldn't work with his mother—that she was unscrupulous. Greg was now stuck in the middle between me and his mother and that was tough.

Unknown to me, a friend of mine did do a sneaky thing. He called Greg's mom to say that he wanted a wedding for 500, they had a $100,000 budget and could she arrange it, but "I only want Nancy Hillis to manage it." I hadn't worked for her for several months and out of the blue I get a call on a Sunday morning to meet her and Greg for breakfast. The two of them were "already on the causeway to St. Simons and we'll take you anywhere you want to go." They told me about the reception and that they had a contract in hand and would I sign it. She wanted to divide the contract four ways – I get a piece, Greg gets a piece and she gets two pieces (one for the business and one for her). I started thinking about this and how big it would be, and told them it could be a catastrophe if we didn't plan well; I'd have to think about it. Then I gave the man a call. It was my friend and he confessed that it was a set up to show what a thief she was; he wanted me to know and he said he told her he wanted no one but Nancy to do the wedding. I told Greg it was a set up and that I hadn't known. He told me to tell his mother that the people changed their mind so she wouldn't know the real truth. In the meantime, she had five other weddings, and Greg told her to give them to me, but she wouldn't. I had been her wedding planner and she was taking the weddings, I found out later, and giving them to a person she was training. I quit, again.

Greg found a job in St. John, Virgin Islands, teaching sailing for the season. It was to last December through March. Jacob was in the place in Miami that was just wonderful. He received expert care and I felt he was content, so I could relax a bit. Greg asked me to come to St. John and I went with him for a couple of weeks at a time after visiting Jacob. It was probably the most wonderful time in my life; the water was so blue and jewel-like; 98% of St John was a state park with animals running free (Ziggy the pig is particularly famous); and it was so peaceful—plus we were on the sailboat every day, and we had all the fresh seafood we could eat. It was almost as good as Disney World.

Chapter 35

Charles Re-enters Stage Left

One day I received a strange phone call from Edna Simmons. She had been the nurse when Charles had his practice and she remained friends with all of us after the practice split up. She said she had been visiting her father in the hospital, talking about good doctors and he talked about Charles. "Sure wish he were here," her dad said, "he'd fix me up." The lady in the next bed leaned over and asked if they meant Charles Hillis. "Yes," Edna said, and the lady proceeded to tell her that Charles was in an insulin coma and didn't have long to live. He wasn't diabetic, but evidently somehow he was given some kind of insulin shot which sent him into the coma.

Hattie soon called Wes to say that Charles was very ill, and the boys should come to say goodbye. They went and evidently it was quite sad, and we awaited the news.

We didn't hear and we didn't hear, then Edna calls me to say that Charles had recovered somewhat and was in an assisted living home. He had dementia and some physical problems, but he had recovered and was now a ward of the State of Alabama. She told me that Hattie had cashed in all the insurance policies and Charles was living off of the only remaining one, and soon the money would run out and he'd have to go to Section 8 Housing. (I knew a lot about Section 8 Housing and it wasn't good.)

"Nancy, you should think about taking him in. Maybe he and Jacob could salvage a relationship."

"Are you out of your mind?" I said.

"You're a good person, and remember what the Bible says, if you don't forgive, how can you expect to be forgiven?"

"God, Edna, think about what he did!"

"You've always done the right thing,"

"God is going to have to work on it," I said, and He did.

I was reminded that Charles had been the only person who believed in me. He said I could do anything I tried to do, especially when it came to purchasing the Hamilton-Turner House. Nobody believed in me or the project, but he did; he was my cheerleader and champion. "I've watched you," he said, "and you can do anything you put your mind to." At that point, he did owe me some money, but he didn't have to give it to me for this House, but he did. Remember that he later put the property totally in my name when it looked like there'd be trouble with Hattie.

I also thought about my mother and grandmother who were living in our house in LaFayette when we separated. He was going to sell the house, but when he realized they were still there, he let them stay. They were happy there and he left it alone for several years, even visiting them upon occasion, and he didn't have to do that. He also loved them and took care of them medically, and helped them financially.

I thought of all the money Charles had put up for Wes and Jacob's education at private schools, especially after we separated. I thought of all the good years we had had, and that for most of them, he had been a terrific father, loving my son Wes as if he were his own. He was good to me, the best doctor and a terrific minister. I blamed Hattie for bringing sin to the table. I'm not excusing Charles; he definitely was involved and he evidently enjoyed it, but if not for Hattie, I don't think the molestation would have happened.

You be my judge and jury, but I considered taking him in. It was a very hard decision but it was like I had someone sitting on my one shoulder saying, "Remember this and remember that," and someone on my other shoulder saying, "But how can you forget what he did to his own son?!" I also knew if Charles lived alone he would not remember to take his meds; he would not remember to eat; where would he get food and how would he get it?

Before anything could happen, I went to Jacob's therapist, Todd, to talk about it. He thought it might be a good idea and suggested we go and have lunch first, so Edna, Jacob and I went. Jacob was very excited.

Edna and I walked in first and Charles did not know me.

"Who are you?"

"I'm Nancy Hillis."

He got up and looked and looked at me and said, "You've changed; you're a little thicker in the middle and your hair use to be dark and now it's blonde like that magazine cover."

"You've changed, too," I said.

I went and got Jacob and he walked in. They hugged and cried together and it was quite touching. Jacob was glad to see his father in spite of everything. As they ate, Charles kept staring at me.

"You're the prettiest wife I had."

"Thank you, Charles."

I went back to Todd and he thought that given how the lunch went, it might be a good thing for Jacob to have Charles with us. He thought they could salvage some kind of relationship. We petitioned the court (who at this point was Charles' ward) and the lawyer at first said no. "You just want the money," he said, but I was already receiving $2,000 a month out of his $2,600 a month social security check, and I wouldn't be doing it for the additional $600. I told them what the therapist said about Jacob having his father close again, and I talked to caseworkers, social workers, and judges to present our side. The judge finally ruled in our favor, and we brought Charles home. This was in 2010, and Charles was with me until my ALS illness became really serious. At that point, his friend took him and cared for him until his death, in the nursing home where she worked. He had Alzheimer's, but he still knew me at times. He'd see my mail and say, "I see here that your name is Hillis; that's my name, too. How am I related to you?" I'd tell him again and again that I was one of his wives, and that Jacob was his son. One time he said with tears in his eyes, "You've been real sweet to me; I must have been awful; you're so good to me and I'm really sorry for whatever I did." I said it was all in the past. "What did I do?" he said. I said that he had run around on me with other women. "Who?" he asked. "Our next door neighbor," I said. "Well she must have been something 'cause you're pretty."

Charles died in December of 2012.

Chapter 36

Something's Wrong

In 2009, at St. John, my ALS (Lou Gehrig's disease) began rearing its ugly head although I didn't know what it was at the time. We went snorkeling one day and I went in like I always did and all of a sudden I couldn't move and I couldn't hold my head above water. I also had trouble breathing. Greg saw I was in trouble and got me—he saved my life and I didn't know what was wrong. I had to put on a life belt just to be in the water. Looking back, I now know it was the beginning of the ALS, so I'm doubly grateful for that wonderful time on St. John.

We came home but Greg didn't let his mom know we were back; and we were doing great until a month or two later when he called her. He didn't know what he was going to do for money. He had been a caddie at Sea Island but was fired because he tried to convince them that there was a better way to do things—they weren't amused. He managed Huey's on the River for a time but that didn't work out because he told the owner that he could get steaks cheaper and could make him so much more money. The boss told him that "I would rather have more time on the boat with my family than worry about making another $500 per month." This was a man who realized the importance of family, and Greg couldn't get it because all he knew his whole life was work.

He called his mom for help and she asked him to come and photo-graph a wedding "this one time." (Greg was a talented photographer.) I knew if he went he'd never be back and I begged him not to go. He went. Then there was another time, and another and our relationship began going downhill.

One day we saw an ad in the paper advertising that the gambling boat in St. Simons needed a captain. Greg applied and said he got an interview which he went to and felt good about. Then he said he had to go to Savannah—something about his mother. Before he left, he said to me, "Nancy, for my part in everything, I'm truly sorry." I was puzzled and told him he had already said that. "Just know that," and he kissed me on the forehead and left. The next day I was in the shop, The Swing Set (they have the cutest children's clothes anywhere) and he called me at two in the afternoon and said he was at the Los Angeles airport on his way to Singapore to build and manage an historic cultural center. I asked him if that meant that he'd move there, and he said yes, and it'd be like St. John where I'd come every so often, but I knew it wouldn't be like that. He said he had to check it out and he'd contact me soon. Then he said, "I love you."

I didn't hear from him for a few days. It was close to Valentine's Day, and I hadn't given him the glossy book of photos and special moments that I had made of our four or five years together—that was his present, so I was waiting to see him to give it to him.

I was walking the dog and one of the ladies who knew me and Greg said she had received an e-mail from the Savannah Beach Inn that said they were opening a restaurant on River Street, much like the one they had had in Key Largo. It was happening because "Greg has found the love of his life (who lived in Tahiti) that he had been looking for 30 years and she will be dancing at the new restaurant." My friend forwarded the e-mail to me and there was a YouTube video attached, so I looked at it and it featured this woman singing a song. In the video you saw feet, and a woman writing in the sand, "my love Greg" with a heart around it. A bird flies from island to island, finally going to a waterfall, and under the waterfall is Greg and this Tahitian woman. It turns out he wasn't in Singapore, but in Tahiti. He had gone to find this woman that he knew 30 years ago in Key Largo. Back then he had taken her to his high school prom and they were lovers, but they'd lost track of each other. He now had found her and went to her, and they were going to be married right away. I sat there and just kept looking at the video of them over and over. Then I looked at his valentine that had just come that very day. It professed how much he loved me. Why this valentine? Maybe he was afraid it wouldn't work out with his lost love and he was hedging his bet. I was so shocked, I didn't know what to do.

Sheila, my daughter-in-law, said she could find her number. She called a hotel in Tahiti to say she was looking for the singer, using her last name. There were only six singers in the city with that name, and the person gave her the numbers. I called them until I found her, and told her who I was. She couldn't believe it and said she had wondered about some things. I told her about us, that he had no money and was working with his mother, and that he professed to love me, too. She said she couldn't talk, because Greg was Skyping her that moment on the computer. She called back later and said he told her I was nothing and that she should believe in him; he loved her, wanted to marry her. He was bringing her ticket and had the restaurant ready for her. He didn't have it ready—he had the business plan, but needed investors.

I didn't know at the time what the status was with the two of them; it's not easy to get married in Tahiti, but I decided I would go ahead and give him the Valentine I created, and so I called to see him again when he finally came home. I had lost weight and I got all dressed up in my "holey" jeans (with holes in all the right places) and felt so sexy, and I went over. I was cool as a cucumber, and he looked shocked. I gave him his book and said I wanted to end on a good note, and I told him I hoped he would have a wonderful life. He told me I looked good, I said thanks and take care, acting happy and in a hurry as I walked out. I went to Lin's house (we became friends again after she sent messages through her associate saying she didn't like being mad with me, and hated how it was), and in 20 minutes he was out front. I called him and said I saw him outside, and I didn't know why he was here, but I wanted to end on a nice word rather than a lousy lie.

"I've met someone who's 44 and who loves me to death and there's nothing like somebody who really loves you, and I just wish you'd been honest with me—we might've worked it out. Maybe one day you'll realize you are manipulated by your mother; I'm sure she paid for your trip to Tahiti and back, but I wish you well. Bye."

I never saw him again and I had the last word.

Greg and his mother did lease a restaurant on River Street, the one with the pineapples out front, and they hired Hawaiian girls to dance.

Wes went to see them once but they weren't around. I heard through the grapevine that she was a good singer with a manager, and when she came to Tybee, she and Greg lived on the sailboat. But I think she realized that his mother was supporting him, and I heard that it didn't work out. The lease on the restaurant ran out in a month or two, and they didn't renew. Last I heard, he was doing some kind of weather research at the equator.

The Inn eventually went into bankruptcy.

Greg and I dated about five or six years, and one thing we did do when we were together is produce a show called the *Spirit of Old Savannah*. We did it at Cha Bellas restaurant on Broad Street, and the play itself was just great. My great friend, Jeffery Hall, wrote it (including all of the original music) and he played General James Edward Oglethorpe, founder of Savannah, and we had a person playing Minerva, the voodoo priestess from *Midnight*, and me playing myself. We did a CD and it featured the great song by Rick Burris that I had tried to sell to Zuckerman, the producer of *Midnight*. It never got off the ground, though, as no one really had any money, and we just didn't have the expertise to pull it off. It was a shame, because it was a great little play.

Chapter 37

Near Death

Jacob's doctor had decided to change his meds and he started to slide. I saw the change and he was going back to his old ways; then one day I got really sick and drove myself over to the ER because I couldn't breathe.

The doctor said my chest was clear and there was nothing wrong with it, and I was just having an anxiety attack. I told him he didn't know me, that I had sung before thousands of people, sat with Nancy Reagan, had a son who was schizophrenic, had an ex-husband who was a doctor and who molested my son, and I knew it wasn't a panic attack. I said, "I know about panic attacks; I had had them in the past and I know what they feel and look like. That's not what this is. There's something really wrong with me." I said this over and over to this ER doctor and finally, he said he'd put me in for observation, but he wanted me to see a psychiatrist.

"Great, I'll be glad to see a psychiatrist. I want to find out what's wrong with me just like you do. If it's in my head then I am one sick puppy."

No one recognized I was physically sick.

The next day, Lin Walsh came to see me. She asked the nurse to give me something because I was having trouble breathing. The nurse was a smart aleck, saying they couldn't do anything without a doctor's approval. "She has to see a psychiatrist," she said. I don't remember a lot of that time, but I know I got out of bed and fell.

When I was a little better, the psychiatrist came to see me in the hospital. She said that I was getting "secondary gain" from Jacob's illness. She explained that there were some people that got their only place in the sun by taking care of their sick child. I was the busiest person there was, with all kinds of jobs, I didn't need Jacob for my place in the sun. It was ridiculous. She also said I was co-dependent on my ex-husband, Charles. How could you be co-dependent on someone you hadn't seen or talked to in years until recently, and he had dementia? There was no way.

Then less than 24 hours after I was admitted, I quit breathing. I woke up in a tremendous amount of pain and I was tied down in a hospital bed. I had blood pressure cuffs on my arms and ankles and I had a respirator down my throat.

"Blink if you know where you are," someone said. I blinked and she told me that I had pneumonia in my lungs. There were IV's everywhere and they kept me in a drug induced coma for a week as I would have been in too much pain with all the tests and such, to stand it.

I clearly remember that at one point, I thought there were big red and green balls coming out of my mouth and if I could just break them, the pain would go away; it hurt so bad. I was lucid enough to pray to God.

"I've had enough, just take me. I can't handle any more, it hurts too much."

About that time there appeared five little angels, like little fairies or Tinkerbelles, with angel glow around them and for a while I had no pain whatsoever; it all went away and I was pain free—I remember that so clearly. I knew that I now had a choice; the tiny angels never said a word, but I knew I could stay or I could go. I could hear Brian's (my boyfriend at the time), Wes's and Jacob's prayers and I was astonished because they all had a hard time with God.

I thought, "Wow, they are praying."

I had to leave or stay; and I chose to stay and the pain came right back in my body with a vengeance. For the first time ever, though, I felt totally forgiven for any bad things I had done, especially the one thing I wanted forgiveness for most—the abortion.

I woke up and there was my current boyfriend, and he was praying and crying. Wes was there, and later they brought Jacob over and he went to his knees. Evidently, I had been close to death.

This was in February 2011 and I couldn't talk. I had a ventilator to keep me breathing, and they weren't sure what was wrong with me. Out of a list of about ten things, they told Wes I had seven or eight that could kill me. I had double pneumonia, staph that turned into MRSA, I was septic, and it was bad. I couldn't talk and I was so weak I couldn't expel the mucous and phlegm that accumulated in my throat and lungs, so I had a suction thing that did the job for me. That thing saved my life. If the suction thing fell out of my hand I had to call for help with my "magic wand," and they retrieved the suction device. I was in a bed that shook me to keep the blood and muscles going, and I never had had so much medicine in my life but I survived, and I spent three weeks in ICU.

I was on the respirator (it hurt so badly), and they had to wean me off of the strong drugs (one of which was the one that killed Michael Jackson), and all pain meds so I could breathe on my own. Kathleen and Lin were there one day, telling me I had to breathe. Lin was tough and she became my cheerleader.

Lin would say, "All right Nancy, I know it hurts, but you're never going to get that respirator out until you breathe, now when I run up here it's time to breathe," so she'd run up and I'd breathe, and it hurt so badly.

"Deeper" she'd say, and I'd breathe deeper.

Kathleen said, "They've got all your eyelashes off; doesn't that make you mad? You've got to wake up and put your eyelashes on. You've got to breathe." It felt like they were there for days, telling me to breathe. Finally, they were able to take the respirator out.

I moved out to the CCU floor and was there another few weeks because I still had infection in my body—three "picc line" sights were in me. I also needed therapy because my left leg would just not work and they didn't know why. I was in isolation and everyone had to put some purple gloves on and a yellow gown and mask. Jacob would bring Charles, who had dementia at this point, to the hospital to visit even though Charles really didn't know me. He touched my foot and said, "You're sick." He'd start pulling the gloves off with his teeth and then he'd chew part of them like gum. Next, he'd rip off the gown and he wouldn't wear the mask to start with. After he got everything off, he'd start saying, "Let's go," every five minutes. Jacob would have to take him home. During this time Jacob was wonderful—he took care of our dog, he took care of our house, and he alone took care of Charles who was living with us at the time; he was just wonderful.

I went to another nursing home in St. Mary's, Georgia, a beautiful seaport town with a lot of history, to totally recover and receive physical therapy. (This is where many people who were guests at the John Kennedy,

Jr. wedding caught the ferry to Cumberland for the ceremony. The week of the wedding the boat went several times a day loaded with everything for the wedding and reception.) They were wonderful and they found out who I was. Jeffery brought copies of the *Midnight* movies for me to give the nurses, and they asked me lots of questions—I felt as if I was on tour—and it was wonderful. I also received letters, especially one from a granddaughter of one of the nurses. She had seen the movie and she loved Mandy. She wrote me a letter, and came to see me, and she told her teacher she had met a movie star; she was so pretty and so sweet. She wrote, "You are so pretty and I enjoyed meeting you. Much love." It was a lovely and awesome moment in an otherwise difficult time.

The physical therapy wasn't working—I was doing better, but my leg wasn't working. They changed the way they gave me my meds, from IV's to pills, and I couldn't tolerate them. I threw up; I couldn't walk on my own; and they kept testing me, on and on, but they couldn't find out what was wrong.

It was time for St. Patrick's Day in Savannah, and I had attended Linda Odom's private party for over ten years, and had not missed a parade in 15. I wanted to go and the administrator said no and then got mad when I insisted. She (and others) didn't understand that I would be in my wheel-chair, at a private party, and escorted by people who would care for me and I wanted so badly to go, so I just went.

I asked them for an oxygen tank and they said no, so I had to get my own. I went to the St. Patrick's Day celebration, Jacob and his friend took me, and I had a wonderful time. I was tired the next day, but I went and I sang my signature song, *Hard Hearted Hannah The Vamp of Savannah*; that was about all I could do. Jeffery had some CDs of the song and people actually bought some of them. It was great.

When I returned to the nursing home, they asked me to leave the next day. "If you can go to that, you don't need to be here," they said. I said I couldn't do that so quickly because I needed to put my bed downstairs and arrange some things at home, including Charles' care. I didn't have Medicare, and I couldn't get it until I was diagnosed (I also wasn't old enough yet). They were being ugly to me, but I just couldn't leave so I had to fight. I called the ombudsman and she came to help me. She said that was no way to treat someone, and she showed them what the Georgia

State Law said: that they did have the right to evict me, but that they needed to give me a little time. I got my time to prepare and soon I came back to my house.

I began seeing Dr. Lori Trefts, a wonderful neurologist, and she did a test that confirmed I had amyotrophic lateral sclerosis (ALS), a progressive, neurodegenerative disease that causes weakness (predominately) of the motor neurons (the cells in the brain and spinal cord that control the body's muscles). It can affect either the lower or upper motor neurons. When the lower motor neurons are affected, the muscles atrophy or shrink and twitch; when the upper motor neurons are affected, patients' muscles develop stiffness with hyperactive reflexes. To absolutely confirm that I had the disease, she referred me to Dr. Kevin Boylan, head of the Neuro Center at the Mayo Clinic in Jacksonville, Florida. My boyfriend took me, and Dr. Boylan confirmed it. He also said I had a forty percent reduction in my lung capacity.

He explained the disease to me in detail and in words that I could understand. The disease resembles multiple sclerosis, and the brain's neurons, for some reason, quit telling your involuntary muscles what to do; so it's like a storm in your brain. Eventually muscles weaken, and you lose ability in different parts of your body little by little. For me it was my legs first, and I can now only travel in a wheelchair—it's hot pink, of course, my favorite color. I also have difficulty breathing, and because I don't always have muscle strength to exhale, carbon dioxide gets built up and I lose consciousness. I can, of course, die if not given treatment right away, and doctors say this will probably be the way I will go.

No one is sure what causes ALS, but there are different theories about environmental factors and for reasons not yet known, it appears to be more prominent in professional athletes and those who have served in the military. About ten percent of ALS cases are genetic. (If someone in your family developed the disease, you may want to be tested.) None of these variables fit me, except that I was a twirler, but I wouldn't say that was necessarily an athletic sport, so who knows.

The illness, also known as Lou Gehrig's disease, Charcot's disease, and motor neuron disease (MND), is not contagious, but there is no cure. There are medications that can slow the progression of the disease, and therapists can focus on strengthening and stretching the muscles, but it eventually slowly takes your life.

I had a boyfriend during this time who took me to the emergency room. I met him at the Sonic where I always went to get a limeade. He was the manager, 6'2", almost 300 pounds, had played football in college, and I thought he was flirting with my friend. He asked me to pull over one day, and I asked him if he wanted my friend's number; he said, "No. I want yours." That's how it started. He asked me for a date and that was it. We, of course, went to Disney World about three times, sometimes taking his daughter and Jacob. We had a wonderful time.

He was funny and fun, but then I got sick. Every time I talked about the disease, he'd tell me to exercise; he just didn't get it. On my valentine he wrote, "I love you and will be with you forever through this. I love you." But I think my illness was more than he could handle, and he just quit calling. So much for love.

Chapter 38

The Last Days at Home

Twice I have had Hospice come in. The first time Dr. Boylan (from the Mayo Clinic) wrote saying that I needed daily care. The letter said, "Expected time of life is six months." I was absolutely shocked and called right away to verify this.

"Don't worry, Ms. Hillis, we say that so Hospice will come." I cried for days.

They did come and it was wonderful. But after a while the doctor in charge decided (rightly so, I suppose) that I wasn't sick enough, that "the disease progression was not felt to meet the criteria for Hospice services," so after ten months, I "graduated," and the care stopped (as a matter of fact, he didn't believe I had ALS). My nurse friend then started coming on weekends to help me out and that was great. I had offered her and her husband, the whole upstairs to live for free in exchange for my care and I thought it might work out, but he ended up not wanting to and she finally stopped coming. She had a husband, a job and a life.

Another Hospice group came again shortly thereafter and it was a nightmare. First, the doctor insisted I immediately sign a DNR form (Do Not Resuscitate). I already had one of those filled out, and I didn't want to sign another one. My original form, which Wes has, allows for some resuscitation. For example, if they find me unconscious from the carbon dioxide buildup, they will resuscitate; but if I'm gasping for every breath, or in a great amount of pain, the order is to not resuscitate. This doctor also told me I was in the last phase of my illness and "your family will suffer if you do not sign this form." If I had signed their form, for the last episode I had, they would have let me die. Obviously, I was nowhere near death. I was still going out with friends to eat, to shop, to church and I was writing this Book.

Next, the doctor said he'd start a morphine drip "to keep you out of pain," but I'd be in a stupor and my life would slowly drip and slide to its demise. I just wonder how many people accept this diagnosis, and end up sliding away when they aren't ready to go. Anyway, I was appalled and I finally said, "You know the front door you came in? Well, you can go out it right now."

All of this happened in less than a month. It seemed so strange that one doctor said I wasn't sick enough, and the next one said I was and wanted to take me out!

In February of 2014 I went for my regular check up at the Mayo and the doctor said "Ms. Hillis has ALS with global functional impairment and needs assistance in home to manage daily living." I was able to get home health care back in, but temporarily—just one month; that was all allowed by the government. They came in and it was great, but then the month was over. I did the best to care for myself, depending on friends.

Jacob's been ill for a long time now. Medicines help him the most, but they are strong and they make him feel weird, so he doesn't always take them, and it's not the best. They also take away his "umph" and he says he can't concentrate. I notice that sometimes his illness will spiral down for no reason; the meds get out of whack or something. But he's been to just about every hospital and treatment center in the state, and no one's offering much hope. I wish I could put Jacob back in the Miami facility where he did so well, but I found out the doctor died and it shut down. It's such a shame because that was the only place that really got a handle on Jacob's situation and care. He improved tremendously there, and became as near a normal person as he could get.

Todd Stanley (Jacob's therapist), Jacob, Wes, Sheila and I met for lunch so we all could be supportive when Todd told Jacob that indeed my illness would kill me; we just didn't know when. Jacob "deflected" the news—he heard it and promptly changed the subject. Todd asked him if he heard what he said, and did he understand, and Jacob just said yes and changed the subject again.

The health care system in the United States for mentally ill people is atrocious, especially for those that have little or no money. Money can buy a lot, and I used all of mine to help Jacob all I could. Once I ran out, though, there was nowhere to go. Our system just doesn't offer many choices and they aren't that empathetic to mental health problems. People in my situation just live crisis to crisis, engulfed in paperwork. They are shuffled around, going places where they put a "bandage" on the person and then throw them back into the community where they have no business being; and there's very little empathy or help from anybody. People fear, minimize or deny things they don't understand. (I have thought about precious Joe and he probably would have been called bi-polar today.)

Senator Creigh Deeds from Virginia, who was stabbed by his mentally ill son, has lobbied for better mental health care laws and plans. "The issue is much bigger than any one person's experience," said Deeds, and he frequently touches on his family's experience with the state's mental health system, and the need to end the stigma around mental illness. He is determined to push for additional reform.

Proponents say, "You don't just give up when somebody is diabetic," they explain; "Do you send a cancer patient home and tell him to come back when he's reached stage four? No! Why not have the same attitude toward mental health? Treat the brain like any other part of the body; mental health is a disease of the brain. Go after it like you would heart disease or cancer."

The singer, Demi Lovato, who is bi-polar, leads marches concerning mental health issues and coming up with a plan. She stated recently, "We know that mental illness has no prejudice. It affects people of every race, age, gender, religion and economic status. It doesn't discriminate between Republicans or Democrats, either," and she's right. Treatment is a lot of work; you may have to try several drugs before you get one to work, but you can't give up. There is life after diagnosis, too, if the person gets the right care, and it's consistent and precise. I would hope legislators, health care workers, psychiatrists and psychologists, hospitals and doctors would work on real reform for the mentally ill.

The last year I was still living in my house, Jacob lived with me (he is not capable of living on his own). We visited doctors and therapists, trying all different medications and treatments, but he would still have "episodes" where he'd go off the deep end. I gave him a little money every day so he could have some autonomy and he'd drink it up and get in trouble, or spend it frivolously. Sometimes he'd be gone a couple of days and I didn't know where he was. It was scary.

His anger and frustration over his illness spilled over and he became angry with me. He'd take my little dog, Jack away from me, knowing it upset me; he'd yell at me and threaten me; he'd sneak in my room when I was sleeping and steal money and my credit cards. It was stressful, and I ended up putting a padlock on my bedroom door.

As I mentioned, I had a hot pink motorized wheel chair with which I tooted all over St. Simons and it was just beautiful. I did run out of power once right in the middle of the town; a gentleman turned it off for a moment, then back on and I was able to get to my destination. I asked a friend to get my battery at my house and he did, and while I had a meeting about Jacob's illness, I charged my chair. I have to say, that was a very scary situation, but I kept going. It is amazing how kind people are, and I'm amazed when people rush out to help. One man asked to help me load groceries in my car. "This is my car," I said, and he was astonished.

One day one of my friends came in and asked if I'd seen my bathroom. Jacob had taken a Sharpie and written all over the walls and countertop, as well as all over the walls in his room and all over the tiles on the porch. He wrote strange things about being God, power and death—really scary stuff. I hired a cleaning lady to clean it up and told Jacob he'd have to pay for it. I also immediately took him back to the program in Brunswick called Gateway. "You've been here three times in a month," said the administrator. I said yes, but what could I do? We were at a standstill, but I had an appointment with a probate judge, a doctor from the A.C.T. team (they come to the house everyday and administer the drugs so a patient is sure to get them) and social workers to see what could be done. I ended up in the emergency room the night before this meeting, but I couldn't miss it, so I went home.

The next day, Jacob and I went to the meeting. They explained to him that he was guilty of parental abuse and if he continued, he could go to jail. Jacob listened and I thought we'd finally get some help as they were sending him to a doctor for a diagnosis. The physician asked lots of questions, but ended up saying he doubted Jacob had schizophrenia—which was the worst thing he could have said. Now Jacob was convinced there was nothing wrong with him. I called immediately and asked how he could say this when I'd been dealing with him for 20 years. "You don't know what you've done," I said. The doctor met with him again, and determined he did indeed have symptoms of schizophrenia.

The group informed me that the problem was that he wanted to control his own disability money ($1,500 per month) and I should let him. I told them "been there, done that" with disastrous results; his money, that had to last a month, would be gone by the tenth or so.

"How does he spend that much money that quickly," they asked.

"Drugs, alcohol, prostitutes, strip clubs, watches—you name it. How much does a lap dance cost? How many can you get in an evening? Who knows?"

They decided that I needed to get a payee that would monitor his money and divvy it out. I said great, and signed the paper, but it never came to fruition.

They decided it would be best if I relinquished guardianship and he went to a group home. "Been there, done that," I said. It was like I was the enemy and to Jacob, I was. "But I will do anything to help my son; tell me where to sign."

As usual, things moved slowly and because of my illness, I was not able to get around following through and keeping his case at the forefront.

Jacob continued to be angry. He'd threaten me, slam doors, come home drunk and yell obscenities. I ended up calling the police four times in one month.

One time two officers came and stood out in the hallway by Jacob's room. Jacob was in there and had the door locked. "Come out, Jacob," the one officer said.

"No," said Jacob, "I'm not letting you in, you sorry son of a bitch. The only reason you're a cop is because you are so stupid. Everybody knows you are cops because you're so stupid and just like to be bullies. You can't touch me and what's more, my dick is bigger than yours."

I could hear all of this and I was so embarrassed, but couldn't help but laugh a little, especially over Jacob's comment over the size of the police officer's member. They continued arguing for about 20 minutes and finally the officer came to my room and said he didn't have a right to break down the door as Jacob hadn't used force with anyone. They left and I was praying for an answer.

One day I went to the kitchen with Jack in my lap to get him some food. I was in the wheelchair and Jacob began shaking my chair, picking it up and yelling, "I hate you so much I could just kill you. My life would be perfect if you were dead." Little Jack jumped down and ran under the bed; he knew this was trouble. I told Jacob, "That's a shame, 'cause if you wait a little while I'll be gone anyway and you won't have to spend the rest of your life in jail—that's what will happen if you kill me." His face got blood red, his teeth were grinding and his whole body was ready to pounce. "It'd be worth it," he yelled, "I'll do the time for the crime," and he walked out.

I called the police and they came yet again, but this time he admitted to them that he had made the threats and shook my chair, so they arrested him for terroristic threats and parental abuse. This turned out to be good, because a day or so later I was rushed to the emergency room.

I had fallen in my hallway, and I didn't have my phone and couldn't get up, and my arm was hurting. My dog, Jack, heard the thud and came running, jumped on my chest and just looked at me. He knew something was wrong. He ran upstairs, barking, to try and get Jacob but no one was there. He ran back down and he barked at the patio door thinking Jacob was out in the yard smoking. He finally came back and sat on my chest for the whole four hours until my friend found me. The EMT's let Jack stay on my chest while they put me on the gurney and took me to the ambulance. Then they finally took him and gave him to my friend so they could transport me to the hospital. My little four-pound dog was so faithful that day. I miss him more than I can say; no nursing home will let him stay, of course.

I went to the hospital, haven't been home since, and probably never will be home again.

Chapter 39

No Where to Go

While in the hospital, it was determined that I needed constant care and access to a breathing machine. There was some talk about doing some surgery while I was still able to have it to put in a feeding tube so when the time came that I couldn't swallow, they could feed me. They also said they could do surgery to have a machine breathe for me. I refused both—I just wasn't ready to give up. I could still eat and breathe (with my oxygen) so I said no. It is now too late to do such surgeries as my ALS has progressed to the point where surgery would kill me.

There was talk of hospice; talk of a nursing home. Several nursing homes could take me and I opted for the one at Tybee Island, Georgia as my friends were there and it was easy to get to for them. Most people were wonderful and indeed, I did see my friends often. I was also able to have my little dog, Jack, with me for most of the day. Mary Anne took care of him and would bring him most days, picking him up in the late afternoon. But the Tybee home was not equipped to care for someone with advanced ALS—they didn't have the right personnel, the proper breathing machines, the proper bed and the proper rehab facilities. One night I had to be rushed to the hospital as I couldn't breathe.

I stayed in the hospital while doctors and administrators tried to decide what to do with me—Tybee was now out of the question and where could I go? The hospital gave me great care, but they were not equipped to take care of someone long term, and I had to go. We opted for a health center in Port Wentworth, Georgia. They accepted me with my own breathing machine called a Trilogy. (The machine does three things: it can be a by-pap; it can be a c-pap, or it can serve as an outside, non-invasive ventilator.) Most nursing homes in Savannah and Brunswick would not accept the Trilogy machine; I had no idea why this home could, but those were the facts. The nursing home did have the rehab facilities and the bed I needed to help me breathe.

I was not your normal person in the nursing home. I was alert, involved, looking for things to do, and therefore, in the staff's eyes, a pain in the butt. I was social and I questioned, and I was able to be assertive when it came to my care. I even got myself together to attend two *Midnight* parties to which I was invited.

The first was in the fall of 2014. It was called "Midnight in the Garden of Good and Evil Garden Party" which showcased the best of the best in Savannah, and was sponsored by the *Savannah Magazine*. My hairdresser and good friend, Judy Mullin, came and did my hair; I did my eyelashes; got my nails done; Linda Odom brought me some clothes and jewelry; Miss Anita from my nursing home even went home to get me an evening bag and jacket to wear; and the social worker, Hallie, and Missy, my nurse, helped me get ready. Mary Anne acquired a special handicapped van, I brought my oxygen, and several of us, including Wes and Sheila, went to the gala.

It was packed and I saw many friends from the good old days. Natalie Hendrix interviewed me for her television show, I got to have a real drink, eat some goodies and I generally had a great time, until my oxygen ran out. We were panicked for an instant as we couldn't find the second tank, then we didn't have the "key" to hook it up. A lady attending the soiree finally was able to switch the tanks out and I was saved ("leave it to a woman," she said). Wes was very close to calling the EMTs, but the tank was hooked up and I had a great time.

The other event was even more interesting. I received an invitation to the Jepson Center where John Berendt was appearing to announce a new app for the *Midnight* book. I got all dressed up again, another good friend got transportation for me, Judy came back to make me pretty again, and Wes escorted me to the gala. I saw John from across the room and he made a beeline over to me. I didn't know what to expect. He bent over, kissed me on the cheek twice, and said, "Nancy, I'm so glad you are here." You could have knocked me down with a feather. It was the first time he had ever been nice to me. I went back to the nursing home.

Nursing homes suck! Most patients have dementia or Alzheimer's; they aren't alert, many sit in a chair or bed all day, they aren't social, and they are there just waiting to die. The care facilities are hard places to be, especially for someone like me who has all her mental capabilities, who is still "with it," but who has no money. If you have all kinds of cash you can opt for a "country club" type home where standards are high, people are paid well, staff are treated well and it all trickles down to the patient who gets good care. But facilities that take people in who have no money are a different breed. The staff is overworked and underpaid, there aren't enough staff to start with, and it's easy to get burned out when you spend day after day taking care of the critically ill and mentally unstable.

In short, you get what you pay for and if you have no money except for social security (which they take most of) and only Medicare and Medicaid…you get the picture. The elite nursing homes, that give the best care because the staff is well paid and well trained, cost $7-25 K a month.

Because I cannot get up to use the restroom, I wear pads. I am not incontinent, but you turn your light on for them to come and help you, and an hour (or two or three) later they come, but you just can't hold it that long, so you go and now the entire bed needs changing. I finally gave up and now wear pads.

The pads obviously need changing and, again, it may be two or three hours before they come to do it. I have contracted more than a few bladder infections because I am not cleaned in a timely manner. If I complain, I am a trouble maker, which just makes it worse. For example, at one point I had waited two hours to get changed, and when the person finally came, I made the remark that I felt she could've gotten to me sooner (big mistake). I said, "How would you feel if you had to sit in your own urine and feces for over two hours?" And with that she replied, "Well, I'm not incontinent, and I can wipe my own butt." Then she walked out. It was mean.

Then there was another person who came in because I had a problem with my Trilogy machine. It has to have water to help moisten my nose so it won't bleed (as much). About every three hours it had to be refilled. This particular nurse had never refilled the machine before and she grabbed it by the top not knowing that that would spill the whole thing. As nicely as I could, I told her that raising it from the top would cause problems, and I asked to help her fix it as I was worried about something happening to my breathing equipment. She sternly and angrily said, "I am the nurse and you are the patient; I know what I'm doing." (Never mind that I had taken care of it at home for three years.) She started to put the top on wrong as I thought would happen, and I tried to stop her again before it got worse, so I repeated that I'd like to help. She said, "Miss Hillis, you are not to touch this; I am the nurse, and I'm the only one who can touch it in this nursing home tonight; and you're kind of in trouble, aren't you, because it's not going to work so well because you don't have any water. Well, my goodness," and with that she walked out the door. In other words, you may die because you can't breathe and I'm not going to touch it now. I was scared to death. I sat there a few minutes, wondering what I was going to do now, but I was able to pull the table toward me, grab the heavy bottle of distilled water and refill and fix my machine. I spilled the water all over, but I got the job done. What she did was mean spirited, hurtful and depressing.

She was eventually let go, but there are just some people who do not belong in the business of taking care of the sick and the elderly.

I know my own body, and several times I've known that I was really sick, sick enough to go to the hospital. I've told the staff that I needed to go and they hemmed and hawed around, as they aren't supposed to call the EMTs for various reasons. For example, one time the nurse made me transfer from the shower chair to the wheelchair, and the floor was very wet. I told them I felt weak that morning, but they insisted. I stood up and took one step toward the wheelchair and down I went. They held me by my arms (which hurt very much) and I went down again slowly, but landed on top of my right foot that went up behind me. The foot was badly scratched and cut by something on the floor. A couple of weeks after the incident, my foot was still hurting. The supervisor felt it and kept saying it was OK, that there wasn't much heat and not much swelling. I knew it hurt too much to be OK, so I asked for an ambulance. They hesitated, saying I was going against medical advice, and I got worse, so I called the ambulance on my own. The ER doctor said the foot had a staph infection.

I've done this twice now and both times I was in the hospital for at least a week as they brought my body back to a safe state. I was right about something being wrong, and I believe I saved my own life. But they got upset, and this last time, when it was time to go back to the nursing home, I was told I couldn't return. All of a sudden they "can't take care of the breathing equipment" that they've been dealing with for months now. They thought I owned the Trilogy machine, but I don't (it is rented) and it costs $1,800 to pay for and take care of it. So far Medicare had paid it, but when that runs out, someone else will have to pay. It all comes down to money, and if you don't have it....

I had no idea where I was to go. The hospital care coordinator called several other homes who also didn't have people, a respiratory unit, and/ or equipment to take care of my needs, so for two months, I was in limbo.

By the way, I cannot say enough wonderful things about the doctors and staff at St. Joseph's Hospital. They were so attentive and loving, and the care they gave me was superb. I would have loved to have stayed, but hospitals are for the very sick; they aren't nursing homes, so I had to go.

Finally, one day I was taken to a health and rehabilitation home in Statesboro, Georgia which had a respiratory unit and a Trilogy machine which is a state-of-the-art, exterior, non-invasive vent that pushes air through my nose and into my lungs, and which I need to live. The one I had been using before had been ordered by my ALS doctor at the Mayo Clinic and it was rented from Barnes Equipment and paid for by Medicare. At first, I only used it at night, but as the disease progressed, I had to use it more and more.

When I arrived at the new home, I had to change to the equipment they had which was rented from a different company, but it was also state-of-the-art, so all was well. I began using their machine and receiving therapy 24/7. I became totally dependent on oxygen 24 hours a day (The Trilogy Machine), and needed help with just about everything I did. My feet curled up, and I lost most of the use of my left arm and hand.

The disease was progressing but I was getting care and therapy.

When I thought all was on an even keel and nothing could get worse (except the disease), I had another unfortunate incident take place in the world of healthcare.

One night, I couldn't sleep because when I nodded off, I would wake up gasping for air. I finally just ran out of energy and went to sleep around 6:00 am. When they tried to wake me for breakfast and later, for meds and therapy, I just couldn't wake up except to say "no" and tell the nurse something was wrong. She thought so too, and called an ambulance. As the ambulance was picking me up to go, I explained that I had to have my Trilogy vent to breathe. The respiratory therapist said, "No, that is our equipment and it can't go with her; Statesboro will have one, I'm sure." I explained that the only hospital I had been to that had them and used them was the Mayo Clinic in Jacksonville, Florida, and the Statesboro hospital would not have one. They all assured me that the Statesboro hospital would have one, and because I was too sick to keep arguing, off we went without it.

The emergency room, of course, did not have one. I was put in a mask thing, a miserable "helmet" that covered my mouth and nose. They said I had pneumonia in my lower lungs and I had to be admitted, so they started me on an IV and nasal cannula to be transferred to a room. I told them I could not tolerate a nasal cannula or laying down for any length of time, and I needed my machine to get me from the ER to the room.

Wes' friend, Jenna had come to be with me, thank God, because I needed help. She tried again to explain about my vent, and she called the nursing home to say I needed it. The nursing home administrator said they understood and it would be there in two minutes. Shortly thereafter, Jenna gets a text back that says they can't bring the machine and would the hospital administrator come to the phone. She informs the hospital that the insurance company would not allow the machine to come there. Jenna explained that every time before, when I had to be admitted to a hospital, the (Barnes) machine came with me. They still said no. So, the machine that replaced my Barnes one (which I had used for over four years, and that had been several times to three different hospitals), could not be brought to me. (By the way, I was never told I could not take it to a hospital.)

The ER people tried everything they could to get a machine that might work for me, but to no avail. Finally, the ER doctor called my lung doctor in Savannah and he thought my numbers were good, and said that I always tended to have a little pneumonia in my lungs because of the ALS and he thought I could be treated at the nursing home. So since the nursing home was holding my machine hostage, it was a consensus that I should go back there. The poor EMT took me back and immediately put me on the Trilogy.

Here's the thing: at one point I got Barnes on the phone and they said they would be glad to bring me a machine anywhere I needed it, but it would take a day or two because Medicare would not pay for two machines for me. The nursing home would have to cancel their contract and use Barnes, a different company. Everyone said that nothing could happen very quickly so the whole thing was moot.

It again boils down to the bottom line: m-o-n-e-y. When did health care workers, nurses, administrators, therapists, care more about a machine than they did their patients? If I get really sick again with something that requires a hospital visit or stay, I'm out of luck. The nursing home has to use the Barnes product or figure out how to make it OK to take their machine out. I do know the respiratory department at the nursing home has to have a back-up machine; it's the law, but I know they don't have one.

I just wish I could go home!

A note here; if you ever have to put a loved one or yourself in a nursing home, please have a family member or good friend go by everyday and serve as an advocate, especially if the patient has Alzheimer's or dementia. Patients need advocates to monitor care.

Chapter 40

I Ain't Down Yet

I have a new definition of ALS: A for Aggravation; L for Loneliness and S for Scared.

It is so aggravating not being able to do anything. If I want to brush my teeth, I have to get someone to get the items for me, along with a basin, before I can brush. The disease has progressed to the point where I need a bedpan (why can't someone invent a device for women to urinate into without making a mess?). I can't reach for something unless it's within an arm's length. I can see the brush, pen, book and/or straw, but I can't reach it; and if you can't reach it, you can't have it. I have to call someone. And when you lay in a bed, dependent on other people—some you've never met—to take care of you, it's very frightening.

I want to do things for myself and I can't. I want my dog; I want my eyelashes; I want my make-up and a good bathroom mirror; and I can't have them. I want to help people whom I have known for years, and who have been kind to me, but I can't. Aggravating!

It is lonely in this disease. All my friends have a life—children, vacations, places to go, jobs, and I'm excluded. I understand it all, but it hurts. I also can't do anything that puts me in the middle of people any more, and I was so use to that. Friends visit, show me pictures, and I am grateful for that, but I'm excluded from the excitement of living life.

I am scared, but it's not the dying I mind; it's giving up this wonderful life. Also, death doesn't scare me so much as the mechanics of it—how one dies. Does it hurt? What happens afterward? From my near-death experience I feel like I'm forgiven for the bad things I've done, but I find it hard to forgive myself. I have a strong faith, and I know I am going to heaven, but how do you get there? Are you zapped straight into heaven? Is there a "courtroom" where judges reside and review your life? Do you do like Rose in the *Golden Girls* and go to the holding station's gift shop, only to be told you have to go back? I'm scared of the unknown and I dwell on this, as death is coming.

My ALS definition gets me down sometimes, but I rally and try to go on. I do my best to stay "in the game." I have hope that they will find a cure just any day, and I'M NOT GIVING UP!

I worked on the Book but some of it was difficult as I had a hard time concentrating with so many issues regarding Jacob. When he was in jail, of course he wanted to get out. He called me most days, crying, "Mom, get me out of here," but I was in no position to do that. Besides, I would not have gotten him out—he needed time in jail and some treatment because he had been convicted of a felony and needed some stability. It upset me to be so helpless though. Then, on top of it all, Medicare and Medicaid informed me that they could no longer pay for his care and treatment, and he would be released. I began calling places and thought I found one in Statesboro, Georgia, which did seem promising, but it didn't pan out. At this point, some days I would call the DA's office and the Victim's Advocate's office three or four times a day—I was at my wit's end.

Now things were dire, and one night I was fervently praying for some kind of answer. "Dear God, it's your will; I'm at the end of my rope and I can't help him anymore. Please help us."

The very next day I got a call.

A friend who was a manager at a phone service company had a customer and she struck up a conversation with her when she was fixing her phone. The customer mentioned that she was involved with mental health and placing folks who needed a place to go. She had a brother who was schizophrenic and had had a lot of experience with trying to find good places for him. My friend mentioned Jacob and my dilemma and the woman called me right away. She gave me a list of numbers to call, and she took another list of numbers and we started our search and found a place in Waycross. The woman went to court with Jacob to tell the judge he had a place to go, and Jacob was released from prison (where he had been six months), and taken to a facility in Waycross. But he was in treatment only one month and then he was released. He went to our house at St. Simons.

You get so much faith and hope in the system when you tell the whole story, but at the end, after all that time, there's something wrong and they can't help, so you start over again with another agency—over and over again. Sometimes they accept your family member and then, boom, they let them go, because there's not enough money, or they can't handle the illness, or some other reason. You get beat up over and over.

Jacob lasted a while at home and then checked himself into the mental health clinic at St. Simons because he was having trouble. He just couldn't make it on his own and it was at this point we received another miracle.

The person who had tried to help me find a place for Jacob needed a place for her family to live. She asked if they could rent the upstairs area at my house in St. Simons. They'd pay rent and would be there for Jacob, giving him stability and structure. This has worked out beautifully so, as of this writing, all seems well.

As for me, I'm fighting the good fight. All have assured me that I will not recover from this disease, and as the illness progresses, I think more and more about what will happen to Jacob. I have been assured that The State of Georgia cannot take my house in St. Simons as long as Jacob lives there, but who knows.

With so much time on my hands, I am reflecting back on my life, and I want to take my mess and turn it into my message through this Book. I ask myself if all this pain is for a greater purpose. Maybe my life can be a message to other people who are suffering, and I think I should not "waste" this pain—I am now uniquely qualified to help others with theirs. It may be presumptuous to think I could help, but I will try to in my own small way.

I wonder what in the heck caused Nancy Hillis to be such a hit. I was Mandy Nichols in The Book and my character didn't have much coverage in it, either. Yet people found me, wanted my autograph, wanted to meet me—they would be lined up out the door to meet me and talk with me and sometimes I'd have to sneak out the back door to have some peace; my life was so overfilled with meeting people. I had three and four jobs, running back and forth from places, and was so busy I often didn't have time to go to the bathroom. I was on Oprah, for goodness sake. They called to say I had "charisma," and I had "a lot of life to me," and I should be on the show. That's all stopped and it's so difficult to cope with the snail's pace that is my life now.

I still have very good friends who come and visit: Darlene, Evie, Melissa, Robin, Cherise, Lin, Jeffery, Judge Barry, Bruce, Lois, Mr. G., Linda, Tara; as I name them I realize how very fortunate I am, but it's feast or famine. Wes comes almost every day, and John Brown faithfully comes every week. Jacob comes to see me when he can. It's a two hour drive for him but he manages to make it. He still goes up and down in his daily living.

So many kind and wonderful people have done so much for me. One of the best dentists ever did some much needed dental work for me and did not charge me a penny! Thank you, Dr. Durham. When my cars bit the dust, my friends gave me a car—a car that Jacob now drives. Friends have paid for special transportation for me and have come to the nursing homes to fix my hair and get me ready to go to the few events I have been invited to. The list goes on and on.

I have The Book. It's given me purpose and a reason to use my brain. It's brought me back to life and given me a chance to tell my story.

Do I have regrets? Not many. There's the abortion, of course; I've labored over that many, many times, and I still think of it with great remorse. I also regret not being there more for my first son, Wes. I missed his basketball games and school events when he was in high school because I usually was scrambling, trying to get out of messes, starting a new business, and take care of Jacob whose care became all-consuming. My Wes is just a dear boy and now a fine man, but I wasn't there for him like I wanted to be. Forgive me, Wes.

Concerning the Hamilton-Turner House, I think I was a woman before her time. I pushed through the battles (public opinion, the Gods in the Marble House) to make it easier for the next owners. I loved it and I feel I saved it. It was so rundown and little by little over the course of three years, I brought it back to life and given a few different twists, I would've been successful as the owner of the best bed and breakfast in Savannah. I met people from all over the world and gave thousands of Girl Scouts the opportunity to spend the night in a grand Mansion, an experience they'll never forget. I've told my Mandy story and shared my faith with thousands of people. The House is in my soul, and I mourn for it still. I had found my niche in it, and I was happy there. It was to be my retirement home, giving me everything I needed to get to the end of life, but I had a choice: the house or Jacob, and there was no choice.

I'm proud of my drug and alcohol abuse work, and I think I did all I could at the time; but the whole business, the big picture, is pretty hopeless. First, there's a lot of money in drugs. For example, one time a police officer of a small little town said that his job was to check the dirt airstrip once an hour every night. A person came and offered him $40,000 if he'd miss just one run. That's difficult to resist: one night can equal his kids' college education. That's just one small town; multiply that by a million small towns and you can see the dilemma.

Second, drugs work. For some the only way to handle anxiety, stress, peer pressure, expectations and so forth are drugs. They help and become a great coping mechanism. Tough stuff.

In my opinion, we have to keep on fighting. Even foreign powers who want to do us in say they don't have to worry about doing it because, "America will implode all by themselves." America's appetite for drugs and alcohol, and our need for immediate gratification will simply destroy us if we don't keep fighting.

I knew I wasn't going to save the world, but I thought I could save all the kids in Georgia. I didn't, so I said I'd save all the kids in the county. I didn't, so I finally decided to try and just save one kid at a time, and I did help save a few. If I only helped save one (and I know I helped some) it was worth it.

What can I recommend to parents? Tell your children very early about drugs and alcohol. There will be someone who will tell them how much fun they are; or how much better they will be at an activity if they use a drug; or if they need to stay awake and study for that exam, a drug will help them do it; or just one little joint will help them relax and be calm for that tryout. Show them the facts—don't give them some big story for scare tactics—stick to FACTS.

Keep your children busy; make them get into an extracurricular activity at school—it doesn't matter what, just something they excel in and enjoy that keeps them busy. And when they are old enough to get a job, make them get one. Jobs will keep them out of trouble. Most of all, make sure you have your hand on the pulse of their lives.

I know I'll get criticized for taking Charles in, but he had no one to care for him, so I took him into my home (at this point he didn't really know me). I know this is so hard to understand, especially after what he did to Jacob, but I had compassion for him and decided to forgive him. He had been a love of my life, and an unbelievable person; if you just could have seen him with his patients—he was just a wonderful doctor. When I finally got over our marriage breakup, and got over the hate from the incidents with Jacob, there was nothing left but pity for him. And I hoped that he and Jacob might yet have a father-son relationship that was good, and that's what happened.

I believe in a higher being and in my case, that's God, and I know He blessed me with enough foolishness to think I could make a difference in this world. My faith has brought me through and been the source of my strength, and I know I'll go to heaven but, as I said, I'm afraid of the unknown, the mechanics of death. I guess I'm not ready yet. I see value in life; I can enjoy the sun, birds, squirrels, trees and life and I don't take one single thing for granted. I certainly don't think I have all the answers to all the questions—sometimes I don't even know the questions—but every day is a wonderful gift no matter how bad it seems. Bloom where you are planted, I say, and as Forrest Gump said, "Life is like a box of chocolates; you never know what you're going to get."

I hope my Book will impact other lives in a way that will inspire people, especially women, to stay positive, and to never give up. I hope it will remind people to be kind; not to judge people by their faith, color, sexual preference, nationality or how much money they have or don't have; that God is the judge and our job is to care for and accept people.

I had decided to donate my body to Emory for research for ALS, hoping that maybe my body would be the one that produces the cure, but guess what? When I read the paperwork it said that if I died obese, they wouldn't take my body! (So guys, in death we fat folks are still discriminated against.) As food is one of my last pleasures, I doubt I'll be skinny enough; but who knows what this illness will do to me yet.

I have a bucket list. I've had to drop some things because I don't think they are possible, like go around the world. (I always wanted to visit other cultures.) I would still love to meet Dolly Parton and Betty White. I would love to get a motor home and go with my family (and nurse, I suppose) to see Grand Canyon. I'd love to do one more trip to Disney World and stay in Cinderella's castle. I'd love to have my doggie, Jack, to love again, and I wish I could start an ALS support group.

(Note: Jack died September 1ˢᵗ. Nancy said she knew the exact moment he died as she "felt" him stir next to her as he always did. She whispered, "it's all right, Jack" and turned to see him vanish.)

My Grandmomma said to me several times that if ever I was someone of importance, I should try and do something about unfair things that happen to children and helpless people. I'm not necessarily important, but it's on my bucket list to try and do something.

We are only here for a short time, and I wake up every morning and try to see some magic, to try and find the wonder and amazement in my day and leave behind a little memory. The only way you can really fail at life is to not participate every day, no matter the circumstances. I also think about my former precious roommate at the first nursing home I was sent to, who reminded me everyday how lucky I am. At 17 years old she was hit by a drunk driver and suffered a lot of neurological damage. It has affected everything from her speech, to her walking, to her cognitive abilities, and now at 53 she is still in the nursing home and probably will be for the rest of her life. I am blessed!

I've been knocked down a lot lately and this last fall has been a tough one, especially because my legs don't work and it's hard to get up, but I'm not out. I'm hanging in there and fighting the good fight. And you should stay tuned; I ain't down yet!

Regardless, I am touched that you read my Book. It's been a long process.

And most of all, I'm sure glad I got to be here!

CPSIA information can be obtained at www.ICGtesting.com
Printed in the USA
LVOW06*1825021215

463982LV00002B/3/P